Anastasia V. Mitrofanova

THE POLITICIZATION OF RUSSIAN ORTHODOXY

Actors and Ideas

With a foreword by William C. Gay

ibidem-Verlag
Stuttgart

Bibliografische Information Der Deutschen Bibliothek

Die Deutsche Bibliothek verzeichnet diese Publikation in der Deutschen Nationalbibliografie; detaillierte bibliografische Daten sind im Internet über <http://dnb.ddb.de> abrufbar.

∞

Gedruckt auf alterungsbeständigem, säurefreien Papier
Printed on acid-free paper

ISSN: 1614-3515

ISBN: 3-89821-481-8

© *ibidem*-Verlag
Stuttgart 2005
Alle Rechte vorbehalten

Das Werk einschließlich aller seiner Teile ist urheberrechtlich geschützt. Jede Verwertung außerhalb der engen Grenzen des Urheberrechtsgesetzes ist ohne Zustimmung des Verlages unzulässig und strafbar. Dies gilt insbesondere für Vervielfältigungen, Übersetzungen, Mikroverfilmungen und elektronische Speicherformen sowie die Einspeicherung und Verarbeitung in elektronischen Systemen.

Printed in Germany

Anastasia V. Mitrofanova

The Politicization of Russian Orthodoxy

Actors and Ideas

With a foreword by William C. Gay

Cover picture: Red banner with an image of Christ. 1 May 2005. ©Anastasia Mitrofanova.

To my parents: Nina and Vladimir

Contents

Acknowledgements	9
List of Abbreviations	11
Foreword	13
William C. Gay	
Introduction	15

I Between Ideology and Religion — 21

I.1 Political Religion: A Definition — 21
I.2 The Difference Between Political Religion and Fundamentalism — 24
I.3 Political Religions vs. Ethnic and Nationalist Religious Ideologies — 26

II Political Orthodoxy as an Ideology — 31

II.1 General Characteristics and Historical Background — 31
II.2 Five Versions Of Political Orthodoxy — 37
   Political Fundamentalism — 37
   Contemporary Pan-Slavism — 44
   Neo-Eurasianism — 51
   Orthodox Communism — 60
   Russian Nationalism: Quasi-Orthodoxy and Neo-Paganism — 66
II.3 Political Orthodoxy Between Universalism and Particularism — 74

III Political Orthodoxy as a Subculture — 77

III.1 Self-definition, Language and Symbols — 78

	III.2	Art	84
		Music	84
		Literature	90
		Visual Arts	94
	III.3	Mass Media	102
		Television and Radio	102
		Newspapers and Journals	108
		Internet	110
	III.4	Hangouts and Dress Code	114
IV	**The Political Orthodox as Believers**		**121**
	IV.1	Ideological Religiosity vs. Traditional Religiosity	121
	IV.2	Religiosity of the Political Orthodox	132
V	**The Political Orthodox as Intellectual Community**		**143**
	V.1	New Orthodox Intellectuals and Their Style of Writing	143
	V.2	Political Religion and Para-Science	148
	V.3	New Intellectuals and the Established Academic Community	156
VI	**The Politicization of Orthodoxy, the Church and the State**		**165**
	VI.1	The Russian Orthodox Church and Politicization of Orthodoxy	165
	VI.2	Civil and Uncivil Religion: Transformations of Official Nationalism	176
VII	**Political Orthodoxy at the Micro- and Macropolitical Level**		**187**
	Concluding Remarks		**203**
	Glossary of Names, Organizations, Events and Mass Media		207
	List of Illustrations		223
	Illustrations		227

Acknowledgements

This book was to a great extent made possible thanks to support from the Research and Writhing Initiative of the Program on Global Security and Sustainability of the John D. and Catherine T. MacArthur Foundation, which provided funding for my initial theoretical study of politicization of Orthodoxy and for some of the empirical research.

I would like to express my gratitude to Michael Howard who provided invaluable assistance in editing the manuscript with exceptional speed and quality and to Professor William Gay who read the entire study and gave me useful comments and suggestions.

I am also indebted to the Centre for Information and Analysis "SOVA" headed by Aleksandr Verkhovskii for its extremely useful mailing lists on religion and xenophobia.

Besides, I would like to thank everyone who, in this or that way, assisted me in collecting empirical data needed for this publication.

List of Abbreviations

AKIRN –	*Assotsiatsiia po kompleksnomu izucheniiu russkoi natsii* (Association for Complex Studies of the Russian Nation)
CEBs –	*communidades eclesiales de base* (basic Christian communities)
CIS –	Commonwealth of Independent States
DOTU –	*dostatochno obshchaia teoriia upravleniia* (Reasonably General Theory of Management)
ECOSOC –	UN Economic and Social Council
ESM –	*Evraziiskii Soiuz Molodëzhi* (the Eurasian Union of Youth)
FSU –	Former Soviet Union
GOC –	the Georgian Orthodox Church
GRU –	*Glavnoe razvedovatel'noe upravlenie* (the Main Intelligence Department of the Army)
ITN –	Individual Taxpayer's Number
KOB –	*Kontseptsiia obshchestvennoi bezopasnosti* (Concept of Public Security)
KPRF –	*Kommunisticheskaia Partiia Rossiiskoi Federatsii* (the Communist Party of the Russian Federation)
MGIMO –	*Moskovskii gosudarstvennyi institut mezhdunarodnykh otnoshenii* (Moscow State Institute of International Relations)
MSU –	Moscow State University
NDPR –	*Natsional'no-Derzhavnaia Partiia Rossii* (the National Etatist Party of Russia)
NAMAKON –	*Nezavisimoe Agentstvo, Marketing i Konsalting* (Independent Agency, Marketing and Consulting)
NIMB –	*Fond natsional'noi i mezhdunarodnoi bezopasnosti* (the Fund of National and International Security)
RKRP –	*Rossiiskaia Kommunisticheskaia Rabochaia Partiia* (the Russian Communist Worker's Party)
ROC –	the Russian Orthodox Church

RNE –	*Russkoe Natsional'noe Edinstvo* (the Russian National Unity)
SMI –	*sredstva massovoi informatsii* (mass media)
TsIK –	*Tsentral'naia Izbiratel'naia Komissiia* (the Central Electoral Comission)
VTsIOM –	*Vserossiiskii Tsentr Izucheniia Obshchestvennogo Mneniia* (the All-Russian Centre for Studying Public Opinion)
WTC –	World Trade Center
ZAO –	*zakrytoe aktsionernoe obshchestvo* (joint-stock company)

Foreword

This publication is a new brilliant work of Anastasia Mitrofanova that continues her original research on religious politicization. This groundbreaking study has been evaluated so highly that a more condensed preliminary exposition of this thesis was selected for publication in the *Global Studies Encyclopedia* (English edition) published in 2003 simultaneously in the Russian and English languages. However, most of the findings of the research have so far been published only in the Russian language; significantly, thanks to *ibidem*-Verlag, these outstanding theoretical conclusions and empirical data, are now available for the English-speaking scholarly community of Europe and the United States.

The Politicization of Orthodoxy provides seminal research on Orthodoxy-based political ideologies (what the author calls "political Orthodoxy") in all their diversity – from fundamentalism to religion-impacted versions of communism. This broadness of scope distinguishes Mitrofanova's work from the majority of previous publications that are mostly limited to analyzing fundamentalism (or, sometimes, also religious nationalism) as if it was the only form of politicization of Orthodoxy. Moreover, the author deliberately avoids paying too much attention to ecclesiastical issues (focusing instead on religiopolitical movements of laypeople), and this restraint allows her to avoid repeating what has already been stated in other publications.

Knowing the interrelations between Orthodox Christianity and politics with regard to Russia is of primary importance due, first, to the enormous role religion plays in Russian politics, culture, and everyday life, and, second, to the tremendous part that Russia still plays in world political affairs. Obviously, Orthodoxy will influence all further developments related to the Russian Federation. Understanding what politicization of Orthodoxy means and what impact it may have on the broader world situation can not be overestimated; this book contributes greatly to understanding the issues in question.

A distinguishing feature and the most significant achievement of *The Politicization of Russian Orthodoxy: Actors and Ideas* is its being focused not only on ideas, but on actors as well. To the best of my knowledge, this book provides the only research (published either in Russian or English) describing and analyzing what may be called "the subculture of political Orthodoxy", its language, symbols, communication channels, networks, etc. This analysis correlates with recent trends in philosophical and political studies on language and symbols wide-spread in Europe and the U.S.A. with regard to the ideas of Pierre Bourdieu. Significantly, the author was able to collect unique empirical data on the subculture of political Orthodoxy including observations of events, that have been hard to admit, and interviews with people, who have been hard to contact. This empirical data provides for scholars of the politicization of Orthodoxy a new basis for their further research.

Of equal importance is the valuable contribution this publication makes to contemporary discussions of civil society, nationalism and religion. The author considers the latest developments in nation-building with regard to Russia and the CIS countries (so called "orange revolutions" and their possible impact) and draws rather pessimistic conclusions about the future of democracy in Russia. If Russia experiences a democracy-building failure, this may most likely lead to an abrupt growth of the influence of politicized Orthodoxy. These considerations make the book even more topical.

This book definitely deserved being published by any serious academic book series. I am genuinely pleased to see it published in the series "Soviet and Post-Soviet Politics and Society" initiated by such a distinguished academic publisher as *ibidem*-Verlag. By publishing this very thought provoking and empirically rich text, *ibidem*-Verlag allows all who read this book to see that not only is Mitrofanova's work in the mainstream of contemporary philosophical and political theory but also her work extends this theory. Moreover, her application of these theories to the politicization of Orthodoxy provides insights and sets standards that other scholars will find difficult to match.

Professor William C. Gay
University of North Carolina at Charlotte

Introduction

This book is not about Orthodox Christianity as such. Instead, it will focus on Orthodoxy-based political ideologies which only slightly resemble the religion from which they arise. Politicization is understood as a process through which a "normal" religion turns into a religious ideology. The supporters of such ideologies see the world as the arena of confrontation between "us" and "them," but this distinction is not so much between "the Orthodox" and "the non-Orthodox" as between the supporters and the opponents of political Orthodoxy. Even the Orthodox Church hierarchs, not to mention ordinary believers, are often seen as "them." At the same time, many who are formally non-Orthodox (Muslims, Communist atheists, Catholic Slavs, etc.) are often counted as "us" and therefore as "the Orthodox *honoris causa*." Backers of religion-based ideologies often have no religious faith in the traditional sense; they profess religious ideologies rather than religions.

The fact that politicization in most cases transforms the original religion beyond recognition often prevents scholars from acknowledging Orthodoxy-based ideologies and movements as religiopolitical phenomena. Some scholars simply exclude from their analysis the ideologies of political Orthodoxy most differing from the official doctrine. As a result no substantial publication has thus far examined politicised Orthodoxy as a complex ideology embracing a spectrum of variations from Communism to Nationalism. What unites all of them is their appeal to Orthodoxy as *ultima ratio* whenever the validatation of political action is needed.

The Communist Party of the Russian Federation, for instance, has never been regarded as a relgiopolitical organization. Stephen D. Shenfield, nevertheless considers it to be an organization which is almost fascist in orientation.[1] Although we in no way support Shenfield's assessment of the party or his broad definition of "fascism," his flexible approach generally corresponds with the one we advocate. We also support problem-oriented ap-

---

[1] Stephen D. Shenfield, *Russian Fascism: Traditions, Tendencies, Movements* (Armonk, N.Y.: M.E.Sharpe, 2001), 51-59.

proach utilized, for example, by Vadim Rossman when he demonstrates that such diverse ideologies as Neo-Eurasianism, National Bolshevism, Orthodox Nationalism, etc. have at least one thing in common: namely, their anti-Semitism.[2] He, however, does not unite these ideologies under any common name like "political Orthodoxy."

Most publications remain focused upon specific versions of political Orthodoxy, of which political fundamentalism is the most substantially studied (due to its obvious closeness to the Church and to the canonical doctrine).[3] Studies on political Orthodox fundamentalism have been undertaken by Konstantin Kostiuk, Stella Rock, Aleksandr Verkhovskii and others. There are also publications about separate organizations and/or personalities not envisioned as a part of the process of politicization of Orthodoxy. One may name publications by Alan Ingram, Madlene Laruelle and Andreas Umland on Eurasianism; by Viacheslav Likhachev and Vladimir Pribylovskii on *Russkoe Natsional'noe Edinstvo*; by Vladimir Shnirel'man on political Neo-Paganism; by Aleksandr Tarasov on skinheads and so on. There is also a substantial amount of literature on nationalism and right-wing extremism in Russia but most of them don't relate the issues in question to religious politicization.

Unwillingness to acknowledge that political Orthodoxy, in spite of all its internal differentiations and dissimilarity with the canonical version, is, in fact,

---

[2] Vadim Rossman, *Russian Intellectual Anti-Semitism in the Post-Communist Era* (Lincoln, NE: University of Nebraska Press and SICSA, 2002).

[3] See, for example, the following works by the authors mentioned below: Konstantin Kostiuk, "Pravoslavnyi fundamentalizm," *Politicheskie issledovaniia* no. 5 (2000); Stella Rock, "'Militant Piety': Fundamentalist Tendencies in the Russian Orthodox Brotherhood Movement," http://www.georgefox.edu/academics/undergrad/departments/soc-swk/ree/rock_mpf_01.html (as of 4 December 2003); Aleksandr Verkhovskii, *Politicheskoe pravoslavie: Russkie pravoslavnye fundamentalisty i natsionalisty. 1995-2001 g.* (Moskva: Tsentr "SOVA", 2003); Alan Ingram, "Alexander Dugin: Geopolitics and Neo-Fascism in Post-Soviet Russia," *Political Geography* 8 (2001); Madlene Laruelle, *Ideologiia russkogo evraziistva* (Moskva: Natalis, 2004); Andreas Umland, "Die Herausbildung einer faschistischen 'neoeurasischen' Intellektuellenbewegung in Russland," http://www.boschlektoren.de/a-sites/projektterasse/fertigeprojekte/csteck/andreas.html (as of 18 November 2003); Viacheslav Likhachev and Vladimir Pribylovskii, *Russkoe Natsional'noe Edinstvo: istoriia, politika, ideologiia* (Moskva: Panorama, 1997); Vladimir Shnirel'man, *Neoiazychestvo i natsionalizm: Vostochno-evropeiskii areal* (Moskva: IEA RAN, 1998); Aleksandr Tarasov, "Britogolovye," http://lucky-angels.narod.ru/articles/skin.htm (as of 23 October 2003).

an organic whole, renders scholars unable to utilise theoretical approaches worked out by those who have studied other religiopolitical ideologies, such as Islamism or progressive Catholicism. We, on the contrary, think that these approaches are of the highest methodological value. By applying theoretical concepts worked out by scholars of Islamism to Orthodox relgiopolitical movements, a scholar acquires the ability to trace otherwise undetectable trends and to predict their development in the foreseeable future. This approach does not imply that, for example, Islam and Orthodoxy are "the same" but that religious ideologies and religiopolitical movements based on these religions have, indeed, very much in common.

This book presents political Orthodoxy as a complex of ideologies among which, based upon their vision of Russia's place in the world, we distinguish political fundamentalism, Pan-Slavism, Neo-Eurasianism, Orthodox Communism and Russian nationalism. However, in spite of their external diversity, all of them make a single ideology of political Orthodoxy characterized by a specific set of ideas. Any of these ideas may be pivotal for a given version of political Orthodoxy while, at the same time, remaining peripheral for the other versions.

There is no reason to assume that contemporary studies of religious ideologies in Russia should be limited to analysing texts.[4] In this book we try to support textual analysis, which we still think necessary, with a description of "the political Orthodox" (i.e., people who profess ideologies of political Orthodoxy) as a cultural, religious and intellectual community. This allows us to characterize not only the ideas of political Orthodoxy but also the actors producing and consuming such ideas.

The specific subculture of political Orthodoxy – language, music, dresscode and the like - has so far been neglected by most scholars in spite of the fact that this topic is currently researched with regard to the other "Orthodox" countries, such as Greece or Serbia. Although the political Orthodox community is not a genuinely clear-cut subculture, most political Orthodox are aware of their differences from the mainstream, thus defining themselves as a spe-

---

[4] On limitations of this approach see: Mikhail Gabovich, "Russkii natsionalizm: razmyshleniia o sostoianii issledovanii," (Paper presented at the conference "Russkii natsionalizm v politicheskom prostranstve: ot radikalnykh grupp do partii," Moscow, 21 February 2005).

cific group of "Orthodox patriots" or "national patriots." Here the author has mostly relied on her own empirical studies based on methods such as observation and interview.

To understand who the political Orthodox are and why they are at odds with the canonical version of their religion, we find it necessary to examine the nature of the religiosity of those who initiate and support religiopolitical movements. Empirical data here is partly taken from reliable sociological surveys and partly collected by the author through interviews and observation. Combining this empirical data with theoretical conclusions previously reached by scholars of Islamism and the other religious ideologies, we are able to challenge the notion that because people in Russia are not religious in the canonical sense, Orthodoxy is therefore unlikely to become politicised. This book clearly demonstrates that the non-traditional religiosity of the political Orthodox and their hostility to the Church is precisely what makes their active participation in religiopolitical movements possible.

The book also contains some empirical observations on the political Orthodox as an intellectual community and on their relations with the traditional academic environment. We designate the knowledge produced by the political Orthodox as para-scientific while sharing features with the previous tradition of Soviet social sciences.

We have found it necessary to demonstrate that the Russian Orthodox Church (the ROC) is in no way a pro-politicization force and that religiopolitical movements operate outside the Church as an institution (although some clerics may support political Orthodoxy). The book also includes a subchapter discussing penetration of Orthodoxy into the official project of national ideology. This subchapter aims to demonstrate that these developments have nothing to do with politicization and that the role for Orthodoxy here is fully instrumental.

Finally, we intend to move beyond empirical description and primary analysis so as to determine the extent to which political Orthodoxy is able to affect modern Russian politics. Based, once again, upon the experience of the Islamic world and Latin America we shall focus more on the micropolitical than the macropolitical level, demonstrating that only those organizations who initiate a network of alternative social institutions are able to win mass support and to infiltrate mainstream politics with their ideas.

Ultimately, we would like to stress that our task is not to compare ideologies of political Orthodoxy with those of the official doctrine of the Russian Orthodox Church. We think that religious ideologies are dangerous not because they distort the "original" dogmas but because they define religious differences in terms of "us" and "them," thus clearing the way for xenophobia and religiously-motivated violence.

I Between Ideology and Religion

I.1 Political Religion: A Definition

We suggest referring to the religiopolitical ideologies in question as political religions. The term political religion, as more commonly used, has a slightly different meaning. It dates back to Eric Voegelin's book *Die politischen Religionen* (1938) where he defines totalitarian ideologies such as Communism, Fascism and National Socialism as political religions. Such ideologies establish grounding for national unity by providing a quasi-religious dimension to the political order.[5] For Voegelin and his followers a political religion is not a religion as traditionally defined, rather, it is an ideology which does not necessarily imply a belief in the supernatural. Ideologies are secular phenomena (unless we consider "supernatural" such concepts as "nation," or "state" in the framework of totalitarian ideologies). Voegelin considered deification of these entities a feature of political religions.[6] Nevertheless, deification here is simply a metaphor, and Voegelin's political religions are thereby religions only in a figurative sense. However, when an ideology includes genuine references to the supernatural and justifies political activities through an appeal to the other world, it is, in our opinion, not an ideology as such but a "politicised" or "political" religion.

Our usage of the term correlates with the "classical" one because we, following, for example, Juan Linz, understand a political religion as worldview which claims to be the absolute truth and which is not compatible with existing religious traditions.[7] However, our concept of political religions also closely resembles what Linz defines as "theocracy," stressing that politics are

---

[5] Hans Maier, *Politische Religionen: Die totalitären Regime und das Christentum* (Freiburg, Basel, Wien: Herder, 1995), 29.
[6] Ibid., 30.
[7] Juan J. Linz, "Der religiöse Gebrauch der Politik und/oder der politische Gebrauch der Religion: Ersatzideologie gegen Ersatzreligion" in Hans Maier, ed., *"Totalitarismus" und "Politische Religionen": Konzepte des Diktaturvergleichs* (Paderborn: Ferdinand Schöningh, 1996), 130.

used for religious purposes, and not vice-versa.[8] A "theocracy," for Linz, is not a political religion (which he considers secular ideology) but a form of "politicised religion" somehow correlated, nevertheless, with political religions.

The term "political religion" is commonly used by many scholars to designate religious ideologies both directly (for example, in an article "Political Religion in the Twenty-first Century" by Peter van der Veer)[9] and indirectly (widely used constructions like "political Islam," "political Hinduism," etc. may easily be reshaped into constructions like "political religion of Islam" and "political Hindu religion"). We also suggest that "theocracy" is a misleading terms because one can hardly imagine a polity that would be based directly on religious principles (except, may be, very small communities); we prefer to describe polities governed by political religions as "ideocracies".

Political religions understand the events of this world as a part (or reflection) of sacral cosmic events. Aims of religiopolitical movements are Aims with a capital "A," vital human endeavours are thought to be sanctioned by supernatural forces. Those who are motivated by political religions do what they do not because they want to do so; instead, they see themselves as following the decree of God or some other supernatural force. It is important to understand that political religions should not be confused with the use of religion for political purposes. Religious politicization implies that political means are used for religious purposes, such as to build God's Kingdom on Earth, an Islamic state, etc. Political power is in thereby only the means by which to achieve an ultimately sacral goal.

American scholar of political religions Mark Juergensmeyer describes "religious wars" (as opposed to "wars justified by religion") in the following manner:

> These religious activities are not just political exercises justified by religion, they are perceived by the faithful as facets of a more fundamental confrontation. Conflicts of the real world are linked to an invisible, cosmic war: the spiritual struggle be-

---

[8] Ibid., 138.
[9] Peter van der Veer, "Political Religion in the Twenty-first Century" in T.V. Paul, John A. Hall, ed., *International Order and the Future of World Politics* (Cambridge: Cambridge University Press, 1999), 311-327.

tween order and disorder, light and darkness, faith and doubt.[10]

This means that any worthwhile war is seen as a "holy" one, or as an earthly reflection of the conflict between Good and Evil in the other world. In many instances, though, a cynical use of religion by politicians can become the first step towards religious politicization.

Sacralization of political conflicts entails the demonization of enemies, who become personifications of universal Evil. No sacrifices are too extreme and negotiation with the enemy becomes impossible. "We are not fighting so that the enemy recognizes us and offers us something. We are fighting to wipe out the enemy," states Hussein Mussawi, the former leader of Lebanon's Hezbollah.[11] This approach often results in indiscriminate acts of religious terrorism or in suicide terrorist attacks.

Thus, political religions can be understood to include not only totalitarian ideologies, but also ideologies which justify political actions through appeals to the supernatural. In other words, political religion is a hybrid of religion and ideology. Most scholars distinguish between political religions and the religions upon which they are originally based by using special terms to designate the former: for example, a political religion based on Islam is called "Islamism;" some authors also use "Orthodoxism" (*pravoslavism*) to define political Orthodox Christianity, although this term is not commonly accepted[12]. Liberation theology or progressive Catholicism is also a political religion in our opinion.

---

[10] Mark Juergensmeyer, "Sacrifice and Cosmic War," in Mark Juergensmeyer, ed., *Violence and the Sacred in the Modern World* (London: Frank Cass, 1992), 112.

[11] Quoted in: Bruce Hoffman, *Inside Terrorism* (New York: Columbia Univ. Press, 1998), 96.

[12] This term may be found in: Vitalii Mal'kov, "Pravoslavnyi radikalizm i budushchee Rossii," www.islamnews.ru/utl/affichage.php?idprim=337&cat=3 (as of 12 February 2004).

I.2 The Difference between Political Religion and Fundamentalism

Although some authors, for instance, Bassam Tibi, use these terms as synonyms we think that to confuse these two ideas reflects a deeply rooted misunderstanding. Fundamentalism literally means "the adherence to the fundamentals," i.e. the most essential and established principles of a religion. When we speak of fundamentalists, we are typically referring to "theologically literate" people who know and practice the dogmas of their religion (for example, a Russian Orthodox fundamentalist is expected to take communion regularly). Unlike fundamentalists, adherents of political religions hardly pay attention to the rituals of the religions upon which they are based. They may develop their own rituals instead; notwithstanding, even the strongest devotion to a political religion does not necessarily entail the practice of the original religion.

Unlike political religion, fundamentalism is focused on the past, and thus it can also be called traditionalism or religious conservatism. On the other hand, political religions aim not at revitalization of the past; rather, they seek to address the most vital issues of modernity. This difference can be illustrated by the example of an Iranian scholar Ali Shariati, who is considered one of the forerunners of Khomeini. Shariati was in no way a Shii fundamentalist because his main concern was the Shii interpretation of the revolutionary ideas of the Latin American guerrillas. It is, then, no surprise that his views were opposed by traditional (i.e., fundamentalist) Shii theologians and that they condemned him as "Marxist," "atheist" and "Wahhabist."[13] John Esposito mentions, that "Shariati's 'return to Islam' was not a retreat to the medieval Islamic worldview of conservative *ulama*, but a revolutionary vision of early Shii Islam which provided the inspirational basis for a modern reinterpretation of Islam."[14]

Fundamentalists are not always non-political; likewise not all of them try to preserve the status-quo. The status-quo is mostly preserved by the religious establishment. Some fundamentalists may join it; others don't want to

---

[13] See: Vladimir Iurtaev, *Iran: studenty v islamskoi revoliutsii* (Moskva: Nauka, 1993), 9, 11.

[14] John L. Esposito, *The Islamic Threat: Myth or Reality?* (New York; Oxford: Oxford University Press, 1992), 107.

admit that the world has retreated from the traditions of the past. Even though fundamentalists want to return to the pre-modern world, they must nevertheless live in a modern world that shapes their worldview. Their vision of the past is influenced by contemporary ideologies; moreover, in order to reach their goals they must employ use modern tactics. Non-political fundamentalists prefer to encapsulate themselves in closed communities and compounds; political fundamentalists participate in political battles in order to transform the rest of society according to their principles. Political fundamentalism, thus, may sometimes be considered among instances of political religions although fundamentalists normally condemn the latter as heresies and distortions of faith.

Both fundamentalism and political religion are inspired by social change, whether it is that of modernization or of transition. Fundamentalism always confronts modernization as an external influence. Political religion is not so much a reaction to modernization as its sometimes unexpected result. Opposing Westernization it aims at conducting "another" modernization, reaching "another" world unity. Of course the supporters of political religions are often more fundamentalist than fundamentalists themselves. They call for "returning to the fundamentals," "purifying the faith," "liberating from Western domination," etc. This, however, does not make them less modernist. In summary, we can distinguish between fundamentalism and political religion by stating that fundamentalism uses the concepts of the past to change the modernity while political religion uses modernity to change the concepts of the past.

I.3 Political Religions vs. Ethnic and Nationalist Religious Ideologies

The universal appeal of political religions allows them to undermine state sovereignty in the same way global secular ideologies (like Communism) do. In response, states create national religious ideologies. For such nationalist projects religion sooner or later becomes secondary because strengthening national community is their primary task. This is why such national religious ideologies may not be equated with political religions: religion is for them the means rather than the goal. Such projects may evolve into civil religions providing moral legitimacy to nation-states. With time civil religions become more secularized, gradually reducing their appeal to the supernatural. Civil religions are thereby compatible with democracy and religious freedom. In spite of their references to various otherworldly forces (God, gods, saints, Providence, etc.) they more closely resemble secular nationalist ideologies than religions.

Instead of evolving into respectable civil religions, national religions sometimes sanction ethnically and religiously homogenous states, excluding the members of the other ethnoreligious groups from the "national body." Such ethnoreligious movements may be called "uncivil religions," analogous to the wide spread term "uncivil society" (civil society based on non-liberal principles), because, instead of consolidating civil nations, they intend to get rid of the other ethic groups and to form ethnically homogenous nations.

Uncivil religions are professed, for example, by various Protestantism-inspired white supremacy organizations such as the American religiopolitical movement "Christian Identity." Their ideology is based on so-called "British Israelism," or "Anglo-Israelism."[15] Its supporters in the 19th century claimed that Jesus had been an Aryan, not a Semite, and that Anglo-Saxons were the Biblical Jews, while contemporary Jews had usurped this name. This ideology had been imported to the United States where it acquired overtly racist characteristics and became a basis for various right-wing organizations (the Aryan Nations and other Christian Patriot paramilitary groups).[16] This ideology understands the white race (first of all, Anglo-Saxons) as the Chosen People.

---

[15] See: Mark Juergensmeyer, *Terror in the Mind of God: The Global Rise of Religious Violence* (Berkeley: Univ. of California Press, 1999), 33-34.
[16] See: Hoffman, *Inside Terrorism,* 111-120.

The idea that a particular ethnic group is the Chosen People is a characteristic of uncivil religions. This idea is dominant in most ethnic groups historically professing Orthodoxy. For example, ethnonationalist Serbian intellectuals often draw parallels between Serbs and Jews. In 1985 a well known Orthodox Serbian nationalist Vuk Draskovic published an open letter to the Israelis where he calls Serbs "the thirteenth lost and the most ill-fated tribe of Israel." Dobrica Cosic, a writer and the first president of post-Tito Yugoslavia also drew parallels between Jews and Serbs as two martyr nations and innocent victims of genocide.[17] The same comparisons are drawn in the Russian Orthodox political literature portraying Russians as the Chosen People. The idea of being chosen by God inevitably leads to growing xenophobia and garrison thinking.

Let us repeat that national religious movements are able to evolve into both respectable civil religions and xenophobic ethnocentric ideologies. They, however, have one thing in common: their particularism and anti-universalism. Neither ethnocentric ideologies, nor civil religions can be exported. Their ideal is a religiously and ethnically homogenous state (e.g., Hindustan for Hinduists, Khalistan for Sikhs or Russian Republic for Russian nationalists). They aim at consolidating a community rather than fulfilling a "cosmic" plan related to universal struggle between Good and Evil.

Political religions, on the contrary, are primarily concerned with achieving purely religious goals. Such goals are not geographically confined and are determined to be universal. Political religions are adversaries of nationalism, which places them at odds with national religions or national expressions of universal religions.

The universalism of political religions does not entail full correspondence with the principles of religions from which they descend. Their opponents thus have many sound reasons for calling these ideologies "heretic." Let us briefly summarize features common to all political religions, distinguishing them from "traditional religions."

First, political religions are oriented towards the present. They mix "this world" with "the other world" in a manner that fundamentalists or traditional religions rarely do. Most traditional religions pay little attention to the present,

---

[17] See: Vjekoslav Perica, *Balkan Idols: Religion and Nationalism in Yugoslav States*

because all religiously significant events are thought to have happened in the past or are expected to happen in some unforeseeable future. For example, they suggest that the ideal society can be achieved only after the coming of a Messiah or in the afterlife. Political religions are based on the supposition that the ideal society (the caliphate, the Christian kingdom) can be created on Earth by human efforts. Political religions equate political struggle with martyrdom while genuine religions do not. Progressive Catholicism (liberation theology), for instance, views revolution as a sacral activity and the heroes of revolution as "martyrs," whereas the official Catholic Church resisted this approach by defining those people as "false martyrs."[18]

Second, political religions readily alter dogmas and the corpus of sacred texts. For traditional religions these texts are not only complete and unalterable, but authoritatively interpreted as such. The supporters of political religions, on the other hand, feel free to interpret sacred texts anew and to edit or amend them. They also freely borrow ideas, methods and symbols from the other religions and secular ideologies (such as Communism), resulting in a very eclectic outcome, i.e., political religion itself. This loose approach to dogmas may lead us to incorrectly assume that religious faith itself is not important for the backers of political religions. On the contrary, political religions justify all their political moves by references to religion, although at any given point in time the contents of the sacred corpus may vary.

Third, all political religions have a very specific definition of who belongs to their religion and who does not. Those seen as "us" are automatically understood as something like "*honoris causa* members" of their religious community. If all Muslims are "us," then all "us" are Muslims. For example, Khomeini in his Last Will wrote that "My divine political testament is addressed not only to the great Iranian people; it is a recommendation to all Muslim peoples and the oppressed of the whole world of all nationalities and confessions."[19] Even atheists from the viewpoint of political religion can be considered "Muslims" or "Catholics." For the supporters of political Orthodox

---

[18] (New York: Oxford Univ. Press, 2002), 124.
"III konferentsiia SELAM i papa Ioann Pavel II (obzor)" in *Katolicheskaia tserkov' v sotsial'no-politicheskoi bor'be v stranakh Latinskoi Ameriki: Referativnyi sbornik* (Moskva: INION AN SSSR, 1983), 52.

[19] Velikii Aiatolla Imam Khomeini, *Zaveshchanie* (No publisher. No year), 9-10.

Christianity, for example, all "our friends" are automatically Orthodox, even when they are atheists or agnostics. As for the enemies, they are considered non-Orthodox even if they are Orthodox bishops.

Due to their "heretic" nature political religions are often criticized by scholars for various deviations from "traditional" religion (even in such cases as Hinduism, where, in fact, no traditional version exists). "Ironically, non-Muslim scholars sometimes sound more like mullahs. When faced with new interpretations or applications of Islam, they often critique them from the vantage point of traditional belief and practice," John Esposito mentions.[20] This trend is even more visible in case of Orthodoxy. For example, Aleksandr Verkhovskii does not count Neo-Eurasianism and Orthodox Communism as Ideologies of political Orthodoxy because they are "far from Orthodoxy."[21] It should be admitted, however, that for political religions being "far from" their original versions is a norm.

---

[20] Esposito, *The Islamic Threat*, 205.
[21] Aleksandr Verkhovskii, *Politicheskoe pravoslavie: Russkie pravoslavnye fundamentalisty i natsionalisty. 1995-2001 g.* (Moskva: Tsentr "SOVA", 2003), 9.

II Political Orthodoxy as an Ideology

II.1 General Characteristics and Historical Background

Political Orthodoxy as a whole shares the features of all the other political religions.

Firstly, it is focused on the present, revealing the symbolic meaning of contemporary events and directly connecting "the other" world with "this" one. Backers of political Orthodoxy readily portray ordinary political activists as saints and martyrs (for them it is not a metaphor). For example, Stanislav Tereknov, the leader of *Soiuz Ofitserov* (the Union of Officers), portrays the defense of the parliamentary building in October 1993 as a spiritual battle.[22] Writer Aleksandr Prokhanov designates as saints everyone who sacrificed their lives for the "Russian Elysium," such as heroes of the second World War, Soviet soldiers who took part in overseas conflicts or sailors from the "Kursk" submarine.[23] Modern political conflicts are seen as a direct reflection of the struggle between Good and Evil taking place in the other world.

Secondly, the theorists of political Orthodoxy freely interpret dogmas. When continually referring to Orthodoxy, they are not mentioning its official, Church-approved version, but their own. This, of course, perturbs many scholars. Research on political Orthodoxy often turns out to be a demonstration of various departures from the canonical dogmas. As a result, the xenophobia of political Orthodoxy is often ignored as misinterpretations of dogmas receive more scholarly attention. Its actual dangers are left unattended.

And thirdly, political Orthodoxy maintains a very broad definition of who is Orthodox and who is not. Along with other political religions, it divides the world is into "us" and "them;" all of "us" are automatically considered Orthodox even when they are members of another religious group or even atheists. As Aleksandr Dugin once said, "it is the Kingdom of 'us' and the Church of

---

[22] "Podvig dukhovnyi i podvig ratnyi," *Moskovskii zhurnal* no. 4 (2001): 25.
[23] Aleksandr Prokhanov, "Krasnaia Paskha – Krasnaia Pobeda," *Zavtra*, 6 May 2002.

'us.'"[24] Thus, for instance nearly all versions of political Orthodoxy define Communists as "us," and Catholic Slavs, Muslims or simply (as in Khomeini's Last Will) "the oppressed of the world" are considered "the Orthodox *honoris causa*." At the same time, "them" (e.g., Jews, anti-Communists, liberals, etc.) have no right to call themselves Orthodox even when they are bishops of the Russian Orthodox Church. Even political fundamentalists, who generally do not support this broad vision of Orthodoxy, find groups of allies in the outside world.

Political Orthodoxy embraces numerous ideas; we will focus on those related to Russia's place in the world and to the notion of "the Orthodox world," or "the Orthodox civilization" directed by Russia. These issues are central to contemporary political Orthodoxy as well as to its predecessors; they also let us distinguish between various versions of political Orthodoxy. We estimate the number of such variations as five: political fundamentalism, contemporary Pan-Slavism, Neo-Eurasianism, Orthodox (i.e., Orthodox Christian) Communism and nationalism. All of them (with the exceptions to be discussed later) descend from early Orthodox political ideologies such as Pan-Slavism and Eurasianism.

According to classical Pan-Slavism of the 19th century, represented by Nikolai Danilevskii, Fëdor Tiutchev, Konstantin Leont'ev and others, Russia's mission was to politically unite the Slavic-Orthodox world. "Slavic" and "Orthodox" are synonyms for classical Pan-Slavism. For Pan-Slavists, ethnicity was much less important than religion; since they readily defined all the Orthodox (e.g., Greeks, Romanians) as "Slavs." According to Pan-Slavists, Catholic Slavs (Poles, Czechs) were prepared to return to Orthodoxy at any moment; otherwise they would not have been considered to be among the "Slavic" community.

Pan-Slavist movements were strong in Russian society of the 1870s and elicited some response from the other Slavic peoples of the Ottoman Empire. Nevertheless, soon after the Balkan states had gained independence they professed no wish to form a union with Russia. Orthodoxy became the "national" and even ethnic religion of Greeks, Serbs and others. The ideology of Russian ethnic nationalism, or *chernosotenstvo*, was one of the by-

---

[24] Aleksandr Dugin, *Konspirologiia* (Moskva: Arktogeia, 1993), 130.

products of this dissolution of Pan-Slavism. Although the ideologists of *chernosotenstvo* (especially their elder generation) continued to emphasize their links with Pan-Slavism and Slavophilism of the past century, for them consolidating a Slavic union meant multiplying the domestic enemies of Russia.[25] A Pan-Slavist idea of Russocentrism (that Russia should be the leader of the Orthodox-Slavic Union) devolved into the idea of a homogenous Russian Orthodox state needing no external alliances.

The Eurasianism of the 1920s, which is the second major ideology of political Orthodoxy, positioned Russia between Europe and Asia, opening the way for the reconciliation of Orthodoxy and Islam. Early Eurasian theorists – Pëtr Savtskii, Georgii Vernandskii and Nikolai Trubetskoi, for example, advanced the idea of a Eurasian "continental state," or *empire*, uniting many ethnic and religious groups. Their vision of Orthodoxy was so broad that any difference between "Orthodoxy" and "non-Orthodoxy" disappeared. In fact, all religions originating outside the West were counted as "Orthodoxy." Savitskii wrote that Buddhism and Islam express two different facets of Orthodoxy – its "passivity" and "contemplation" (Buddhism) and, at the same time, its "activity" and "aspiration to transfigure the world" (Islam).[26] The entire Eurasian empire was seen as "potentially Orthodox."

In spite of their disagreements with canonical Orthodoxy, Eurasianists called for the total "Orthodoxization" (*opravoslavlivanie*) of society, which can be compared with the notion of Islamization. This idea implied that religion was to penetrate all spheres of social life, thus becoming a total(itarian) ideology. Eurasianists envisioned a Eurasian continental state as ideocratic, rather than clerical, meaning that the ruling elite should be selected on the basis of its devotion to the ruling idea.[27] This concept of an ideocratic state still predominates Orthodox political thinking in Russia.

Classical Eurasianists could not help sympathizing with the USSR, which seemed to embody the very continental ideocratic state they dreamed of. So-called National Bolshevism, or left-wing Eurasianism, in a way, reflects

---

[25] Sergei Stepanov, *Chernaia sotnia v Rossii (1905-1914 gody)* (Moskva: Izdatel'stvo VZPI, A\O Rosvuznauka, 1992), 22.

[26] Pëtr Savtskii, "Pravoslavie kak osnova ideologii," in Pëtr Savitskii, *Kontinent Evraziia* (Moskva: Agraf, 1997), 28.

the dissolution of the Eurasian movement. It provided further development of the Eurasian ability to neglect religious dogmas in behalf of sustaining and enlarging the state territory. For National Bolsheviks Orthodoxy played no significant role; they were ready to approve any other ideology (Communism, for example) that would allow "the continental empire" to prosper and grow. Thus, National Bolshevism is the first manifestation of now wide-spread ideology of *derzhavnost* (*derzhava* means "great state" or "great power"). For this ideology the first component of the "empire/idea" dyad is much more important than the second one. This ideology contributed to the formation of contemporary Orthodox Communism.

Nearly all above-listed ideologies of Political Orthodoxy descend from Pan-Slavism and classical Eurasianism. The only exceptions are extreme fundamentalism and extreme nationalism. Political fundamentalism is, of course, genetically related to *chernosotenstvo*, which we define as a result of the decay of Pan-Slavism. Most topics discussed by contemporary political fundamentalists were key issues for *chernosotenstvo* as well (i.e., the people's monarchy, the legal recognition of the ROC highest authority, etc.). However, fundamentalism is also directly linked to the ultraconservative trends inside the Orthodox Church resulting from its "shift to the right" after the revolution of 1905. Many concepts of that period have been preserved intact by the most conservative elements of the clergy who emigrated after the 1917 revolution and by some religious dissidents within the Soviet Union.

Some extreme versions of Russian nationalism (or, rather, racism) exist which are unrelated to these two ideologies. Their racism (i.e., Russians were seen as a superior race) and Neo-Paganism had been borrowed from German National Socialism. This ideology had been established by the end of the 1960s. In the mid-1960s *Nauka i religiia* (Science and Religion) magazine began publishing fragments from *The Morning of the Magicians,* a famous book by Louis Pauwels and Jacques Bergier dedicated to Nazi occultism and Neo-Paganism.[28] It was also an era in which new fiction movies about Nazis began to appear which were more realistic than the accusatory films of the

---

[27] Nikolai Trubetskoi, "Ob idee-pravitel'nitse ideokraticheskogo gosudarstva," in Nikolai Trubetskoi, *Nasledie Chingizkhana* (Moskva: Agraf, 2000), 518.

[28] See: Louis Pauwels, Jacques Bergier, "Kakomu bogu poklonialsia Gitler?" *Nauka i religiia* no. 10-11 (1966).

1940s-50s. While these movies did not necessarily romanticize the Nazis, they certainly provoked interest in them.

Of such films a famous TV-series *17 moments of the spring** was the most significant. Unlike films of the previous two decades, the series paid no attention to Nazi atrocities in the occupied countries, showing instead how state offices worked in Berlin under constant air-raids of the Allies. A Soviet agent working in disguise as an SS top-officer is the main character, played by Viacheslav Tikhonov. Posters with Tikhonov wearing SS uniform are still on sale among the other Nazi accessories. Sergei Troitskii, leader of a nationalist rock-band "*Korroziia metalla*" (Corrosion of Metal), gave the following answer to the question about his National Socialist world outlook:

> When I was at the elementary school, the series *17 moments of the spring* was being screened. Naturally, we were all mad for it. We made for ourselves Nazi papers like 'SS-Oberführer Sergei Troitskii, Nordic temper, etc.' What is most interesting [is that] it was not mockery but something subconscious, something deeply in our blood.[29]

We, of course, don't wish to assert that movies about Nazis led to the spread of Nazi ideology in the USSR. This happened as the result of numerous social and economic circumstances. But its specific forms had been primarily determined by the information provided by accusatory films. The influence of *17 moments of the spring* can still be traced in ideologies and activities of many radical nationalist movements. The biography of an extreme nationalist Vladimir Popov located at the web-site of *Russkaia Respublika* organization (The Russian Republic), includes, for instance, the characteristization: "Genuine Russian. Stands well with comrades-in-arms. Merciless to the enemies of the Russian people."[30] This is a direct quotation from the series, where SS-officers are characterized in the same way: "Genuine Aryan. Stands well with comrades-in-arms. Merciless to the enemies of the Reich".

---

* Shot in 1972-73. Director: Tat'iana Lioznova, screenplay: Iulian Semënov, starring: Viacheslav Tikhonov, Leonid Bronevoi, Ekaterina Gradova, et. al.

[29] "Beseda Konstantina Kasimovskogo s Sergeem (Paukom) Troitskim. 1997," http://korrroziametalla.inc.ru/stat/97/kasim.htm, (as of 20 February 2002).

Various white supremacy organizations such as the American religio-political movement "Christian Identity" are, beyond dispute, another source of ideological doctrines and practical strategies adopted by extreme Russian nationalists. This influence from external sources only proves that racist nationalism is not only the most recent of Orthodox political ideologies (although such ideologies retain very little Orthodoxy) but also one which is quite alien to Russian traditions.

---

[30] "Vladimir Popov. Biografiia," http://www.rusrepublik.narod.ru/bio.htm (as of 5 February 2004).

II.2 Five Versions of Political Orthodoxy

Of course, in practice it is not possible to clearly distinguish between various versions of political Orthodoxy; they can be isolated from each other only as Weberian ideal types. In fact, they are ultimately different versions of a single ideology. This issue will be discussed at the end of the chapter. At the moment, however we shall attempt to separate various ideologies from one another on the basis of their vision of Russia's place and mission in the world.

Political Fundamentalism
Political Orthodox fundamentalism is in no way the official ideology of the Russian Orthodox Church, although of all the versions of political Orthodoxy it most closely resembles the viewpoint of the Church. Aleksandr Verkhovskii suggests that "Orthodox fundamentalism" should be distinguished from "normal intra-Church conservatism, which does not intend to change anything within the Church even in the direction of the 'pious old days.'"[31] This is correct in that political fundamentalists are not conservatives. They are true revolutionaries – "revolutionaries from the right."

The initial period of political fundamentalism is associated with the name of Ioann (Ivan Snychev, 1927-1995)[*], Metropolitan of St. Petersburg and Ladoga. During his lifetime the Metropolitan was often accused of being too "politicized." He denied this accusation, responding that: "It is true, peace should, above all, be upheld… But is every sort of peace God-given; is every sort of peace acceptable for an Orthodox?"[32] Metropolitan Ioann even used (with regard to Serbia) a term such as "Orthodox revolution," which is fully analogous to "Islamic revolution."[33] In his fundamentalist vision Ioann was

---

[31] Aleksandr Verkhovskii, Ekaterina Mikhailovskaia, Vladimir Pribylovskii, *Politicheskaia ksenofobiia: Radikal'nye gruppy. Predstavleniia politikov. Rol' tserkvi* (Moskva: Panorama, 1999), 65-66.

[*] There is a persistent whisper that all political articles signed by Ioann have actually been written by his press-secretary Konstantin Dushenov. So far we have no reliable information on this.

[32] Ioann, mitropolit Sankt-Peterburgskii i Ladozhskii, *Bitva za Rossiiu* (Saratov: Privolzhskoe knizhnoe izdatel'stvo; Pravoslavno-patrioticheskoe obshchestvo Georgiia Pobedonostsa, 1993), 107.

[33] "Pravoslavnaia revoliutsiia protiv sovremennogo mira. Interv'iu s mitropolitom Ioannom," *Elementy* no. 4 (1993): 19.

closer to the Russian Orthodox Church Abroad than to the ROC, although his revolutionary ideas alarmed both churches.

Fundamentalists tend to praise religiopolitical violence. Konstantin Dushenov, one of the leaders of *Soiuz Pravoslavnykh Bratstv* (the Union of Orthodox Brotherhoods) and press-secretary of Metropolitan Ioann in 1992-1995 made the following comment regarding the destruction of the WTC on 11 September 2001: "Christian ethics approves any form of righteous struggle against Evil. In this case for me personally the question is open – what is the bigger evil: so-called 'international terrorism' or the delirious policy of the United States?"[34] Political fundamentalists commonly use peaceful methods of political struggle, such as meetings and so-called "worship-ins" (i.e., when a group of people publicly worships in the street in response to some political event). Nevertheless, some of these organizations are paramilitary.

It is unclear whether they practice peacefulness as a matter of principle or whether they simply lack resources for violent acts. It was fundamentalists, for instance, who committed some extensively publicized violent acts, such as the vandalism of an art exhibition entitled "Beware, religion!" in January 2003 at the Moscow Sakharov Museum. It seems that in recent years the number of such violent acts has grown. This issue will be discussed later.

Fundamentalist organizations include *Soiuz Pravoslavnykh Bratstv*, *Soiuz Pravoslavnykh Khorugvenostsev* (the Union of Orthodox Gonfalon-Bearers) lead by Leonid Simonovich, *Pravoslavnoe obshchestvo (bratstvo) "Radonezh"* (Orthodox Society (brotherhood) "Radonezh") lead by Evgenii Nikiforov, *Soiuz Pravoslavnykh Grazhdan* (the Union of Orthodox Citizens), *Soiuz "Khristianskoe Vozrozhdenie"* (the Union "Christian Resurrection") lead by Vladimir Osipov, *National'no-patrioticheskii Front "Pamiat'"* (the National Patriotic Front "Memory", now hardly existing), *Obshchestvennyi komitet "Za nravstvennoe vozrozhdenie Otechestva"* (the Public Committee "For Moral Resurrection of the Fatherland") and various separate Orthodox brotherhoods. Of course, not all of them are equally radical. Some fundamentalist organizations and activists (*Soiuz Pravoslavnykh Grazhdan*, for example) are relatively moderate and able to participate in a civil dialogue.

---

[34] "Est' li istina v chuzhoi vine. Glavnye sobytiia oseni glazami rossiiskikh religioznykh deiatelei," *Novaia gazeta*, 12-14 November 2001.

In spite of its modern vision of the role of religion, church and believers in contemporary world, political fundamentalism, unlike the other versions of Political Orthodoxy, denies modernity altogether. The aspect of modernity which has been most vehemently rejected by political fundamentalism is globalization. It should be emphasized that the anti-globalism of political fundamentalists does not involve advocating the plurality of cultures and civilizations. They don't object to world unity, rather, they object to the fact that it has not been achieved on the basis of Orthodoxy. Globalization is understood by them as the reign of Satan or of the Anti-Christ. All international organizations, including the UN, are considered to be pro-US agents of enslavement (it is interesting that American Protestant fundamentalists consider the same institutions anti-US).

The world is thus seen as hopeless, estranged form God. The Orthodox doctrine, as Father Aleksii (Prosvirin) explained to Gennadii Ziuganov, includes the idea of apostasy, or the alienation of the world from God. He thus stated: "The Church teaches that as a result of gradual rejection of the moral ideals of the Gospel... the world will finally be united under the power of Anti-Christ... This development of victorious Evil will only be stopped by the second coming of Christ the Savior..."[35] Only the Orthodox Kingdom – Russia (sometimes "the Orthodox world" as a whole) – is considered as an exception from this world fated to death.

This opposition of the Orthodox kingdom and the apostate world resembles the Islamic fundamentalist concept of the world of Islam (*dar al-Islam*) and the world of perdition (*dar al-harb*). Fundamentalists place no value on other, non-Orthodox cultures. Their project is not local but global; the globe, however, is limited to the Orthodox Kingdom. All the rest is not "the globe" but the kingdom of the Anti-Christ which is destined to death. Thus, it is not accidental that extreme fundamentalists have much in common with extreme Russian nationalists: they have nearly the same concept of Russia's uniqueness and isolation.

If the idea of world apostasy was the final point for political fundamentalists, they, most likely, would have to settle in compounds to wait for the

---

[35] "Volia k bor'be. Beseda igumena Aleksiia (Prosvirina) s liderom Narodno-Patrioticheskogo Soiuza Rossii G.A.Ziuganovym," in Gennadii Ziuganov, *Vera i vernost'. Russkoe Pravoslavie i problemy vozrozhdeniia Rossii* (Moskva, 1999), 59.

Doomsday. Instead, they prefer political activism, suggesting that the Orthodox world in general and Russia in particular still have a chance to escape the rule of Anti-Christ. This is where the difference between apolitical and political fundamentalistm lies. Political fundamentalists have a political project of rebuilding Russia as the Orthodox Kingdom, the center of Orthodox resistance to disastrous global developments.

No plurality of civilizations becomes possible: God's Kingdom on Earth emerges in the Orthodox region; the rest of the world perishes. Orthodox fundamentalism thus resembles the eschatological doctrines of religious groups such as Aum Shinrikyo. These doctrines imply a global catastrophe or a war after which only the members of the group in question survive to create a new civilization. Nevertheless, no fundamentalist theorist in Russia (unlike some radical Protestants in the US) calls for the annihilation of the doomed world. They imply that it will most likely disappear on its own.

In a way, the Orthodox Kingdom is equivalent to God's Kingdom on Earth. Fundamentalists suggest that Russia may avoid the destiny of the rest of humankind and that it will escape the power of Anti-Christ. This means that God's Kingdom on Earth will be built before the Second Coming, though only on a small piece of the globe. However, as many fundamentalist authors have acknowledged, this idea appears to be a deviation from accepted dogma.[36]

All fundamentalists support the economic autarchy of Russia. Their political ideal is usually described as an "Orthodox people's monarchy with a free state structure based on estates and corporations."[37] No fundamentalist authors have developed a theory of Orthodox revolution or have suggested any practical means by which such a revolution may be implemented.

Most fundamentalists neglect foreign policy topics. This would seem to be the natural outcome of their view of the outside world, which for them is nothing more than a source of danger. "For us, the most important concern is to furnish our own home," Metropolitan Ioann wrote.[38] Fundamentalists would like the Ukraine and Belarus to re-join Russia, though not all of them insist on

---

[36] Aleksandr Kazin, *Poslednee tsarstvo (Russkaia pravoslavnaia tsivilizatsiia)* (Sankt-Peterburg: Izdatel'stvo Spaso-Preobrazhenskogo Valaamskogo monastyria, 1998), 35-36.
[37] Ibid., 133.

rebuilding the USSR. Russia's foreign policy, Ioann thought, should be exclusively based on national interests, remaining isolationist, (or self-sufficient) and fully neutral (i.e., all "geopolitical claims" must be declined).[39] To be sure, some authors support resurrecting (under Russian leadership) the Byzantine Empire. They dream about "bringing back" Constantinople and erecting the cross upon the Saint Sophia Temple. But this is not the position which currently prevails.

Evident unwillingness to pay attention to modern developments reveals that contemporary fundamentalism has directly descended from conservative elements within the ROC of the end of the 19th and the beginning of the 20th century. These ideas have been preserved nearly intact. In the USSR, of course, such ideas could not evolve, since there was no Orthodox intellectual milieu, while abroad the Orthodox community was too small. For many years Russian Orthodox Church Abroad has been the keeper of fundamentalist positions. We should not be surprised, then, that politicised laymen – members of this Church – were prone to idealize the pre-revolutionary period, becoming monarchists and adoring the last Csar's family. The same characteristics (although transformed) are typical of the supporters of political fundamentalism inside Russia who are members of the ROC. Fundamentalists are the strongest supporters of the re-unification of the two churches.

Monarchy is, beyond doubt, the most archaic of all archaic ideas put forward by political fundamentalists. Some of them believe it to be an unachievable ideal, which was the position of Metropolitan Ioann.[40] Others, on the contrary, want monarchy to be immediately reinstated. They, however, fail to name the future monarch. Fundamentalists do not recognize Georgii, a grandson of Vladimir Kirillovich Romanov, as a possible candidate, but so far they have not suggested any other candidate. A famous sculptor and Orthodox activist Viacheslav Klykov has once mentioned that the Romanovs have no rights to the throne and that the monarch should be elected by *Zemskii Sobor* (Country Assembly) from some notorious family, such as the family of

---

[38] Ioann, mitropolit, "Tvoreniem dobra i pravdy," in M.N.Liubomudrov, ed., *Russkii front: sbornik statei o russkom etnose i tsivilizatsii* (Sankt-Peterburg, 1998), 27.
[39] Ibid., 29.
[40] Ioann, "Bitva za Rossiiu," 49.

Marshall Georgii Zhukov.[41] However, this idea appears to be overtly utopian; it is quite unlikely that the author himself was serious about it.

Militant anti-modernism isolates fundamentalists from all possible allies in the outside world, transforming this movement into a "sect." Contacts with Catholics and Protestants, as well as with Muslims, are considered to be sinful. Some authors sharply criticize Eurasianism as "hidden anti-Christianity,"[42] and it is interesting that the most extreme fundamentalists demonstrate a more positive attitude towards Islam than non-Orthodox Christianity. For example, Konstantin Dushenov said in an interview that in spite of the fact that Islam is in many aspects wrong, "should we not consider whether it is possible that Muslim countries, geopolitically speaking, are strategic allies of Russia?"[43] This peculiarity is explained by the fact that the most radical and politicized fundamentalists are typically the furthest from traditional Orthodox conservatism.

Orthodox fundamentalists think of Russians as the Chosen People whose universal mission involves protecting the Orthodox enclave in a world destined to death. For the most radical political fundamentalists the destiny of the Russian people is of special significance because it maintains the right faith *per se*, regardless of the formal religion through which this faith is professed. Political fundamentalists, however, seem to percieve no theological problem here: they equate being Russian with being Orthodox. No one either affirms or denies that there are non-Russian Orthodox Christians.

It is worth mentioning that all fundamentalists support the idea of a "triune" of Russian people uniting Russians, Ukrainians and Byelorussians. Large fundamentalist organizations operate throughout the three Slavic republics of the former USSR. There are also Ukrainian and Byelorussian fundamentalist organizations whose ideology is a mixture of fundamentalism and Pan-Slavism. Such organizations don't see themselves as "foreign" in relation to their Russian counterparts. One of the most well-known organizations of this sort is ZAO *"Pravoslavnaia initsiativa"* (the stock-company "Orthodox Initiative") operating in Belarus (headed by Vladimir Chertovich). Its headquar-

---

[41] Viacheslav Klykov, "Istinnyi svet monarkhii," *Zavtra* no. 37 (September 1996).
[42] See, for example: Svetlana Flegonova, "Atlantida i grad Kitezh," in *Russkii krest* (Sankt-Peterburg: Bel'veder, 1994), 40; Kazin, *Poslednee tsarstvo,* 25.
[43] "Est li istina v chuzhoi vine".

ters boldly displays the slogan: "The Orthodox of the world, unite!" *ZAO "Pravoslavnaia initsiativa"* is among the strongest supporters of president Lukashenko and of the Union of Russia and Belarus.

In spite of their closeness to the Russian Orthodox Church, some fundamentalists profess that Russian (and only Russian) Paganism had some positive features. "Moving towards the true God, Russian people firmly rejected the brutal cults and rituals of the ancient faiths... Attracted by the light and the good the Russian people came to the idea of monotheism before adopting Christianity," fundamentalist author Oleg Platonov writes.[44] He thinks that before the Baptism Russians worshipped not gods, like common Pagans, but the moral foundations of existence.[45] It seems impossible to clearly ascertain when fundamentalists are admiring Russians because they have preserved Orthodoxy and when they are admiring Russians simply as they are.

In general, Orthodox fundamentalists suggest that the idea of "the Russian people" is to be understood as more of a cultural community than a community of blood relations. Metropolitan Ioann, in particular, emphasized that "the Church does not discriminate among its children on the basis of nationality."[46] In recent years, however, the most extreme fundamentalists seem to have departed from this loyalty to the non-Russian Orthodox. Konstantin Dushenov in his newspaper *Rus' Pravoslavnaia* (The Orthodox Rus) even objects to the ordination of Orthodox Jews. "I am sure that any Jew who has candidly rejected the unholyness of Yids and has candidly repented of the horrible crime of his tribesmen, will not feel offended," Dushenov writes.[47] Moreover, fundamentalists have recently demonstrated some symptoms of so-called "caucasophobia" by not discriminating between Orthodox and non-Orthodox "Caucasians."

This loss of Orthodox universalism naturally leads to the rejection of the traditional idea of Russia's universal mission to save the whole of humankind.

---

[44] "Iazychestvo," in *Sviataia Rus': entsiklopedicheskii slovar' russkoi tsivilisatsii* (Moskva: Entsiklopediia russkoi tsivilizatsii, 2000), 1013.

[45] Oleg Platonov, "Russkaia tsivilizatsiia: poniatie, vozrast, dukhovnye parametry," in *Russkii front*, 98.

[46] Ioann, mitropolit, "Tvortsy kataklizmov," in *Russkii front*, 232.

[47] Konstantin Dushenov, "Revniteli v ermolkakh," *Rus' Pravoslavnaia* no. 73 (July 2003).

Many extreme Orthodox fundamentalists have openly converted to the nationalist position, abandoning the idea of Russia as the Third Rome that preoccupied Russian Orthodox political thought of the last four centuries. Denying the Third Rome concept appears to be a significant step for fundamentalists.

The attitude of fundamentalists living in Russia towards Communism is rather dubious. On the one hand, as church-goers familiar with Orthodox dogmas, they must reject Communist ideology. On the other hand, most non-émigré authors refuse to conceive of the entire communist period as a black hole. They, following to some extent the Eurasianists and even the National Bolsheviks, consider the Soviet empire as a version of their Orthodox Kingdom. Dushenov's *Rus' Pravoslavnaia* was initially an inset of a communist newspaper *Sovetskaia Rossiia* (Soviet Russia).

Some fundamentalists see nearly no difference between the Orthodox Kingdom and the Soviet empire. Thus they join the supporters of Orthodox Communism while distancing themselves significantly from the official position of the church (not to mention "pure" fundamentalism). For example, Nikolai Lisovoi, a poet, scholar and nationalist writer, said in his presentation delivered at the Moscow-Crimea Conference on East Christian Civilization in the Global World (18-22 September 2000), that Orthodoxy is not separable from the empire regardless of the latter's relation to Christianity[48]. This is apparently the idea of *derzhavnost'* per se. Consistent fundamentalists reject Communism altogether. Such people, however, are as a rule either émigrés or former religious dissidents.

Contemporary Pan-Slavism
Modern Pan-Slavists uphold their predecessors' ideal of a Slavic-Orthodox world headed by Russia and coexisting with the other civilizations. Unlike political fundamentalists, Pan-Slavists place some value on other civilizations and acknowledge their right to exist. Most Pan-Slavists view Russo-Slavic, or Slavic-Orthodox civilization as a local one. Evgenii Troitskii even mentions

---

[48] See: Sergei Antonenko, "Trevoga i otvetstvennost' za sud'bu tsivilizatsii," *Moskva* no. 12 (2000): 143.

that universalistic concepts are "vulgar."[49] This positive view of other civilizations is a distinguishing feature of Pan-Slavism.

Pan-Slavists are not conservative; neither do they support the full encapsulation of Slavic civilization or its partition from the other world. Unlike political fundamentalists, they don't think that the world is evil and apostate. Even Western civilization is considered an adversary only because it (according to Pan-Slavists) initiated attacks on the Slavic-Orthodox world.

It may be said that Pan-Slavists think of regionalization as of the means by which the negative impact of globalization may be diminished. Kim Smirnov, rector of the International Slavic University, and his co-author Ol'ga Kataeva envision the All-Slavic Economic Union where "every Slavic country will have its own currency for domestic use and the new, convertible, ruble will be used for accounting outside the Union."[50] It seems that such a Union would, if realized, be an improved version of the Council for Economic Cooperation.

Unlike their predecessors of the 19th century, contemporary Pan-Slavists must admit that some Orthodox people happen to be non-Slavic while some Slavs are non-Orthodox. For them Slavic unity is more important than a universal profession of Orthodoxy. "The attempts to reject the very opportunity of Slavic-Russian unity or the reality of the Slavic-Russian civilization under the pretext of the existence of several confessions among Slavic nations are invalid," Troitskii writes.[51] He points out that many great civilizations have been multiconfessional and that there are no obstacles to uniting Orthodox, Catholic or Muslim Slavs. "The fact that I am a Slav is more important that my being Orthodox, Catholic, Protestant, atheist or Pagan," Boleslav Tejkovski, a Polish Pan-Slavist, says.[52] This evident priority of ethnicity over religion differentiates Pan-Slavism from political fundamentalism, which insists that Catholic Slavs are heretics.

---

[49] Evgenii Troitskii, "Kontseptsiia russko-slavianskoi tsivilizatsii," in Evgenii Troitskii, ed., *Russko-slavianskaia tsivilizatsiia: istoricheskie istoki, sovremennye geopoliticheskie problemy, perspektivy slavianskoi vzaimnosti* (Moskva, 1998), 21.
[50] Kim Smirnov, Ol'ga Kataeva, *Istoricheskii vyzov slavianskomu soobshchestvu* (Moskva, 2000), 123.
[51] Evgenii Troitskii, "Pravoslavie i slavianskoe edinenie," *Mir Bozhii* no. 2 (1999): 32.
[52] See: *Russko-slavianskaia tsivilizatsiia*, 254.

There are signs that the focus of Pan-Slavist ideology in its contemporary interpretation has blurred so that, in many respects, it has begun to resemble Eurasianism. Thus, one may clearly distinguish between Pan-Slavist writers moving towards Russian nationalism and those preferring so-called "Slavic Eurasianism."

The terms "Slavic Eurasian Union" and "Slavic Eurasianism" were introduced by Boris Iskakov (Dr.habilitat in Economics), the president of *Mezhdunarodnaia Slavianskaia Akademiia* (the International Slavic Academy). He insists that "the concept of Slav-Eurasianism is thoroughly different from the concepts of Eurasianism and Pan-Slavism…. For example, 'Eurasianism' diminishes the role of Slavs, while 'Slavic fundamentalists' ignore the fact of Russia's deep penetration into the East…"[53] Iskakov admits that "Slavic fundamentalists" criticize him, but in his own opinion all Eurasian nations are "partly Slavic."[54] This position is apparently not purely Pan-Slavist, although Iskakov's reputation among Pan-Slavists is firmly established.

Generally speaking, Pan-Slavists place value not only on Islam but on Hinduism. They actively borrow concepts from so-called Russian Cosmism, an ideology that has been rejected by the church as a heresy, and see nothing objectionable in the occult teaching of the Roerichs, which has been condemned by the church as "Satanism." Most contemporary Pan-Slavists stress that their project of uniting all Slavs is only a part of a bigger (Eurasian) geopolitical enterprise. This idea was expressed, for example, by Boleslav Tejkovski in his presentation at the IX *Vsemirnyi Russkii Narodnyi Sobor* (World Russian People's Assembly) in Moscow in March 2005.

The basic problem of contemporary Pan-Slavism, as well as that of its predecessor in the 19th century, is its unwillingness to accept that there is no single "Slavic," not to mention "Orthodox Slavic," civilization. Using such terms as "Slavic community," "Slavic world" or "Slavic Orthodox civilization" implies an entity that not only understands its unity, but also acts at the international arena as an integrated force. For example, Smirnov and Kataeva write about "the Slavic community" consisting of 12 Slavic states.[55] The lead-

---

[53] Quoted in: Troitskii, "Kontseptsiia russko-slavianskoi tsivilizatsii," 66.
[54] Boris Iskakov, "Super-etnos na pereput'e," http://stepanov-plus.ru/literator/interviews/iskakov.htm (as of 5 March 2005).
[55] Smirnov, Kataeva, *Istoricheskii vyzov slavianskomu soobshchestvu*, 4.

ers and populations of these states would most likely be surprised to learn that they are members of some "community."

The "Slavic world" of Pan-Slavists exists not at the level of states, but at the level of non-governmental Pan-Slavist movements and private contacts between Pan-Slavists from various countries. This "Slavic civilization," of course, has no significant political influence. Due to this fact contemporary Pan-Slavists have to speak about both the "Slavic world" as an integrated community and about an unfinished "Slavic project."[56] Moreover, they admit that the Slavic world, at best, consists of three countries: Russia, Belarus and Serbia.

Serbia plays (or, rather, played) a significant role in the political mythology of contemporary Pan-Slavism, not only as a natural ally of Russia, but also as a sanctuary of truly Slavic and truly Orthodox values now lost by Russia itself. Nikolai Kokukhin writes that "Russia and Serbia constitute an organic whole. One can say that Serbia is a small Russia, while Russia is a big Serbia."[57] Nataliia Narochnitskaia speaks in the same manner: "Russia and the Balkans represent the Orthodox world, the post-Byzantine region as distinguished from Western civilization... Russia is its potential strength, and the Balkans – first of all, Serbia – its fortress in the West."[58]

The existence of Serbia (or, "the Orthodox Serbia") is for Pan-Slavists an indirect proof of a single Slav Orthodox world which exists in opposition to the West. The unified actions of the Western world against Milosevic's Yugoslavia and Radovan Karadzic's Republika Srpska are events to which Pan-Slavists frequently refer in support of their theory of the confrontation between "Slavdom" and the "Latin World" (working in cooperation with the Muslim world represented by Bosnian Muslims and Kosovo Albanians).

Il'ia Chislov, the Chairman of the Society of Russo-Serbian Friendship, presents the Orthodox world as a political entity with common interests and policies. "Orthodox Serbia remains the main barrier obstructing hostile European forces, which are attempting to conquer the Balkans so as to make

---

[56] Ibid., 82.
[57] Nikolai Kokukhin, "Belyi Angel. Rasskaz o palomnicheskom puteshestvii v Serbiiu i Chernogoriiu," in *Nad Vostokom i Zapadom. S liubov'iu o Serbii* (Moskva: Rarog, 1999), 149, 223.

them another foothold against Russia," he writes.[59] Pan-Slavists think that NATO's Yugoslavian operations confirm their worst suspicions, considering them to be evidence of aggression against Orthodoxy designed by the West.

It is no surprise that Pan-Slavist ideas are popular with, for instance, Russian Balkan Studies scholars, Slavic languages specialists and translators of the Serbian language. "It is now clear that the US strategic plan, as implemented by NATO, is directed first of all against Russia. But Yugoslavia could have become an obstacle to this," states Elena Gus'kova (Dr. habilitat in History), one of the leading Balkan Studies scholars in Russia.[60] When Aleksandr Krutov, host of the TV-program *Russkii dom* (Russian Home) said that the West had organized a massacre in a "Christian Orthodox country" and that "Orthodox Yugoslavia had suffered military aggression," his guest Gus'kova supported him: "It would be great if we could have helped the Serbs to defend themselves by providing them with modern weapons."[61]

Pan-Slavist enthusiasm regarding Serbia sharply increased in 1999 when Yugoslavia obtained permanent observer status at the diet of the Union of Russia and Belarus. On 12 April 1999 the Yugoslavian diet voted to join the Union (with 6 abstainers and no votes against the measure). Responding to this decision the State Duma of Russia (dominated, in that period, by the opposition) had voted for immediate initiation of all the respective legal procedures. This was the heyday of Pan-Slavism. Pan-Slavist sentiments reached their peak after the beginning of NATO's operation in Kosovo in March 1999. An international Pan-Slavist movement has organized a so called "International public tribunal on NATO crimes in the former Yugoslavia" headed by Professor Mikhail Kuznetsov (Dr.habilitat in Law). It was initiated by the Fourth Extraordinary Congress of *Vseslavianskii Sobor* (the All-Slavic Assembly) on May 23, 1999 in evident connection with Kosovo events. This tribunal has found the US and NATO guilty in crimes against peace and humanity.

---

[58] Nataliia Narochnitskaia, "Bor'ba za postvizantiiskoe prostranstvo," *Nash sovremennik* no. 4 (1997): 232.

[59] Il'ia Chislov, "Na strazhe Evropy," *Nash sovremennik* no. 6 (1999): 176.

[60] Elena Gus'kova, *Istoriia iugoslavskogo krizisa (1990-2000)* (Moskva: Izdatel' A. Solov'ëv, 2001), 691.

[61] "'Ikh otets – diavol': Iz teleperedachi 'Russkii Dom' 25 marta 1999 goda," *Russkii dom* no. 5 (1999): 2, 3.

The "loss" of Serbia that resulted from the displacement of Milosevic (presented in *Zavtra* newspaper as a "hero of the Slavs") was a shock for Pan-Slavists. Most Pan-Slavists think that Slavic countries of pro-Western orientation betray Orthodoxy and Slavdom. Nevertheless, they still hope that Socialists may return to power in Serbia and make it once again an Orthodox kin-country.

Belarus is another country important for Pan-Slavist mythology: it is the only state where Pan-Slavism is contained in state ideology. *Belaruskaia dumka* (Byelorussian Thought), a journal founded by the presidential administration, is one of the centres of Byelorussian Pan-Slavism. Contents and external features of this journal remarkably resemble oppositional journals in Russia such as *Mockva* and *Nash Sovremennik*. In April 2004 *Mezhdunarodnyi Soiuz Slavianskikh Zhurnalistov* (the International Union of Slavic Journalists) awarded the editor-in-chief of *Belaruskaia dumka* Vladimir Velichko with a Letter of Honor and the medal of the "True Sons of Russia" (*Rossii vernye syny*). "From the initial days of its existence, the journal *Belaruskaia dumka* has been devoted to the idea of Pan-Slavism, meaning the consolidation of consanguineous Slavic brothers," an editorial article states[62]. Terms like "East Slavic civilization" or the "East Slavic world" are commonly used by the authors of the monthly.

Pan-Slavism is one of the pillars of contemporary state ideology in Belarus. The task of working out such an ideology was set by Aleksandr Lukashenko in the beginning of 2003. In his speech, delivered on 27 March 2003 at the Seminar on the topic of enhancing ideological work he mentioned that Russia has ceased to be the centre of East Eurasian (he also calls it "East Slavic" and "East European") civilization. Therefore, Lukashenko concluded, Belarus should become the spiritual leader of this civilization. "Belarus should attract all of the patriotically oriented forces of our whole Fatherland, which is the post-Soviet area. Here people should establish grounds which are free of neo-Liberal terror and attacks," the president of Belarus said.[63] Certainly, *Vseslavianskii S"ezd* (the All-Slavic Congress) to be held in Minsk on 1-3 July 2005 is intended to provide such grounds.

---

[62] *Belaruskaia dumka* no. 4 (2004): 7.
[63] *O sostoianii ideologicheskoi raboty i merakh po eë sovershenstvovaniiu* (Minsk: Akademiia Upravleniia pri Prezidente RB, 2003), 21.

The idea that Aleksandr Lukashenko should become the leader of the Slavic movement and, in the end, the leader of the All-Slavic State, is widely accepted among Pan-Slavists. Pan-Slavist in its origins, the slogan "Lukashenko instead of Putin" dominates the whole spectrum of political Orthodoxy.

There are not very many purely Pan-Slavist organizations at the moment: most of them combine Pan-Slavism with nationalist, fundamentalist or Eurasian ideas. Among them are the following organizations: *Mezhdunarodnyi Slavianskii Komitet* (the International Slavic Committee), *Vseslavianskii Sobor, Mezhdunarodnaia Slavianskaia Akademiia, Slavianskii Komitet Rossii* (the Slavic Committee of Russia), *Slavianskaia Partiia Rossii* (the Slavic Party of Russia), *Slavianskoe Dvizhenie Rossii* (the Slavic movement of Russia), *Grazhdanskii komitet v podderzhku Soiuza Rossii i Belorussii* (the civil committee for promoting the Union of Russia and Belarus), *Mezhdunarodnoe obshchestvo kinematografistov slavianskikh i pravoslavnykh narodov* (the International Community of Film-makers of the Slavic and Orthodox peoples), *Mezhdunarodnyi fond slavianskoi pis'mennosti i kul'tury* (the International Foundation of Slavic Writing and Culture) and various regional and local organizations.

Pan-Slavist movements of Russia interact with similar organizations from the other Slavic states, including "Catholic" ones. Pan-Slavist lobbies exist in all Slavic states, not only in Belarus, Serbia and the Ukraine where they are relatively influential. *Vseslavianskii S"ezd* in Prague (June 1998) has gathered delegates from eleven Slavic countries (Belarus, Bulgaria, Macedonia, Poland, Russia, Slovakia, Slovenia, the Ukraine, Croatia, the Czech republic, Yugoslavia and representatives of German Serbs and the Ruthenians). The next *Vseslavianskii S"ezd*, held in Moscow in April 2001, gathered Slavs from twelve countries. Many all-Slavic cultural events were featured and some of them emphasized pan-Slavist ideology. For example, the International Film Forum *Zolotoi Vitiaz'* (Golden Knight) is regularly held under the slogan: "For moral Christian ideals. For exalting the human soul."

Most supporters of Pan-Slavism in the non-CIS Slavic countries are socialists who regret the collapse of the world socialist system. They also object to their countries' joining NATO and the European Union. For example, Boleslav Tejkovski, the chair of the Polish organizing committee "All-Slavic Union

'98" and of the Polish Slavic Committee, said at the Prague Congress that Poland "should not integrate with the European Union and NATO, which will disunite us with Slavdom and place us at odds with the Slavic countries."[64] The Chairmen of the Congress, Czech Professor Brzetislav Hvala, characterized the emergence of pro-Soviet regimes in Eastern Europe as a "legitimate uprising of Slavic forces headed by the Soviet Union" aimed at establishing a people's democracy and building fundamental socialism.[65] Apparently, East European Pan-Slavists represent certain population groups within their states. While they may be in the minority, these groups should not be disregarded.

Nevertheless, considering the weakness of Pan-Slavism outside Russia, it is no surprise that it has become not so much an ideology of "Slavism" as of Russian nationalism. Sometimes it merges with political fundamentalism, becoming an augmented version in which not only Russia, but the whole "Slavic world" represents the Orthodox Kingdom; in other instances, it is transformed into an outspoken form of Russian racism. Most Pan-Slavists define ethnicity group in terms of culture rather than by means of physical characteristics. "The Russian ideal is not narrowly ethnocentric, but unifying, particularly with regard to our Slavic brothers," Troitskii writes.[66] Meanwhile, the theoretical equivalence of "Russian" and "Orthodox" may manifest its self in an ideology of Russian racism. In its advanced forms it may reject Orthodoxy in favor of Neo-Paganism. In any event, most Pan-Slavists have a positive attitude towards the Pagan past of the Slavs.

Neo-Eurasianism

Eurasianism is perceptibly the most viable of all existing versions of political Orthodoxy. Its orientation towards a union with Asia and the Islamic world as well as its broad interpretation of Orthodoxy permits the consolidation of nearly all non-Western religions under this name. Furthermore, all of these features of traditional Eurasianism have become even more pronounced in its contemporary form. Eurasianism does not turn a blind eye to contemporary demographic and political changes, and in orienting Russia towards union

---

[64] See: *Russko-slavianskaia tsivilizatsiia*, 252.
[65] Ibid., 242.
[66] Evgenii Troitskii, "Kontseptsiia russko-slavianskoi tsivilizatsii," 129.

with the Islamic world, India and China, it allows "the Orthodox civilization" to find allies in the developing world. Unlike Pan-Slavism or fundamentalism, Eurasianism contributes to the consolidation of ethnic groups within Russia and into the integration of Russia and the CIS countries. This ideology thus offers a seemingly realistic solution for the most substantial problems facing the region.

This is most likely the reason why Eurasianism has enlisted so many supporters among respectable Russian scholars and moderate politicians (not to mention radical politicians). Eurasianism is important, not because it has been immediately influential, but because its influence has been growing steadily. Numerous sources such as media articles, political speeches and analytical works by political scientists with established reputations confirm that in recent years Eurasianist ideas have migrated from the margins of the political spectrum to its center. While in the beginning of the 1990s such ideas could only be found in marginal magazines published on cheap paper at the expense of authors, nowadays Eurasianism is constantly praised by many politicians and governmental officials as the only ideology appropriate for Russia (although it is possible that not all of these people share a common understanding of Eurasianism).

For example, Akhmat Kadyrov, the president of the Chechen Republic (assassinated in 2004), once said that "The Russian national idea is best stated in terms of Eurasian ideology, and through Eurasianism it becomes acceptable for the Chechen Republic."[67] Most likely, Eurasianist influence is responsible for an unexpected maneuver made by Vladimir Putin on 16 October 2003. During his visit to Malaysia he offered the Islamic world the unification of its "financial, technological and human resources" with Russia and for the first time mentioned the possibility of Russia's membership in the Organization of Islamic Conference.[68] This sudden appeal to the Islamic world may have been the result of a disenfranchisement with the West as well as a wish to strengthen the unity of peoples inside Russia.

---

[67] Quoted in: Il'ia Maksakov, "Evraziistvo na iuge Rossii: ubezhdeniia i somneniia: severokavkazskie lidery o novom techenii v rossiiskoi politike," *Nezavisimaia gazeta*, 8 June 2001.

[68] Quoted in: Evgenii Verlin, "Pragmaticheskoe izmerenie islama," *NG-religii*, 5 November 2003.

Most Neo-Eurasian intellectual projects have been initiated by Aleksandr Dugin. *Obshchestvenno-politicheskoe dvizhenie "Evraziia"* (the sociopolitical movement "Eurasia") emerged in April 2001. In May 2002 it was transformed into a party and on 20 November 2003 ultimately took the form of *Mezhdunarodnoe Evraziiskoe Dvizhenie* (the International Eurasian Movement). As a counterweight to Dugin's radicalism *Evraziiskaia Partiia – Soiuz Patriotov Rossii* (the Eurasian Party – the Union of Patriots of Russia), was created under the leadership of Abdul-Vakhed Niiazov (a converted Muslim born as Vadim Medvedev), who before March 2001 was a member of a pro-governmental parliamentary faction *Edinstvo* (Unity). This party maintains a moderate vision of Eurasianism limited to the idea that Russia's unique geographic position makes it a bridge between Europe and Asia.

Pronounced orientation towards the unification of Orthodoxy and Islam is a distinguishing feature of Neo-Eurasianism. Here Neo-Eurasiansists are much more radical than the founders of the ideology. This, of course, reflects the growing strength of the Islamic world. Dugin accuses the first Eurasians of some residual Orthodox arrogance because they thought of Islam as of something like underdeveloped Orthodoxy. He writes that "the Orthodox Church and traditional (Shi'a, Hanafi, Sufi, in one word – Eurasian) Islam are full-fledged and genuine Eastern traditions, while Protestantism and the Wahhabist heresy are parodies, substitutes, resulting from the apocalyptic distortion of pure spirituality."[69] The idea is that all "traditional" religions easily coexist, while their "profane," degraded versions conflict.

According to Dugin, tradition is a primeval and true world outlook that has been transformed and distorted throughout history. All worldviews based on tradition are religious and never put human beings at the center of the Universe. Dugin thereby does not talk about the conflict between Orthodoxy, Islam or Buddhism, for instance, or about "the clash of civilizations" in the Huntingtonian sense. Instead, he focuses on conflict between various deviations from tradition. The West is the only civilization which has not descended from "real" tradition, and that is why all traditional religions should unite against it.

---

[69] Aleksandr Dugin, "Tret'ia stolitsa Evrazii," in *Evraziiskaia ideia i sovremennost'* (Moskva: RUDN, 2002), 237.

There is, according to Dugin, "traditional" and "profane" Orthodoxy. The latter is represented by the Constantinople Patriarchate "embodying Orthodoxy strictly separated from political implementation."[70] It is a liberal Orthodoxy that has forgotten its universal mission and has come to respect a pluralism of opinions and world outlooks. Islam is also divided. In his article "Islam against Islam,"[71] which has become known far beyond Eurasian circles, Aleksandr Dugin distinguishes at least four different ideological models. The first model is represented by Wahhabism, "an extremely moralistic, puritanical, extremist form of the Arabic Sunna," lacking any spiritual dimension and based on blind adherence to formal rules. It dominates Saudi Arabia and other oil monarchies. The second model Dugin calls "enlightened Islamism," represented by some Westernized and secularized states (Pakistan, Egypt, Turkey, et al.), which professes a kind of "souvenier Islam." These two models are essentially pro-Western (Atlantic-oriented).

The third model is the Iranian Shi'a, a spiritual Islam, where formal rules are of less significance. Sufism, according to Dugin, also adjoins this model. He writes that "pro-Iranian, Shi'a and Sufi branches of contemporary Islam can be generically called 'Eurasian' or 'continental' in the geopolitical sense. As a rule a radical dislike of the West or Atlanticism is their common denominator..."[72] The fourth model is Islamic socialism (mostly in the form of Ba'athism) represented by Iraq (before the fall of Saddam Hussein, of course), Libya, Lebanon and others. Models three and four are what Dugin calls "Eurasian" Islam. He also describes Tatar Islam (Sunni) as Eurasian defining it as "a typical variation of Eurasian continental Islam."[73] Properly speaking, Islam in Tatarstan should rather be characterized as Westernized, though Aleksandr Dugin definitely does not want to disrupt relations between the peoples of Russia, as is reflected in his classification of Islam.

The task of Russia is to establish contacts with the Eurasian varieties of Islam. Practically speaking, this means promoting contacts with Iran, which is considered to be a bastion of Eurasian Islam ("the Moscow-Tehran axis"). In

---

[70] "Geopolitika pravoslaviia," *Elementy* no. 8 (1996\1997): 43 (later reproduced in Aleksandr Dugin's book *Osnovy geopolitiki*).

[71] Aleksandr Dugin, "Islam protiv islama," http://www.arctogaia.com/public/dug7.htm (as of 14 July 2000).

[72] Ibid.

our opinion, the appreciation of inner differentiations within the Islamic world is a strength of contemporary Eurasianism, attracting many supporters from academic and political circles.

The concept of empire (or "continental state") remains in the focus of contemporary Eurasianism. This concept has no monarchical connotation stressing, instead, "the unity in diversity" of many ethnic and confessional groups having some common spiritual ground. The most important aspect of empire is not its territorial limits or administrative organization, but its sacral nature as opposed to rude earthliness of nation-states preoccupied with their self-interests.

It is hard to say whether Eurasianists place any value on the other, non-Orthodox, civilizations or whether they wish to work out a universal ideology. It seems that we should not be deceived by their pronounced formal respect for other cultures. Most of them (excepting the most moderate) do not aim at constructing "a multipolar world." The Eurasian project is not local; it is universal, meaning that it intends to spread Eurasian ideology throughout the whole world. For example, Geidar Dzhemal', an ideologist of Muslim Eurasianism, defines the concept of "dialogue between civilizations" put forward by Khatami, the president of Iran, as a repetition of the Soviet idea of peaceful coexistence between the two systems and as a program of pacification advanced by the "Big Satan."[74] "Real struggle against mondialism may be conducted only with the help of another mondialism, with a completely opposite sign and orientation," Dzhemal' wrote.[75] An article entitled "Geopolitics of Eurasianism," located at the web-site of the Byzantine-Eurasian Club "Catechon" openly states that Russia should "unite all Eurasian countries and ultimately all countries of the world into a single geopolitical block on the basis of ideocracy."[76]

The Eurasian political project, in fact, equates the Orthodox world with the "non-West" (or, "the rest," using Huntington's terminology). All Islamic and potentially Islamic countries (such as Turkey), peoples and communities are

---

[73] Dugin, "Tret'ia stolitsa Evrazii," 236.
[74] Geidar Dzhemal', "Vsemirnyi tupik," *Zavtra*, 12 March 2002.
[75] Geidar Dzhemal', "Rossiia i islam," http://www.heydar-djemal.org.ru/Stat/stat0003.htm (as of 20 June 2000).

considered "the Orthodox *honoris causa*." India and China also become "Orthodox," due to their probable anti-Western position. Hidden supporters of Orthodoxy may be found even within the Western world. Assuming that Jesus was the first Communist (see *Orthodox Communism* below) one automatically counts all socialists and communists (from remaining socialist states like Cuba, Vietnam and North Korea to left-wing movements in the West) as among the Orthodox. "All left-wing and revolutionary theories and movements express a certain sacral and traditional essence to the extent that they are oriented against the paradigm of the Modern, the West and the Capital," "Catechon" states.[77] Among "potential" or "hidden" Orthodox believers not only the left but some right-wing movements are mentioned.[78]

A peculiar version of Eurasiansim has been presented by Lieutenant General (in reserve) Leonid Shershnev, the president of *Fond natsional'noi i mezhdunarodnoi bezopasnosti* – "NIMB," which in Russian means "nimbus" (the Fund of National and International Security). He advocates the union of peoples and states in a single civilization, composed of "Russia, India, China and Iran" (RICI). RICI makes, according to Shershnev, a magical square of civilizations. These nations, according to him, should confront the global evil empire (the U.S., Japan, Europe and Israel) and "voluntarily take responsibility for preserving life on earth and protecting the world civilization."[79] Shershnev also puts special emphasize on the fact that RICI sounds (in the Russian language also looks) like the name of the mongoose Rikki-Tikki-Tavi from Kipling's fairy tail. This "little, weak, but spiritual and brave mongoose fights down a huge mighty cobra" – a pattern to be repeated by the RICI in its determination to defeat the global snake.[80]

We have already mentioned the inescapable fusion of Eurasianism and Pan-Slavism. This has resulted in the growing importance of Belarus for contemporary Eurasian ideology. "Eurasian Belarus" is one of the "special pro-

---

[76] "Geopolitika evraziistva," http://www.katehon.narod.ru/geopolint.html (as of 20 November 2003).
[77] "Genealogiia doktriny Vizantistsko-Evraziiskogo Kluba," http://www.katehon.narod.ru/geneology.html (as of 20 November 2003).
[78] Aleksandr Dugin, *Osnovy geopolitiki* (Moskva: Arktogeia, 1997), 369.
[79] Leonid Shershnev, "Tsivilizatsionnyi soiuz Rossiia-Indiia-Kitai-Iran," *Bezopasnost'* no. 7-8 (2002): 10.
[80] Ibid.,18.

jects" at the Eurasian Internet-portal (www.evrazia.org). The unification of Russia and Belarus is seen as a crucial point in the process of building the Eurasian Union. It is interesting that Eurasian ideas constantly reemerge in the speeches of Aleksandr Lukashenko and in the articles being published by Byelorussian state ideologists (including the ones from *Belaruskaia dumka*).

It seems that the Eurasian Union, uniting not only CIS countries, but also Serbia, Greece, Iran, India, Iraq, Syria and Libya,[81] is only a stage on the way towards transforming Eurasianism into a global ideology (perhaps under another name). Universalism is particularly apparent in Aleksandr Panarin's book *Orthodox Civilization in the Global World*, in spite of its misleading name (in the sprit of Huntington-Toynbee). Although Panarin called himself a Eurasianist, his vision of the future is much broader than any of those which have been described as Eurasianist geopolitical utopias.

Panarin rejects the fundamentalist project of separating Russian (or Slavic) civilization from the global world. On the contrary, he considers Orthodoxy a "universal project" and "a universal historical alternative."[82] What is meant is neither "multipolarity," nor a dialogue of civilizations:

> Our discourse of the Orthodox civilization has nothing to do with the paradigm of Danilevskii, Toynbee or Huntington. By Orthodox civilization we do not mean a specific cultural and historical entity juxtaposed to other such entities and doomed to clash with them because of its specificity. We do not mean "a conflict among civilizations" but rather a conflict of humankind with history...[83]

Panarin's vision of the future implies universal realization of the "Orthodox project": "when we speak about the Orthodox civilization we mean a historical project whose mission is...to prepare for the complete replacement of contemporary parasitic civilization."[84] This means that one global project – Western liberalism – is to be replaced with another one – Orthodoxy (or "bad mondialism" with "good mondialism"). Panarin does not explain in detail the

---

[81] See: Aleksandr Dugin, "Izoliatsiia," *Zavtra* no. 50 (December 1998).
[82] Aleksandr Panarin, *Pravoslavnaia tsivilizatsiia v global'nom mire* (Moskva: Algoritm, 2002), 188.
[83] Ibid., 188.

exact characteristics of the Orthodox project, but one may suggest that it opposes the Western project, which is based on a free market, liberal democracy and hedonism. Panarin considered the Western project as racist or Fascist because, in his opinion, its social structure fundamentally involves the segregation of the rich and the poor. Here one may see a link between Eurasianism and Orthodox Communism.

The universality of the Eurasian project is not self-evident. Unlike, for example, Communists, Eurasianists have no cohesive portrayal of the future world order. It is not clear what will happen with various religions in the event that their project is realized world-wide. Most Eurasianists fervently reject the idea of the fusion of all religions. Nevertheless, one may conclude from their statements that "genuine," or traditional, religions need no fusion since, in some sense (it is not clear, in which) they are *already* an organic whole.

Aleksandr Dugin's vision of unity between Orthodoxy and Islam is rather vague, because he stresses that this unity is not dogmatic, but geopolitical, stylistic and sacral: "…traditional Islam is valuable for Eurasia not as "underdeveloped Orthodoxy" but as an orthodox, or righteous, branch of Islam. On the other hand, there is no tradition that would be closer to orthodox Islam than Orthodoxy its self."[85] Dugin admits that both Islam and Orthodoxy claim the universal validity of their dogmas, yet he postpones any doctrinal conflict to the period after their common victory over the Western civilization: "the eschatological dispute between Islam and Orthodoxy can take place only upon the condition of the excluded middle, that means *only* after the Western civilization has been factored out (and this is so far from today that even thinking about it is a utopian fantasy)."[86]

Eurasian ideas are supported by some Russian Muslims. *Islamskaia Partiia Vozrozhdeniia* (the Islamic Party of Resurrection) that existed illegally in the beginning of the 1990s in the USSR was of a Eurasian disposition. As Geidar Dzhemal' writes, had the plans of this party been realized, the USSR (or the Eastern Union of Russia) would have preserved its position as a world superpower which, together with the Islamic East, would constitute "a single

---

[84] Ibid., 246.
[85] Dugin, "Tret'ia stolitsa Evrazii," 238.
[86] "The Rest Against the West," *Elementy* no. 7 (1996): 41 (later reproduced in Aleksandr Dugin's book *Osnovy geopolitiki*).

anti-Western area of Resistance from the Arctic Ocean to the Persian Gulf."[87] This endorsement did not prevent Dzhemal' from criticizing Eurasiansm, demanding that Russia should reject the "Eurasian myth" so as to become "Russia the Asian," or, in other words to eventually become Islamic.[88] This view may be regarded as Eurasianism *"per contra."*

Eurasian ideas are supported by the Supreme Mufti of Russia* Talgat Tadzhuddin. When speaking with Mikhail Chvanov, the vice-president of *Mezhdunarodnyi fond slavianskoi pis'mennosti i kul'tury*, he rejected the very notion of "the Mongol yoke" (this position is typical for Eurasianists). Mufti said that "...Rus did not clash with the Golden Horde; together with the Golden Horde it clashed with the cunning West because by this time Khan Mamai had quite long ago neglected the interests of the Golden Horde, attacking Rus with a Genoese infantry paid with papal money..."[89] Tadzhuddin thinks that "...it is natural, normal and needful for Muslims to call their Fatherland, common for us and the Orthodox, the Holy Rus."[90]

The situation regarding support for Eurasianism outside Russia is more complicated. Nevertheless, proponents of this ideology think that one can be a Eurasianist unconsciously. Ayatollah Khomeini, Muammar Kaddaffi and many other people, both living and dead, thus become Eurasianists. Eurasianists also find allies among the pro-Islamic European intelligentsia (for example, among "the New Right" in France). Nevertheless, it is evident that Eurasianism will never become as respectable an ideology in Europe as it is in Russia.

Eurasianists, due to their universalism, are less prone to Russian racism than political fundamentalists and pan-Slavists. On the contrary, Eurasianists emphasize that traditions of all peoples of Eurasia are of equal value. Eurasianists are not anti-Semitic, even though Judaism is, for them, a collu-

---

[87] Geidar Dzhemal', "Upushchennaia vozmozhnost' na zakate sovetskoi istorii," *NG-religii*, 28 June 2000.
[88] Geidar Dzhemal', "Rossiia i islam".
* We would like to remind the reader that Muslims have no single religious hierarchy and that the title "Supreme Mufti of Russia" does not mean that Tadzhuddin's authority over Muslims is comparable with the authority of, say, Patriarch Aleksii, over the Orthodox.
[89] "Vsevyshnim predopredeleno nam zhit' vmeste," *Moskva* no. 1 (2000): 155.
[90] Ibid., 156.

sion of "Eurasian," or traditional, and "Atlanticist," or profane, beliefs. "Muslims and Hebrews are not just our partners, but our brothers," Dugin said at the first congress of the "Eurasia" movement.[91] Some representatives of political Judaism have already joined *Mezhdunarodnoe Evraziiskoe Dvizhenie*, such as Rabbi Avrom Shmulevich, leader of a Hebrew political movement "For Motherland." Shmulevich is a radical Zionist and former Soviet dissident who immigrated to Israel in 1991.

Nearly all authors close to Eurasianism – from radicals to moderates – oppose Russian ethnocentrism. For example, the Club "Catechon" in its publications equates Russian ethnocentrism with intra-Russian separatism, which plays into the hands of the West.[92] Similarly, Aleksandr Panarin was strictly against the ethnicization of Orthodoxy. He thought that Russians should devote themselves not to realization of their own ethnic project, but to fulfilling some global (universal) mission.

Orthodox Communism
We consider Orthodox (i.e., Orthodox Christian) Communism a version of political Orthodoxy since its constant references to religion disqualify its classification among secular ideologies. The term "Orthodox Communism" is not particularly accurate insofar as this description does not reflect any of the substantial features of this ideology. However, we prefer using it simply to avoid both the old term "National Bolshevism" (now mostly associated with *Natsional-bolshevistskaia Partiia*) and labels such as "the Brown-Reds," or "the Communo-Fascists," which are used mostly by journalists.

Orthodox Communism is currently the ideology of *Kommunisticheskaia Partiia Rossiiskoi Federatsii* (KPRF, the Communist Party of the Russian Federation) headed by Gennadii Ziuganov. Orthodox Communism is also promoted by the movement *V podderzhku armii, oboronnoi promyshlennosti i voennoi nauki* (In Support of the Army, Defense Industry and Military Science) lead by Viktor Iliukhin and other organizations, close or erstwhile close to the KPRF. Apart from the KPRF there are no significant Orthodox Communist organizations; the ideology, nevertheless, enjoys stable popularity and

---

[91] Quoted in: Nikolai Zimin, "Novoe politicheskoe dvizhenie poluchilo podderzhku traditsionnykh konfessii," *Sobornost'*, http://www.sobor.ru/randp.asp?id=1810 (as of 22 April 2001).

penetrates all other versions of political Orthodoxy. *Zavtra* (editor-in-chief: Aleksandr Prokhanov) weekly newspaper may be considered the ideological centre of Orthodox Communism.

Aleksandr Verkhovskii suggests that the KPRF belongs to groups demonstrating a respect for Orthodoxy while "not actually basing their ideological self-definition upon it."[93] We, however, disagree with this idea as well as with the position of scholars who assert that the attitude of the KPRF towards religion is guided, first and foremost, by pragmatic considerations, such as attracting new supporters.[94] This may be true with regard to its leaders, though it does not adequately describe ordinary party members and sympathisers. According to the data collected in the summer of 1996 and the fall of 1997 by the Moscow State University Centre for Sociological Research, 47.2% of KPRF members were believers, 40.2% of whom identified themselves as the Orthodox.[95] The theological position of the leaders may also evolve. While in 1999 Gennadii Ziuganiov said that he "views religious values in a rather philosophical manner,"[96] by 2000 Sergei Glaz'ev (a KPRF faction member then) said that Gennadii Ziuganov "is not an atheist ... He is our man, an Orthodox and he goes to the church."[97] It may be that both Ziuganov and the KPRF as a whole drift from pure *derzhavnost'* when ideology is only the means to preserve the territory towards supporting true ideocratic order.

Initially, modern Communists greatly valued *derzhava* over Orthodoxy. Now Gennadii Zuiganov advocates the idea that "Moscow is the Third Rome," i.e., he proclaims that protecting Orthodoxy is the main task of the Russian state. On November 3, 2000 in an interview aired on the TV program *Russkii dom,* Ziuganov said that he "would not juxtapose" Communist ideology and religion (meaning, in the context of the discussion, Orthodoxy), repeating the popular opinion that "if we compare Jesus Christ's Sermon on the Mount and

---

[92] Panarin, *Pravoslavnaia tsivilizatsiia v global'nom mire*, 265, 266.
[93] Aleksandr Verkhovskii, *Politicheskoe pravoslavie: Russkie pravoslavnye fundamentalisty i natsionalisty. 1995-2001 g.* (Moskva: Tsentr "SOVA", 2003), 7.
[94] Fedor Ovsienko, N.A.Trofimchuk, "Konfessional'nyi faktor v rossiiskom politicheskom protsesse: sushchnost' i mesto (obzor)," in *Religiia i kul'tura. Referativnyi sbornik* (Moskva: INION RAN, 2000), 77.
[95] Ibid., 76.
[96] Ziuganov, *Vera i vernost'*, 63.
[97] "Polugosudarstvennaia tserkov' v polutserkovnom gosudarstve?", *Russkaia mysl'*, 30 March – 5 April 2000.

the Moral Code of the Builder of Communism, they are, in essence, the same."[98] While Aleksandr Krutov, the host, did not voice agreement with this statement, he confirmed the sentiment that "today we should unite our efforts in resurrecting Russia."

Some communists praise liberation theology, regretting that no counterpart exists in Russia. They criticize Ziuganov's connection with the ROC because the church does not confront social injustice. Aleksandr Panarin echoed these criticisms, recommending that the ROC should study the experience of the Catholic Church in Latin America.[99] However, rather than having attempted, persistently though unsuccessfully, to influence the ROC leadership, communists might well have appealed to ordinary clergymen who support socialist ideas.

For example, in the early 1990s, Deacon Viktor Pichuzhkin had already begun to publish an actual manifesto of Orthodox Communism. In an article "Christ was a Communist," for example, he argues that Christ was the first to present the idea of socialism and that this idea has "long been a world religion."[100] Pichuzhkin regularly participates in the KPRF demonstrations having with him a huge metallic cross. (In November 2003 the author of this book saw Pichuzhkin at the October Day demonstration with Stalin's portrait). Nevertheless, Ziuganov prefers official Orthodoxy. The leadership of the KPRF is, most likely, simply unable to establish contacts with ordinary priests, preferring instead habitual and safe "summits."

It has already been mentioned that even Orthodox fundamentalists have no consistent attitude towards the Soviet past. Orthodox Communists face the more complex problem of trying to reconcile Sovietism and Orthodoxy. Having suggested that the Soviet Union inherited the geopolitical mission of Russia they need to reconcile the official Soviet atheistic doctrine with this mission to protect world Orthodoxy. In their attempts to resolve the dilemma, modern communists make the USSR a clandestine "Orthodox kingdom."

---

[98] "Kommuna rodilas' v pervobytnom obshchestve. Interv'iu G.A.Ziuganova teleprogramme 'Russkii Dom' 3 noiabria 2000 goda," http://www.pravoslavie.ru/analit/global/intzuganov.htm (as of 3 November 2000).

[99] Panarin, *Pravoslavnaia tsivilizatsiia v global'nom mire*, 293.

Sergei Kara-Murza, a supporter, in part, of Orthodox Communism, suggests that the Russian revolution was a religious movement and that Bolshevism is nothing but an Orthodox heresy.

> Russian communists did not suppress religious feelings; they never infringed upon them; they themselves were their bearers. Soviet people were (an, as a rule, remain) deeply religious... While market ideologists may build and renovate churches, they nevertheless remain slayers of religion,

he wrote.[101] This position apparently dates back to the National Bolshevism of the past. (At the May Day demonstration in 2005 a KPRF agitator even shouted that "Orthodoxy existed in Rus well before the birth of Christ as the ideal of social justice" – against this background believing in the essential religiosity of the Soviet state does not seem too bizarre).

Aleksandr Prokhanov simply equates "anti-liberal," "Soviet" and "Orthodox." For him not only Kim Jong Il and Milosecvic are Orthodox, but also Fidel Castro, Yasser Arafat and even European nationalists Jean-Marie Le Pen and Jorg Heider.[102] The same broad vision of interconnections between Sovietism and Orthodoxy was expressed in the poetic form by a well-known poet Nikolai Triapkin (1918-1999) whose world outlook combined communism and nationalism:

> For the great Soviet Union!
> For the holiest human brotherhood!
> Oh, Lord! Jesus All-merciful!
> Resurrect our earthly happiness...
> ... Rise our red Union
> To the Cross of Your lectern.[103]

---

[100] Deacon Viktor Pichuzhkin, "Khristos byl kommunistom," *Molniia. Gazeta rabochego dvizheniia* no. 31 (February 1992).

[101] Sergei Kara-Murza, "Kommunizm i religiia: trudnyi vopros k vyboram," in Sergei Kara-Murza, *Opiat' voprosy vozhdiam* (Kiev: Oriiani, 1998), 408, 409.

[102] Aleksandr Prokhanov, "Pokrasim istoriiu v krasnyi tsvet," *Zavtra* no. 18 (2002), http://zavtra.ru/cgi//veil//data/zavtra/02/441/11.html (as of 3 February 2003).

[103] Quoted in: Vladimir Bondarenko, "Nikolai Triapkin," in Vladimir Bondarenko, *Plamennye reaktsionery:Tri lika russkogo patriotizma* (Moskva: Algoritm, 2003), 89.

The Orthodox Communist project should have been universalistic by definition. Nevertheless, an analysis of the position of Gennadii Ziuganov reveals that his dislike of extremes very often prohibits him from drawing out the implications of his own ideas. For example, he writes that the USSR hunted after "global leadership mirages" alien to the spirit of the Russian geopolitical tradition[104] but provides no explanation regarding how Russia will "restore its natural position as a great world power" (a statement appearing in the same book) without hunting after such mirages. According to him, Russia only needs "to occupy a respectable place in the global world of the third millennium" as a leader of a great Slavic-Orthodox and, at the same time, Eurasian civilization.[105]

Ziuganov's interpretation Orthodox Communism increasingly resembles political fundamentalism and its idea of the encapsulation of the "Holy Rus." Nevertheless, it seems unlikely that Orthodox Communism in Russia will ever be able to dispose of universalism so as to become a particularistic ideology (most likely, the abandonment of universalism is one of the reasons why the popularity of the KPRF and Ziuganov himself continues to fall).

The universalistic version of Orthodox Communism is definitely a branch of Eurasianism. Aleksandr Dugin, although not being a supporter of the KPRF, defines its ideology as "left-wing Eurasianism" or "National Bolshevism."[106] Orthodox Communists are determined to be Eurasianists – otherwise, they will not be able to restore "the continental empire," bringing it back into its "natural limits" (e.g., the USSR, the former socialist camp, or even the whole sphere of Soviet influence). The idea of empire is of even greater importance for Orthodox Communists than for "pure" Eurasianists because building the Eurasian empire is for them equal to rebirth of the USSR.

Radical versions of left-wing Eurasianism are currently elaborated by research facilities initiated by the military, namely, by *Akademiia geopoliticheskikh problem* (the Academy of Geopolitical Problems) headed by General Leonid Ivashov and by the Center for Ethnopolitical and Islamic Studies

---

[104] Ziuganov, *Vera i vernost'*, 32-33.
[105] Gennadii Ziuganov, *Globalizatsiia i mezhdunarodnye otnosheniia* (Moskva: ITRK, 2001), 81.
[106] Aleksandr Dugin, "KPRF i evraziistvo," *Evraziiskoe obozrenie* no. 6 (no year), www.eurasia.org (as of 24 May 2002).

associated with this Academy. Addressing the participants of *Vserossiiskoe ofitserskoe sobranie* (the All-Russian Assembly of Officers, Moscow, 22 February 2003) Ivashov articulated his doctrine of a confrontation between capitalist "Anglo-Saxon-Judaic coalition" and the "traditional spiritual civilizations: first of all, Orthodox and Islamic ones."[107] Orthodox Communism differs from "pure" Eurasianism mostly because the former envisions the conflict between the West and the others not only as a religious but also an equally significant social conflict. We would like to stress, however, that contemporary Orthodox Communism draws no line between "religious" and "social" concerns. The West is "Satanic" because it is capitalistic and it is capitalistic because it is "Satanic."

As far as universalism is concerned, concepts of this sort are far ahead of Ziuganov's version of Orthodox Communism. Ivashov openly states that Russian mission is to consolidate all the traditional spiritual civilizations of the East and South to battle with the Western civilization, or, more precisely, with the "golden billion," which is understood as both a class enemy and a religious foe at the same time. Den'ga Khalidov, the head of the Center for Ethnopolitical and Islamic Studies, addressing the Assembly, formulated the quintessence of universalistic Orthodox Communism. He said:

> Not only peoples of Russia, but people of the CIS and people of the Arabic and Muslim world set their hopes on Russia. As long ago as in 1917 Russia presented the idea of social justice, social solidarity and brotherhood to the whole world. This was, in fact, an anti-imperialist, anti-globalist, anti-capitalist idea. That idea united half of the world... But it was based on a shattering godless, atheistic fundament. Time has come to revise our ideas, the ideas used to unite peoples of the whole world, not only of Russia... Russia is able to give to the world the new anti-imperialist, anti-globalist idea.[108]

---

[107] Leonid Ivashov, "O sostoianii natsional'noi bezopasnosti Rossii i pervoocherednykh zadachakh ofitserskogo korpusa strany," http://vos2003.narod.ru/ivashov.htm (as of 8 May 2005). Also: audiotapes distributed by *Soiuz Ofitserov*.

[108] "Vystuplenie D.Khalidova," http://vos2003.narod.ru/halidov.htm (as of 8 May 2005). Also: audiotapes distributed by *Soiuz Ofitserov*.

Similar ideas, with a more or less visible flavor of Russian nationalism, have become prevalent in many organizations, uniting the military, such as *Soiuz Ofitserov, Soiuz Sovetskikh Ofitserov* (the Union of Soviet Officers), many so-called "assemblies of officers" (*ofitserskie sobraniia*) and organizations of Cossacks. The popularity of this radical version of Orthodox Communism will most likely also grow within the KPRF (at the grassroots level) as opposed to the moderate position of Gennadii Ziuganov.

Russian Nationalism: Quasi-Orthodoxy and Neo-Paganism
Extreme Russian nationalism in its present form does not enjoy broad public support. Nevertheless, some elements of this ideology periodically appear across the whole spectrum of political Orthodoxy. Russian ethnic identity is so closely connected with Orthodoxy that being Russian seems to be synonymous with being Orthodox. This idea easily evolves into the belief that Russians are better than any other ethnic group and that the value of Orthodoxy can be reduced to the fact that it is "the religion of the Russian people." At this stage nationalism either transforms Orthodoxy into a totally unrecognizable form or else breaks with it and devolves into political Neo-Paganism.

Most nationalist organizations combine ethnicized Orthodoxy with certain elements of Neo-Paganism. Only a few organizations can be considered as completely or exclusively Pagan and anti-Orthodox, for example, various Slavic Communities. Many martial arts clubs teaching so-called Slav-Gorets wrestling are also based on Paganism (e.g., wrestlers adopt "Pagan" names, so that the founder of Slav-Gorets wrestling Aleksandr Belov is also known as Selidor). Slav-Goretz wrestling is a recently contrived form of hand-to-hand combat including some elements of Russian national wrestling. Belov understands wrestling not just as a method of fighting but as a Slavic national philosophy. According to him, it is especially good for street fighting in large cities.

Neo-Paganism may be both political and non-political. The backers of non-political Paganism are most interested in working out rituals, making clothes and organizing various outdoor activities in "the Pagan way of life," as broadly construed. Their political preferences may, of course, vary but they are not determined by membership in Pagan communities. As for the supporters of political Neo-Paganism, they are much less interested in Pagan rituals or mythology; Paganism is for them the basis of Russian identity rather than an intimate religious choice.

Most radical nationalist organizations are small in number, though they disseminate their ideas very aggressively and publish a great deal of literature. Among them are *"Russkaia Respublika"* (headed by Vladimir Popov); *Russkoe Natsional'noe Edinstvo* (the Russian National Unity, or RNE), which now mostly exists as a virtual community; *Narodnaia Natsional'naia Partiia* (the People's National Party), headed by Aleksandr Ivanov-Sukharevskii; *Natsional'no-Derzhavnaia Partiia Rossii* (NDPR, the National Etatist Party of Russia), headed by Aleksandr Sevast'ianov and Stanislav Terekhov[*]; *Russkoe Deistvie* (The Russian Action, former Russian National Union), headed by Konstantin Kasimovskii; *Slavianskaia obshchina* (the Slavic Community) of St. Petersburg, headed by Roman Perin; *Soiuz Slavianskikh Obshchin* (the Union of Slavic Communities), headed by Vadim Kazakov and others.

A curious movement *"K Bogoderzhaviiu"* (Towards God-Statehood) headed by Major-General (Ret.) Konstantin Petrov can be distinguished from the more ordinary pool of Pagan and semi-Pagan organizations. This movement is based on what adherents call "The Concept of Public Security 'Dead Water.'"[**] According to this peculiar ideology, Russia has been murdered and dismembered. However, it can (and should) be recovered with the help of dead water (meaning "knowledge") and then animated with the help of living water (meaning "action"). The religious basis of this movement can not be identified as Paganism in the strict sense (because it rejects polytheism altogether); it is rather a syncretic occult theory resembling, for example, Scientology.

It is worth mentioning that the movement took part in the 2003 parliamentary elections disguised as *Kontseptual'naia Partiia "Edinenie"* (the Conceptual Party "Unification") and has shown very good (considering that its ideology is, to say the least, bizarre) results: it has won 1.17 % of the national

---

[*] Boris Mironov was a co-chair of the NDPR till 2004 when he was expelled as a "provocateur."

[**] Dead water (*miortvaia voda*) is often mentioned in Russian fairy tales. After a warrior has been killed and dismembered, someone collects his parts and recreates the body with dead water; the warrior is then animated with living water.

vote.[109] Gen. Konstantin Petrov in 1999 ran for Governor's office in the Novosibirsk region where he lives. He won 9.8% of the overall vote, while in some districts of the region as much as 11.6% of the constituency supported him (Kirovskii district).[110] Such a success demonstrates that some people in Russia are ready to vote for an apparently delirious platform as long as it is expressed consistently and firmly.

Skinheads constitute a specific segment of nationalists. Aleksandr Tarasov (of the Center for New Sociology and Practical Policy Studies "Phoenix"), who conducted sociological surveys among them, suggests that initially skinheads had not been religiously orientated. Some of them, nevertheless, thought of themselves as of Aryan Pagans, not even of the Slavic, but German variety. But the new generation of skinheads "has grown up having been convinced that to consider your self Russian and Orthodox is correct and prestigious."[111] Therefore contemporary skinheads, according to Tarasov, may often join Orthodox religiopolitical movements. Unfortunately, it is difficult to establish any precise conclusions regarding skinheads due to the current lack of sociological data.

The contemporary ideology of extreme Russian nationalism is characterized by the racist conviction that Russians are of the most perfect subdivision of the white (Aryan) race, in both cultural and anthropological terms. Vladimir Avdeev asserts that genuine Russians are of Northern (Nordic) racial descent because the word *Rus'*, translated from "the most ancient Indo-European languages" means "fair."[112] Physically, the Russian race is characterized by blonde hair, blue eyes, an athletic body and other racial features, "well-known to the world thanks to Russian folklore and epos."[113] But according to Aleksei Shiropaev, for instance, this pure Russian race has been contaminated by Mongolian and other alien blood. As a result, "the white geno-

---

[109] "TsIK oglasil ofitsial'nye rezul'taty vyborov v Gosdumu," http://www.vibori.info/news/article.php?id=398 (as of 19 December 2003).
[110] *Vechernii Novosibirsk*, 9 June 2003.
[111] "Chelovek, proshedshii skin-subkul'turu, stanovitsia pitatel'noi massoi dlia 'novykh pravykh'. Interv'iu s Aleksandrom Tarasovym", *Vremia novostei*, 21 April 2003.
[112] Vladimir Avdeev, "Belye raby," *Za russkoe delo* no. 1 (2005), http://zrd.spb.ru/zrd/zrd_01-121.htm (as of 1 February 2005).
[113] Vladimir Avdeev, "Geneticheskii sotsializm," in *Rasovyi smysl russkoi idei. Tom 1* (Moskva: Belye Al'vy, 2000), 451.

type is hard to find. And when found, it closely co-exists with the Asian or semi-Asian genotype."[114] It is evident that nationalists themselves admit that their preferable racial type is more ideal than real.

The most radical Russian nationalists intend to replace Christianity with a "truly Russian" Pagan religion (they prefer calling it "native religion," or *rodnaia vera*; instead of "Pagans" they designate themselves as "*rodnovery*"). Neo-Pagan theorist Vladimir Istarkhov writes that "the miserable condition of our Russian people is the fruit of Christian education."[115] He suggests that "Russian...Paganism, unlike Christianity, produces educated, proud, brave, cheerful, spiritually strong and independent persons, people of honor and dignity..."[116] Other nationalists admit that Paganism and Orthodoxy are of equal value. For example, the program of *Russkaia Trudovaia Partiia Rossii* (the Russian Labor Party of Russia) includes a demand for the free expression of "the two traditional religions of the Russian people: Vedic pre-Christian and Orthodox"; the influence of all other religions should be restricted.[117] The majority of nationalists not only acknowledge Orthodoxy but tend to defend it. Meanwhile, they also refrain from rejecting "the pre-Christian tradition."

The Orthodoxy of Russian nationalists significantly differs from Orthodoxy in the canonical sense. It is specifically a "Russian faith" having no universal appeal. Aleksandr Barkashov called himself Orthodox, stating at the same time:

> Our idea of genuine fundamental Orthodoxy is not to be identified with the Moscow Patriarchate, which is not just heretic but simply anti-Christian. Traditional Orthodoxy is preciesly the main fundament for protecting human consciousness, for adjusting human actions to Russian national interests. Genuine

---

[114] Aleksei Shiropaev, "Russkie – belye liudi", http://nationalism.org/shiropayev/art8.html (as of 1 January 2005).
[115] Vladimir Istarkhov, *Udar russkikh bogov* (Kaluga: Oblizdat, 1999), 25.
[116] Ibid., 190.
[117] Quoted in: Roman Perin, "Natsional'nyi instinkt," in *Rasovyi smysl russkoi idei*, 312-313.

Russian fundamental Orthodoxy is a fusion of Christianity and 'Paganism.'[118]

It is not accidental, thus, that nationalist organizations tend to mix various forms of swastika with Orthodox symbols.

Vladimir Istarkhov suggests that Russian Paganism is "genuine Orthodoxy" while the existence of Orthodox Christianity is only justified by the fact that its Christian elements have been dignified by noble Paganism.[119] Aleksei Shiropaev thinks that Russians must reject the traditional vision of Christianity as a religion of love and humility and revert to "Aryan" and "Nordic" Christianity.[120] *Narodnaia Natsional'naia Partiia* is another hybrid organization combining Orthodoxy with Neo-Paganism. While it would like to establish Orthodoxy as the state religion, some members of the party are devoted Neo-Pagans.

Some nationalists oppose the Christianity in Orthodoxy. "It is true that there are many dubious elements in Orthodoxy. It is contaminated with Christianity, bringing with it what never existed in Orthodoxy. In principle, Orthodoxy is 60% non-Russian," suggests Mikhail Vlasov, leader of a military patriotic club *Russkaia Gvardiia* (Russian Guard).[121] Vladimir Pribylovskii demonstrates how in November 1991 the platform of *Russkaia Partiia* (the Russian Party, now ineffective) was changing in the course of debates. Initially their demands were

> to designate Christianity, which preaches that the people of Israel have been chosen, as a religion of slaves descending from Judaism, and to designate Orthodoxy as its branch, to consider Christianity a Jewish ideology and an alien religion that contributed to the establishment of the Zionist yoke in Russia, and to assist in resurrecting the Russian faith where Nature is understood to be God.

In the end, however, the following version was accepted:

---

[118] "Na segodniashnii den' patrioticheskie organizatsii, krome nashei, real'noi sily ne predstavliaiut. Interv'iu s Alexandrom Barkashovym," *Russkaia pravda* no. 3 (1995), http://rnod.h1.ru/int/int_bark.htm (as of 17 November 2003).
[119] Istarkhov, *Udar russkikh bogov*, 136.
[120] Aleksei Shiropaev, "Russkii, oblachënnyi v metall," *Ataka* no. 12 (no year): 37.
[121] Quoted in: Verkhovskii et.al., *Politicheskaia ksenofobiia*, 103.

> To designate Christianity, which preaches that the people of
> Israel have been chosen, as a Jewish ideology and an alien
> religion that contributed into establishing of the Zionist yoke in
> Russia, and to assist in resurrecting Orthodoxy, Islam and the
> Russian faith, where Nature is understood to be God.[122]

This demonstrates that even having rejected Christianity, nationalists do not dare to throw Orthodoxy away completely.

What is the reason for this ideological inconsistency? Vladimir Shnirel'man mentioned that the ambitions of Russian Neo-Pagans are too broad for a limited Russian or even Slavic area. While they may not object to universalizing their ideology, they could not do so without contradicting their emphasis on Russian Paganism as the core of this ideology.

> This is the reason for their ambiguous attitude towards Christianity and even atheistic Communism. The point is that unlike Paganism, these ideologies provide a much firmer ground for building a strong foothold within the country and open the way towards a broader international coalition,

he wrote.[123] For the same reasons many Neo-Pagans insist that "Paganism is just a national version of the religion of Vedism common to all Aryans."[124] Thus, Paganism, as interpreted by nationalists, increasingly resembles Orthodoxy with its autocephalous national churches embraced by the Universal Church.

The Vedism of Russian (as well as Ukrainian) Neo-Pagans is based on the so-called "Book of Veles." It is a set of wooden tables with inscriptions discovered in 1919 (though most scholars consider it to be a fabrication). One of the tables (No. II, 1) describes the principles of a religious and philosophical teaching resembling the ancient Hindu doctrine. It is not polytheistic because various deities are defined as personifications of a single god or as

---

[122] Ibid., 130.
[123] Vladimir Shnirel'man, *Neoiazychestvo i natsionalizm: Vostochno-evropeiskii areal* (Moskva: IEA RAN, 1998), 11.
[124] Istarkhov, *Udar russkikh bogov*, 10.

symbols of natural phenomena. If genuine, this discovery actually discredits the polytheistic aspects of Russian Vedism and its Pagan nature.

Vedism is an artificial religion created in the 19th century by Indian reformers of Hinduism (such as Swami Dayananda Saraswati) who believed that contemporary polytheistic Hinduism resulted from the gradual degeneration of a pristine Aryan religion based on the Vedas.[125] The idea was that this ancient religion had been monotheistic. Contemporary scholars suggest that Vedism emerged as a result of the influence of Christianity on Indian intellectuals, who considered it the basis of the power of the British Empire. Peter Van der Veer suggests that Dayananda attempted to transform Hinduism into a "religion of the book" resembling Christianity or Islam.[126] Modern Russian Neo-Pagans do the same thing: they consider Paganism not so much as a religion of nature or as a worshipping the elements, for example, but as another global "religion of the book," albeit "uncontaminated" by Jewish origins and specially shaped for the Russian people.

It is self-evident that Russian racism is not a universal ideology. This implies the radical rejection of all forms of traditional Russian messianism. Vladimir Avdeev denies any universal notion of humanity and, subsequently, any universal mission destined for Russia: "the image of Russia as a universal benevolent martyr is completely unbefitting for us."[127] What is offered instead? Vladimir Istarkhov asserts that traditional messianism is to be replaced with "sound national egoism." Russia should imitate the United States, who, according to him, "in every corner of the world…is ready to use power and weapons; to kill, to grind out, to crush everyone who cramps its national interests."[128] The false notion that Russia's universal mission is to rescue humankind has, in his opinion, been inspired by Christianity. "There are plenty of such believers in Russia…," he writes with irony, "…not being able to stitch up their own bags, they set forth to rescue all of humankind. This is the fruit of

---

[125] Peter Van der Veer, "The Moral State: Religion, Nation and Empire in Victorian Britain and British India," in *Nation and Religion: Perspectives on Europe and Asia* (Princeton: Princeton University Press, 1999), 36-37.
[126] Peter Van der Veer, *Religious Nationalism: Hindus and Muslims in India* (Berkeley, University of California Press, 1994), 65.
[127] Avdeev, "Geneticheskii sotsializm," 420.
[128] Istarkhov, *Udar russkikh bogov*, 46.

Christian education."[129] The same principle of "sound national egoism" is professed by the other extreme nationalists.

The leading nationalist political project implies establishing within Russia a so-called Russian Republic, or a "republic of the Russian people," which according to nationalists should not simply be one among many republics within the Russian Federation. Instead, it should be isolated from the other (non-Russian) republics, having previously deported from its territory members of all ethnic groups other than Russians.

It is not surprising that nationalists strongly reject Eurasianism, especially its proposed union between Russia and the Islamic world. Vladimir Avdeev disparages the Neo-Eurasianist idea of traditionalism, insisting that it is "a typical analogue to contemporary universal values."[130] Nationalists deny any possibility of physical or spiritual kinship between racially perfect nations (Russians) and racially impure ones (most of the Islamic nations). The idea of a single "tradition," for nationalists, sounds equally absurd in that they believe that human races are separate biological species, while some races (such as Jews or blacks) are considered to be non-human.

It is worth mentioning that in spite of their dislike of universalism, many Russian nationalists are seemingly universalistic. The historical universal mission of Russia and the Russian people, Aleksandr Barkashov wrote, is to create a spiritual civilization and to become a model for all other nations.[131] Likewise, other nationalists may not always abide by their overemphasized anti-messianism. Even Vladimir Istarkhov, in spite of being admiring aspects of US foreign policy, still believes that Russia can and should help all other nations to dispose of the yoke of Judaism, Christianity and Communism. From this viewpoint he criticizes Hitler, who "could have gathered recourses of all nations of the world" but "had never wanted to help other nations."[132] This demonstrates that in spite of all their efforts, nationalists are not entirely able to cast traditional Russian messianism away.

---

[129] Ibid., 43.
[130] See, for example: Vladimir Avdeev, "Novaia Traditsiia i rasovaia modernizatsiia," in *Rasovyi smysl russkoi idei*, 408.
[131] Aleksandr Barkashov, "Krizis mirovoi tsivilizatsii, rol' Rossii i zadachi russkogo natsional'nogo dvizheniia," *Russkii poriadok* no. 1-2 (1995).
[132] Istarkhov, *Udar russkikh bogov*, 277.

II.3 Political Orthodoxy between universalism and particularism

In spite of their different origins and priorities, all versions of political Orthodoxy have much in common. One may thereby conclude that in spite of all of the external diversity apparent in these ideological approaches, there exists a single ideology of political Orthodoxy characterized by a specific set of ideas. Most of these concepts have been supplied by the initial Orthodox conservative political doctrine and by classical Pan-Slavism and Eurasianism. Some important ideas have also been borrowed from Communism, National Socialism and other sources.

Any specific idea may be pivotal for a given version of political Orthodoxy while, at the same time, remaining peripheral for the other versions. For example, the union between Orthodoxy and Islam is a core concept for Eurasianists, though for Pan-Slavists this idea is peripheral and fundamentalists keep only fragments of it. The idea of world apostasy is pivotal for political fundamentalists, but for Eurasianists and Pan-Slavists it is a minor concern used only in support of a union of all civilizations against the West. The idea that the Soviet Union was, in fact, the Orthodox Kingdom is of greater importance to Orthodox Communists than to the others; fundamentalists are the least supportive of this position.

Having examined the versions of political Orthodoxy in their order of appearance in this book, one may notice that borders between neighboring ideologies are nearly non-existent: some versions of fundamentalism are hardly distinguishable from Pan-Slavism; Pan-Slavism merges with Eurasianism; Orthodox Communism is, in fact, a version of Eurasianism. Nevertheless, substantial gap exists between Eurasianism (including Communism) and subsequent extreme nationalism.

At the same time, extreme fundamentalists and extreme nationalists have very much in common: although the former are fanatical adherents of Orthodoxy, while the later stick to Neo-Paganism, their political programs do not differ much. Both reject any alliances with the outside world and call for isolating not even Russia, but a purely Russian ethnic state. Nevertheless, nationalist ideas have gained leverage, eroding Orthodox Communism and even coherently anti-nationalist Eurasianism.

All versions of political Orthodoxy infiltrate one another, often resulting in peculiar configurations of ideas and slogans. We have already demonstrated how fundamentalist concepts and rhetoric influence Orthodox Communism; fundamentalism, in its turn, is affected by Eurasian ideas (such as a possible alliance with the Islamic world). Czar Ivan the Terrible is a very important person for fundamentalists, who for many years urged the ROC to canonize him. This person seemed to be of no significance for the other streams of political Orthodoxy until February 2005, when Aleksandr Dugin called for reviving some of Ivan's political heritage. This call was made during the constitutive congress of *Evraziiskii Soiuz Molodëzhi* (the Eurasian Union of Youth, the ESM) held in the former palace of Ivan the Terrible in the town of Aleksandrov (now a museum).

This demonstrates once again that political Orthodoxy is a pool of ideas emerging and re-emerging independent of apparent borders between its specific versions. The acceptance of all, some, or part of these ideas determines a person's association with political Orthodoxy even in cases where this person does not appear to be a strict "fundamentalist" or "Pan-Slavist," for example.

Extreme fundamentalism and extreme nationalism, however, radically differ from the other versions of political Orthodoxy, though this fact can be easily explained. According to our taxonomy, political fundamentalism differs from all political religions due to its demonstrative denial of modernity. Russian nationalist ideology is not a genuine political religion, but an ethnoreligious particularistic ideology. Thus, we can speak about a single ideology of political Orthodoxy, as one speaks about Islamism as a whole, without paying attention to internal differentiations.

Due to its lack of connections with some universal ideology (except Communism), political Orthodoxy in Russia constantly wobbles between universalism and particularism. All above-listed versions are Russocentric – concentrated on the Russian people, its uniqueness and special mission. Even such universal ideologies as Eurasianism and Orthodox Communism (or "left Eurasianism") are not always as anti-ethnocentric as they pretend to be. The supporters of extreme fundamentalism and nationalism are, at least, ideologically consistent: they think that Russians are the chosen nation and articulate

articulate this. As for Pan-Slavists and Eurasianists, their position seems to constantly waver.

The idea that the Russian people should unite with other nations to fight godless West implies that Russians have to sacrifice the idea of their national (ethnic) supremacy (unless one speaks about conquering and enslaving the other nations, which political Orthodoxy does not do). Messianism does not get along with ethnocentrism. An ideology stressing, at the same time, Russian supremacy and the Russian mission of uniting the other nations seems fairly unpleasant for possible allies.

Of course, Russian ethnocentrism can be explained by the fact that the identity crisis of the Russian people after the collapse of the USSR was quite severe. While the other peoples could, at last, refer to the experience of the third world in the sphere of constructing postcolonial national identities, Russians had no such opportunity. Russian ethnic nationalism appears to be, in the eyes of many Russians, the best reaction to a "sudden" upsurge of national awareness among non-Russian ethnic groups. Such ideas are met by many with sympathy as a new basis for shattering identity.

Since Russia is a multiethnic polity, any particularistic ethnic Russian project would inevitably lead to the dissolution of the federation. This is what radical ethnonationalists and fundamentalists want. But such a solution will most likely prove unacceptable for the majority of the population. There are some signs that even nationalists understand this; below we will see how they constantly "sneak" Eurasian ideas into their platforms to attract broader public support. So far Eurasianism, especially its "left-wing" variation, seems to be the most universal of all versions of political Orthodoxy even in spite of being penetrated by fundamentalist and nationalist ideas.

One should not, of course, exclude the possibility of the emergence of some fully new ideology of political Orthodoxy. It seems that a project of "Orthodox liberation theology" would be attractive for many people in Russia. Discussions of such an ideology emerge periodically across the Orthodox political spectrum. Unlike Orthodox Communism, liberation theology would be able to, following progressive Catholicism, unite revolutionary Marxism with Orthodoxy thus defining a significant and hitherto ignored segment of the world population as "the oppressed." So far, however, no author has offered such a theory.

III Political Orthodoxy as a Subculture

Generally speaking, the lifestyle of a supporter of political Orthodoxy does not differ from the lifestyle of an ordinary, middle-class Russian citizen. In this sense there is no "subculture" of political Orthodoxy. Only fundamentalists and some extreme nationalists (or Pagans) constitute a genuine subculture with strict dress-codes and rules of behavior.

Nevertheless, though seemingly a part of "normal" contemporary Russian society, the supporter of political Orthodoxy watches another kind of TV, listens to another kind of music, reads other books and sometimes even speaks a different language than the vast majority of his or her fellow Russians. Most of these people are aware that they, as a group, differ from the mainstream. Political Orthodoxy has its own megastars and its own great works of art, sometimes seen as marginal by the outside world or remaining simply unknown to it. It is a sort of cultural underworld, although in most cases not legally outlawed. We will try to describe this "underworld" briefly, keeping in mind that the Orthodox political community is not a genuine subculture.

In the sphere of culture we do not see such visible borders between different versions of political Orthodoxy as those existing in the sphere of ideology. While there are more or less clearly distinguishable Pan-Slavist and Eurasianist ideologies, there is no corresponding "pan-Slavist music," or "Eurasianist dress-code." Political Orthodoxy as a subculture is an organic whole where all actors and ideas overlap and interact.

III.1 Self-definition, Language and Symbols

Most of supporters of political Orthodoxy (the political Orthodox) define themselves as "Orthodox patriots" or "national patriots." The latter term dates back to the beginning of the 1990s when it had no religious connotation, but currently being an Orthodox is an integral part of being a national patriot. Very often the political Orthodox define themselves simply as "patriots" (or "radical patriots"). As a result, the very word "patriot" is nearly monopolized by them; even their adversaries refer to them as to "patriots," although they typically put the word in quotation marks when doing so.[133]

The formation of "national" or "Orthodox" patriotism dates back to the period of the unsuccessful uprising in October 1993. Paradoxically, at that moment not many people attached religious significance to the encounter between those who defended the parliamentary building (the White House) and the army. Nowadays nearly all Orthodox patriots understand that collision as a spiritual battle between Good and Evil, God and Satan. In a way, General Al'bert Makashov was right when he said that October 1993 had initiated the awakening of Russian self-awareness[134], since subsequent national patriotism then began to acquire its religious dimension. Now the event is commonly seen first and foremost as a religious event; moreover, choosing the "right" side (even *post factum*) becomes sort of initiation designating a person's membership in the Orthodox political community.

Apart from identifying themselves as a more or less coherent group of "patriots" ("us") the political Orthodox as a community has constructed a shared image of the enemy, or of "them." They all sustain a religious hatred towards the West, which is seen as "godless" and "Satanic," and towards Jews, who are seen as a force which dominates the West and intends to conquer Russia as well. Popular Orthodox tradition maintains that the West is the place where demons live; hell is commonly depicted at the Western walls of Russian churches. A complex group of "Caucasians" or people originating

---

[133] For examples see an article in a liberal newspaper *Novaia gazeta* where patriots (without brackets) are juxtaposed to liberals: Boris Kagarlitskii, "Chei chelovek Putin? Isterika liberalov obostrila paranoiiu patriotov," *Novaia gazeta*, 27 June 2002.

[134] "'Vsem pavshim – tsarstvo nebesnoe'. Dialog Aleksandra Prokhanova i generala Al'berta Makashova," *Zavtra*, 30 October 1997.

from the three South Caucasian republics (Georgia, Armenia and Azerbaijan) and from the Russian North Caucasus has recently become another object of hatred.

Hostility towards Jews is, so to say, a conceptual issue: a long-lasting tradition maintains the position that Jews are destructive for Russia and the whole of humankind.[135] "Caucasophobia" seems to be more instrumental: the political Orthodox don't mind exploiting the anti-migration sentiments of the population but they fail to explain what exactly makes "Caucasians" enemies of Russia and Orthodoxy. All known explanations mostly present "Caucasians" as blind tools of the West and/or the world Jewry. Only some extreme fundamentalists and extreme nationalists transform their "caucasophobia" into conceptual "Islamophobia."

Thus, the West and the South, within the framework of the sacral geography of political Orthodoxy, are juxtaposed to the East and to the North. Russia is seen as a Northern, "polar" state, the land of God and His Mother. The political Orthodox often refer to "Russian Frost" as a sacral phenomenon. The fact that the winter of 1942 was unexpectedly cold is interpreted in religious terms: "Russian Frost" has protected holy Russia from the godless West. What comes from the West or South is seen as "impure," for example, people: inhabitants of the West are considered morally impure ("carrion West"), while inhabitants of the South, including Jews are morally *and* physically impure.

The supporters of political Orthodoxy often use offensive names with regard to Jews (like "Yids"); at the same time they have worked out a system of euphemisms which simultaneously avert legal troubles and identify like-minded folk. Such euphemistic "code" language includes, for example, references to "Zionists" (a term that is not uncommon in the West as well), "Judeo-Fascists," "Masons," "Khazars," or "Sabbatarians." Most "Orthodox patriots" deny being anti-Semites and use such constructions as "moral Yids" or "social Yids," thus hoping to stress that their hatred is not directed towards ethnic Jews. The author of the book recalls how a lecturer Vladimir Mishin, representing *Kontseptual'naia Partiia "Edinenie,"* having said that "the nouveuax

---

[135] More about conceptualized anti-Semitism in modern Russia may be found in: Vadim Rossman, *Russian Intellectual Anti-Semitism in the Post-Communist Era* (Lincoln, NE: University of Nebraska Press and SICSA, 2002).

rich are Yids of various origins," immediately corrected himself, stating, "I mean, social Yids."[136]

Most of the political Orthodox (except moderate fundamentalists) are highly critical towards the ROC and its leadership, counting the latter among "them." It is common practice to call Patriarch Aleksii II by his pre-monastic last name Ridiger (or even "citizen Ridiger" or "Mr. Ridiger") to emphasize that he has non-Russian name (the political Orthodox consider it to be Jewish).

Adherence to political Orthodoxy may normally be revealed through a person's manner of speech and writing. Some subgroups (for example, fundamentalists) speak their own language which is barely comprehensible to the uninitiated. Many terms broadly used by fundamentalists (*sobornost* and "symphony of powers") are used by them exclusively and can not be found in the language of the other representatives of political Orthodoxy. These words are mostly borrowed from ecclesiastical language. In addition, fundamentalist language lacks terminology reflecting contemporary phenomena, i.e. phenomena that emerged after the 1917 revolution.

The language of extreme nationalists (or Neo-Pagans) is also different from the standard Russian language. They, for example, try to use "Slavic" denominations of months instead of Russian borrowed from Latin (*stuzhen', liuten'* instead of *ianvar', fevral'*) or replace words of foreign origins with "Slavic" equivalents: *svetopisi* instead of *fotografii* (photos); *izveda* instead of *interv'iu* (interview). Some Neo-Pagans claim that Russians are superior because they speak the "Aryan language." At the same time, they consider this language distorted by foreign influences and try to reconstruct the "initial" sounds of "Aryan words" (for example, instead of *korruptsiia,* or "corruption," they suggest *skorluptsiia; skorlupa,* in Russian, means "empty shell").

Refusal to use the prefix *"bes-"* in words like *bessmertnyi* (immortal), *besstrukturnyi* (non-structured), *besstrashnyi* (fearless), etc. is a linguistic peculiarity shared by the majority of the political Orthodox. Before the language reform in 1917 these words were written with prefix *"bez-".* The point is that *"bez"* means nothing, while *"bes"* is not only a prefix but a word meaning "devil." To avoid mentioning devil, political Orthodox authors write the above-

---

[136] Public lecture given on 9 April 2005 at the Polytechnic Museum, Moscow.

mentioned words in accordance with the old rules (*bezsmertnyi, bezstrukturnyi*). A nationalist newspaper *Era Rossii* (Era of Russia) proclaims that "This newspaper is published without the prefix 'BES'." Even *Edinenie*, though an anti-Christian organization, insists on non-usage of "*bes.*"

Although *Edinenie* should not be counted among Orthodox political organizations, it has contributed a great deal to the language of political Orthodoxy (for example, the very term "dead water" – *miortvaia voda*). The ideologists of this party insist on using a specific orthography that would express the meaning or words (the absence of "*bes*" is one of its features). They also suggest putting punctuation marks in unusual places in order to enhance understanding of long sentences. General Petrov and his co-authors, who call themselves "The Internal Predictor," have invented a real Orwellian newspeak, thus destroying any attempts at dialogue because they insist upon communicating only in their own language.

Apart from the Internal Predictor (a group of "Russian patriotic scholars") *Edinenie* uses such terms as "the global supra-Judaic predictor" (which the political Orthodox normally call "Judeo-Masons"); "the Euro-American conglomerate" (Western civilization); "crowd-elite society" (modern society), etc. To understand what the followers of Petrov have stated one must virtually learn this newspeak. They also use numerous abbreviations (DOTU, KOB, etc.) making their speech even more confusing. In spite of the fact that hardly anyone outside *Edinenie* uses these neologisms, all supporters of political Orthodoxy are at least familiar with them.

Specific words and ways of using words may be considered a litmus test for people wishing to designate themselves as members of the Orthodox political community. Using specific words instead of a neutral denomination *russkii* ("ethnically Russian") is one of these litmus tests. The political Orthodox often replace it with the archaic words *ross* or *rusich*. There is nothing wrong with these words; nevertheless, they unmistakably permit the identification of a "national patriot." "We, Russians, are hospitable" may appear to be either a neutral phrase or a political declaration depending on the word chosen to designate the subject. The political Orthodox also like using the word "Aryan" (to or off the point).

There is no consent among the political Orthodox about symbols. All of them use various crosses. A traditional Orthodox cross has eight ends; it is no surprise that political Orthodoxy prefers eight-ended symbols. An eight-ended star may be found across the whole spectrum of political Orthodoxy; neo-Pagans prefer an eight-ended swastika. *Mezhdunarodnoe Evraziiskoe Dvizhenie* has adopted "the Eurasian rose" – an eight-ended cross of four arrows (also known as *krestostrel*). The symbol of the RNE is a left-handed swastika embedded into an eight-ended star. According to the RNE documents, this star, or the Star of the Mother of God, was used by both Pagans and Christians as a symbol of the presence of the supreme god. The Swastika symbolizes God's protection in the struggle against material and spiritual enemies. A left-handed swastika is commonly seen as a genuine Orthodox symbol used by icon-painters. Besides, the political Orthodox make symbolic use of ringing bells, axes, swords and torches.

Most totally reject the contemporary Russian banner – the tricolor (white-blue-red). However, it is worth mentioning that Ukrainian pro-Russian movements (many of them have a political Orthodox underpinning) stage demonstrations with Russian tricolors, thus showing their sympathy with Russia. Fundamentalists gather under the black-yellow-white banner of the Romanovs dynasty and they often wear exotic uniforms with medals of unclear origins. Red banners – often with an image of Christ – seem to be the most wide-spread symbol. The red banner has double meaning: on the one hand, it reminds one of Communism; on the other hand, it is considered the ancient banner of all Slavs. It is, above all, bright and noticeable. *Rodina* (Motherland) party made a clever move when it adopted red banner with the party name in yellow on it. *Mezhdunarodnoe Evraziiskoe Dvizhenie* has chosen a black banner with the Eurasian rose.

There is a set of symbolic figures, a sort of pantheon of political Orthodoxy respected by the majority of the backers. This pantheon includes some Orthodox saints (Ioann of Kronshtadt, Serafim of Sarov, saint princes Dmitrii Donskoi and Aleksandr Nevskii), but most of its members are politicians considered "political saints," or saints of a political religion, such as Ivan the Terrible (fundamentalists want to canonize him in the strict sense) or Minin and Pozharskii. Our contemporaries, like a singer Igor' Tal'kov, are often portrayed as saints as well. Stalin is recognized as a member of the pantheon nearly by the whole community with a few exceptions. "Stalin is a saint,"

Aleksandr Prokhanov wrote.[137] On the contrary, Nicolas II is recognized as a saint exclusively by fundamentalists (in spite of the fact that he has actually been canonized by the ROC).

Slobodan Milosevic and Aleksandr Lukashenko are highly respected by the political Orthodox community. We have already examined Lukashenko's significance for the political Orthodox; as for Milosevic, Vladimir Bondarenko has once called him "the consolidator of all patriots in Russia."[138] This is true; if there is anything that all patriots (even non-religious) agree about, it is their admiration of Milosevic.

Colonel Iurii Budanov, sentenced to jail for raping and killing a Chechen girl, is another notorious member of the pantheon. He is seen as a noble Russian warrior unjustly accused of mistreating a woman from the South (we have already mentioned that the political Orthodox consider Southerners "dirty" and thus "untouchable"). During public events, the members of *Soiuz Pravoslavnykh Khorugvenostsev* often carry a broadsheet displaying the slogan "Freedom to Colonel Budanov" with two Orthodox crosses at the sides. One's attitude toward Budanov is one of the litmus tests for distinguishing "us" from "them"[139].

Besides the pantheon, politicized Orthodoxy has its own "anti-pantheon" consisting of symbolic enemies. Names of these enemies are used at random and are easily interchangeable. Among them: George Bush and George W. Bush (there is a slogan "Putin has sold his soul to Bush" – in Russian it is a rhyme: *Putin Bushu prodal dushu*); leading Russian liberals (Egor Gaidar, Anatolii Chubais); Chechen separatists (Dzhokhar Dudaev, Akhmed Zakaev) and the other "enemies of Russia and Orthodoxy."

---

[137] Aleksandr Prokhanov, "Pobeda – religiia, Stalin – sviatoi," *Zavtra*, 5 May 2004.
[138] Vladimir Bondarenko, "Miloshevich – geroi slavian," *Zavtra*, 13 April 1999.
[139] More on Budanov may be found in: Mikhail Sokolov, "Predely primeneniia doktriny prav cheloveka v sovremennoi rossiiskoi kul'ture: sud nad polkovnikom Budanovym i ego protivniki," in O.V. Starovoitova, ed., *Zashchita prav cheloveka v Rossiiskoi Federatsii* (Sankt-Peterburg: Petropolis, 2001), 38-47.

III. 2 Art

The underground art of political Orthodoxy is produced by the same people who produce Orthodox political ideology. It is worth mentioning that most of these personalities are also engaged in political Orthodox activism. Consuming such art is an important marker of being an Orthodox patriot.

Music
Music (and singing) is a prevailing type of art associated with political Orthodoxy. This is partly explained by the fact that singing and making records does not involve considerable expenditures and that musical productions are easier to disseminate than any other media format (most political Orthodox music is currently disseminated in mp3 format via Internet). Singing is also more effective than books for engaging people emotionally. Last but not least, people are able to sing collectively, thus involving a group dynamic that is difficult to obtain by means of printed material. Most Orthodox political singers sing their own songs with guitar accompaniment (or to a phonogram); in Russia this activity is known as "author's songs" or "skiffle songs." There are also rock-bands, choirs and other musical groups.

Political Orthodox music is a complex of overlapping musical subcultures. There are two basic trends in contemporary Orthodox political singing: fundamentalist and nationalist (with Communist flavor or without it). They are represented by two web-sites (these are not the only sites, just the largest ones), respectively: "Songs of the Russian Resurrection" (http://pesni.voskres.ru) and "Songs of the Russian Resistance" (http://www.harchikov.pp.ru). Both contain free music for downloading, lyrics, information about authors/singers, etc.

A politically-oriented Orthodox Christian with fundamentalist preferences will most likely enjoy the songs of Hieromonk Roman (Aleksandr Matiushin, born 1954, took the vows in 1983) performed either by him (to a guitar) or by other Orthodox singers. The poetry of Roman is mostly dedicated to general Orthodox Christian topics with noticeable apocalyptic sentiments (songs like "Jerusalem, Jerusalem…," "Calvary" and others). Roman is popular not only with fundamentalists but with apolitical church-goers as well. Nevertheless, some of his verses are highly politicized. Among them his infamous piece "To General Makashov" published in 1998 by *Rus' Pravoslavnaia* (Makashov is notorious for his anti-Semitic statements). Let us translate a strophe from this verse:

> I am with you, General, carry on!
> You have expressed people's words –
> Allow the Motherland to upraise,
> To endure the yoke of the Khazar rabble!

The phenomenon of "singing monks" seems to be a feature of all supposedly Orthodox countries. In Greece, for example, Father Nektarios Moulatsiotis has organized several monks into a rock-band named "*Eleftheri*" (The Free).[140] One would expect this band to become a pillar of Orthodox liberalism, but Father Nektarious is characterized by extreme conservatism and has been active in the struggle against the removal of religious affiliation from Greek identity cards. He is also the President of the coordinating Committee against the Schengen Agreement. Songs of the group are full of apocalyptic and nationalist sentiments. This is a quotation translated by a Greek scholar Lina Molokotos-Liederman:

> People of all nations unite, the New World Order calls us...
> The godless civilization makes treaties and agreements... The humanists and the policemen of the nations talk about peace, but they bomb us and secure us with threats. Love, truth and justice are ruined by modernisation. Hold my brother, there is a God.[141]

There is, thus, not much difference between singing monks in Russia and Greece. However, so far in Russia there are no rock-bands composed of monks.

Zhanna Bichevskaia is another well-known fundamentalist singer and guitar player (enjoying popularity outside fundamentalist circles). She mostly sings not her own songs but songs by Roman or other Orthodox songwriters

---

[140] Lina Molokotos-Liederman, "The 'Free Monks' Phenomenon: Music and Modernity in Contemporary Greek Orthodoxy" (paper presented at the annual meeting of the Association for the Sociology of Religion, Atlanta, Georgia, 15 August 2003).

(including her husband Gennadii Ponomarëv). Bichevskaia's songs are dominated by an apocalyptic spirit, the admiration of the White Guard and Czar Nicolas II, Russian Orthodox nationalism and other typically fundamentalist topics. A recent convert into Orthodoxy, she nowadays heads a charity organization *Soiuz Pravoslavnykh Zhenshchin* (The Union of Orthodox Women) ideologically close to *Soiuz Pravoslavnykh Bratstv*.

One of Bichevskaia's songs (lyrics and music by Gennadii Ponmarëv) is especially popular among political fundamentalists who listen (and sing) it during their events. The song is called "We are Russians" and it accumulates many popular fundamentalist ideas (Orthodox monarchy, anticommunism, apocalyptic spirit, nationalism and so on). The song is hard to translate because of being mostly written in the above-mentioned "fundamentalist languages"; nevertheless, we try to convey the meaning of at least one strophe:

> Our discussion with the enemy is over,
> We will rise again, lusting after great deeds.
> Russia, the Ukraine and Byelorussia –
> Three warriors of the Slavic people.

Fundamentalist singers are not "cultural underground" in the strict sense: listening to their records as such is not a marker of being a member of the Orthodox political community (as well as listening to church music, such as monastic choirs). This may be explained by their proximity to the respectable "ecclesiastical subculture." CDs and audiotapes of Bichevskaia, Roman and others may be found in church stores and mainstream music-shops.

Another type of Orthodox political music is represented by so called "resistance songs" or what in German is called "*Kampflieder*," or "battle songs" (one may mention that some fundamentalist songs also fall into this category). These are mostly "author's songs," although there are also groups of this type (for example, a rock-band "*Krasnye zvëzdy*," i.e., Red Stars). These records are not found in respectable stores and those who listen to them thereby display their support of some version of political Orthodoxy. To obtain these records, one must know exactly when and where they can be purchased. CDs and audiotapes of resistance songs are available during various

---

[141] Ibid.

"patriotic" events (i.e., demonstrations, meetings) or via the Internet – unless one prefers to download them for free. Free downloading and copying is encouraged by these artists, who sacrifice their own monetary benefits in their efforts to disseminate their ideas.

Among most popular resistance singers one may name Aleksandr Kharchikov, Ivan Baranov, Aleksandr Krylov, Leonid Kornilov and others. We will focus on Kharchikov due to, first, his enormous popularity across the whole spectrum of political Orthodoxy and, second, the scope of his topics. He sings communist songs ("True Communist," "Listen Hear, Comrade"), nationalist songs ("Forward, Russia!," "Russia Waits for Your Will") and simply anti-Semitic songs ("Myth about the Holocaust," "Why Yids Rule Russia"). Some of his songs are apparently Pan-Slavist ("Letter to Serbia," "Slavic Brothers," "Lukashenko, Come to Russia") while a song "Skyscrapers of Manhattan" seems radically Eurasianist. The latter piece deserves to be quoted from:

> Long live the enlightened warriors of the Prophet,
> Who are bravely starting the jihad!
> The angels of retribution will come
> To arrogant America, to mean-spirited Europe.

Kharchikov calls himself Orthodox; however, his attitude to the Russian Orthodox Church and its hierarchy is extremely hostile. In the song "If I Were the Savior" he ruminates:

> If I were the Savior,
> I would set this false saint, this double-tongued Ridiger in the pillory,
> I would rip out his beard; I would tear his cross off,
> I would banish Christ-selling foes from churches…
> … In the end I would build, together with the holy Russian people,
> An eternal state of truth, labour and freedom.

This ability to assimilate all the most important ideas of political Orthodoxy makes Kharchikov popular with all supporters of this ideology, from Communists to extreme nationalists. (A participant of the KPRF web-forum even informs that "one of the comrades" gave Kharchikov's audiotapes to skinheads and they liked them).[142] Responding to critical remarks about Kharchikov's anti-Semitism, an anonymous author at the "Communist.ru" web-site insisted that "Kharchikov's world outlook and creative work combine the two elements which are inextricably connected today – the element of national liberation and the element of Communism, of class struggle ... Let everyone have his own Kharchikov. Nationalist, Communist, Orthodox, etc."[143] (We suggest that the deep emotional involvement in his singing – he virtually weeps – is also responsible for Kharchikov's popularity).

As a political activist Kharchikov cooperates with the KPRF, the NDPR, *Rossiiskaia Kommunisticheskaia Rabochaia Partiia* (the Russian Communist Worker's Party, RKRP); he is also an honorable member of St. Peterburg's *Slavianskaia obshchina* in spite of its being a radical anti-Christian organization. His concerts are accompanied with political declarations: for example, on 19 December 2004 during a concert commemorating Stalin's 125th birthday in St. Petersburg he addressed "all national-patriotic forces of Russia" demanding that no less than 90 % of decision makers must be ethnic Russians and that citizens of Russia should have the right to initiate capital punishment for the president and the members of the parliament. Similar demands may be found in his open letters to patriotic newspapers (who mostly don't publish them) or at his web-site.

The author of the book has personally encountered the evidence of Kharchikov's enormous popularity. His verses are printed on nationalist leaflets or used as slogans during demonstrations. They are also heard during huge KPRF demonstrations on October Day and May Day. At the 8th All-Russian Contest "Songs of Resistance" (28 November 2004) the author observed how the standing audience was cheering Kharchikov's song "Kill the Yid Inside Yourself," which is a hit of radical Orthodox nationalism.

It is no surprise, that even fellow patriots sometimes accuse Kharchikov of Fascism (what he continuously denies). One may not help noticing that his songs are dominated by such words as "blood," "death," "war," "blade," "will," "spirit" (including "Aryan spirit"), "nation," etc. Considering the substance of

---

[142] Posted at http://www.kprf.ru/forum/viewtopic.php?t=5785&postdays=0&postorder=asc&start=15&sid=7dbea0f460b925d0ebff662922bf0a5d on 20 May 2004.
[143] "Otklik na diskussiiu po Kharchikovu," *Communist.ru* no. 98, http://www.communist.ru/lenta/?2362 (as of 28 February 2005).

his work, his popularity seems to be an alarming signal for Russian public consciousness.

At the margins of the Orthodox political music we find extremely nationalist rock-bands and musical groups of skinheads. Among them is a punk-group named "*Korroziia metalla*," headed by Sergei E. Troitskii, popularly known as "Pauk" (Spider). Interestingly enough, he is a son of a Pan-Slavist theorist Evgenii Troitskii. The group is not a skin-band in the strict sense but it is quite similar to real skinhead bands, such as, for example, the band "*Kolovrat*." It hardly makes sense to cite long quotations from Spider's texts, but we shall translate a refrain of his well-known song "Kill the Devils" ("devils" in city slang is an offensive synonym for people of South Caucasian origins):

> Kill the devils, save Russia!
> Kill the devils, save Moscow!
> Tsunar [offensive name for "Caucasians"] was the first to get this knife,
> Your lever jacket saved you – your best friend.
> Nation is with us, God is with us!
> Tsunaref [see above] has fallen bleeding and dropped off!

On the basis of the lyrics of the group (and on the entourage of its concerts) one may conclude that it is more Satanist than Christian ("hell" is one of the most used words). However, Sergei Troitskii (according, at least, to what he says) fights the devil using his own weapons.

> Of course, we have positive regard to religion, to Orthodoxy. All members of the band are the Orthodox, are baptized and, respectively, we need the infernal terminology to provide an allegorical perception of our songs. Through these images the young people will learn about the dangers they may encounter, will learn more about the face of their real enemies,

Troitskii stated in the course of his conversation with Konstantin Kasimovskii.[144] This phrase surprisingly resembles what the above-mentioned Fa-

---

[144] "Beseda Konstantina Kasimovskogo s Sergeem (Paukom) Troitskim. 1997", http://korrroziametalla.inc.ru/stat/97/kasim.htm, (as of 20 February 2002).

ther Nektarios said about his wish to bring young people closer to God by "using the same tools as the devil."[145]

Along with the other politicized Orthodox musicians Troitskii has been actively involved in politics. In 1992 he ran for the Mayor's office in Moscow; in 1998 he was a parliamentary candidate in the Liublino district of Moscow. The concerts of "*Korroziia metalla*" are accompanied by the call "Beat the blacks!" ("blacks" meaning "Caucasians") and "Glory to Russia!" These concerts are often attended by skinheads.

Literature

If compared with music, literary works written in the spirit of political Orthodoxy are not abundant. Of course, all the above mentioned singers are also "poets" who publish their verses and are often (like, for example, Aleksandr Kharchikov, Hieromonk Roman) admitted into *Soiuz Pisatelei Rossii* (the Union of Writers of Russia), which is a "patriotic" organization that emerged after the dissolution of the Union of Soviet Writers. One may also mention Valerii Khatiushin whose poetry should be defined as "resistance verses" where Russia is presented as a country occupied by aliens and needing a purifying civil war. Khatiushin is also known because of his articulated anti-Semitism ("Yids" is one of the most common words in his political verses). As for prosaic works, the majority of ideologists prefer to recite their theories directly, not in the form of fiction books.

We suggest that writing fiction is unpopular due to its insufficient political utility. One may inflame the crowd by singing songs during a meeting but not by reciting books. Fiction books are even of less importance because extracting political ideas from them requires time and mental effort. In the short run direct political propaganda seems to be much more effective. In the long run, however, a gifted author may contribute a lot to the popularity of a political religion, as British Catholic writer Graham Green has contributed into popularity of liberation theology. Thus far, it is an open question whether political Orthodoxy has its own Green.

The author of fairy tales and former religious dissident Nikolai Blokhin (*Grandmother's Glasses*, *Flying on a Stone*, etc.) is praised mostly by funda-

---

[145] Molokotos-Linderman, "The 'Free Monks' Phenomenon".

mentalists. Even though Blokhin's writings are suggested for children, his novels seem too grim and severe even for their parents. For instance, in Blokhin's *Christmas Story* a nine year old boy voluntarily sells his soul to devil. This sounds slightly too horrific even considering that children (according to the Orthodox doctrine) start bearing responsibility for their sins at the age of seven. What is more alarming about Blokhin's books is that parents in his novels are always depicted as wicked and stupid egoists deserving no love or respect from their kids. This makes even fundamentalists hesitate about the actual value of his works.

Another author worth mentioning is Iuliia Voznesenskaia. Generally speaking, she is not a "fundamentalist writer." Voznesenskaia is a former dissident and an émigré; many things she writes seem very liberal even from the official viewpoint of the ROC. At the same time, Voznesenskaia incorporates into her novels some apparently fundamentalist ideas. In the novel *Cassandra's Path* and its sequel *Lancelot's Pilgrimage* the author portrays a world that has fallen under the reign of Antichrist. Only the Orthodox monarchy – Russia – remains isolated and protected from his power. The Antichrist tries to destroy Russia with missiles but they burn away in the air. *Lancelot's Pilgrimage* ends with a scene of the Second Coming.

We suggest that neither Blokhin nor Voznesenskaia fall into the category of "political Orthodox novelists;" they are rather Orthodox novelists with fundamentalist undertone (not to mention that they are not involved in Orthodox political activism).

We would also disagree that *The Lord of this World* by Grigorii Klimov, dedicated to battles between Soviet secret service and Satan, should be considered an Orthodox political novel. There is a great deal of politics and religion in this book, but it is not a "novel." It is a slightly novelized political treatise that should be counted not as "fiction" but as a "propagandist work." The same is true for a notorious anti-Semite "sci-fi" novel *Nameless Beast* by Evgenii Chebalin.

Eventually, the editor-in-chief of *Zavtra* newspaper Aleksandr Prokhanov appears to be the only noticeable author in the domain of literature manifesting Orthodox political ideas. Prokhanov's novels – *Walking in the Night, The Brown-Red, The Chechen Blues, Mr. Hexogen* (2002 "National Bestseller" prize winner) and others – are written from the viewpoint of Orthodox

Communism (with nationalist tincture). Nowadays they are published by the most respectable publishers and may be found in every bookstore. (We should probably mention that Prokhanov donated his prize to the relief fund for Eduard Limonov, who was at the moment in jail).

The success of *Mr. Hexogen* in 2002 can be attributed to two factors: First, Prokhanov is not a bad writer, which even people who do not sympathize with Prokhanov's political ideas will admit.[146] His novels are excessively violent but realistic and bright. In *Walking in the Night*, which describes the war in Chechnya one may find many impressive episodes, such as the one depicting a procession of wounded and semi-dead dogs in the streets of ruined city of Groznyi or the one portraying a dead woman floating along the river. This rude materialism is accompanied by mystical visions and insights revealing, for the author and for his heroes, the hidden meaning of the mundane events.

Second, *Mr. Hexogen* was published soon after two mysterious explosions of apartment houses in Moscow in October 1999. The explanation it provided was completely different from the official one. According to Prokhanov, the houses had been blown up by a clandestine organization aiming at installing "the Chosen" (apparently Putin, although the author never names him directly) as the president of Russia. Public opinion, not satisfied with the official investigation of the explosions, was enthused by the novel.

Prokhanov's novels may serve an illustration of our theoretical remarks regarding political religion and its vision of this world as an arena of a "cosmic" battle between absolute Good and absolute Evil. The protagonist of *Mr. Hexogen* thinks that he is taking part in a "normal" political conspiracy; he is also convinced that the conspiracy aims at restoration of the Soviet Union. It is too late when he finds out that the battle between Good and Evil is being conducted at the level of this world and that he has accidentally taken the wrong side. His would-be friends from the former KGB turn out to be agents of Satan planning unification of humankind under the power of Antichrist.

Here Prokhanov refers to the theory of "two secret societies": one initiated by the KGB and the other one by the Main Intelligence Department of

---

[146] About Prokhanov's literary talent see, for example, an article by Nadezhda Kozhevnikova, the daughter a famous Soviet writer Vadim Kozhevnikov: Nadezhda Kozhevnikova, "Moi sopernik – Prokhanov," *Novaia gazeta*, 2 December 2002.

the Army (*Glavnoe razvedovatelnoe upravlenie*, GRU). While KGB-people intend to submit Russia to the liberal Western civilization (to Satan), GRU-people try to protect Russian strength and spiritual independence. This theory has been explicated in details by Aleksandr Dugin in his early book *Conspirology* (1992). An agent of the world satanic conspiracy explains to the protagonist of *Mr. Hexogen*:

> The explosions you will see are healing explosions curing Russia of "the Russian idea." We explode to avoid an explosion. And we will get what we want. People from the GRU are our adversaries. Like us they have united into a clandestine order. ...they advocate Russian resurrection. They plan the Great Russia. We battle with them and we shall win.[147]

Novelist Iurii Poliakov should not be counted among the Orthodox patriots, although he openly admits his secular patriotism or etatism. Nevertheless, Poliakov's satirical novels are full of Soviet nostalgia and satirize many leading liberals, thus making them popular with most of the political Orthodox. In his novel *I Wanted to Escape...* (*Zamyslil ia pobeg...*) Poliakov outlines simultaneously ironical and epic picture of the siege of the White House in 1993 in a manner which sympathizes with its defenders. Likewise, the "patriotic" personages of the novel evidently enjoy the author's compassion. Poliakov has been interviewed by *Zavtra* and *Den' literatury* (a militantly patriotic newspaper headed by Vladimir Bondarenko); he cooperates with the *Nash sovremennik* journal. Being neither Orthodox nor a political activist, Poliakov is nevertheless active in Orthodox political circles and is seen by the majority as one of "us."

We would like to mention one more literary work (a real literary work, with vivid characters) that gained broad popularity among the Orthodox nationalists: a novel by Dmitrii Nesterov entitled *Skins: Rus Is Awakening*. This book, written with evident positive regard toward skinheads, has been issued by "Ultra. Kultura" publishing house, which specializes in shocking publications. The novel is more about nationalism than about religion; the protagonist defines himself as a "Pagan" but religious issues are not discussed in the

---

[147] Aleksandr Prokhanov, *Gospodin Geksogen* (Moskva: Ad Marginem, 2002), 432.

book. Apart from being available in common bookstores *Skins* was (and still is) sold by people disseminating Nazi literature.

Visual Arts

Since painting is characterized by high level of conventionalization, no one can be sure whether a painter has been influenced by political Orthodoxy or not (unless he/she admits it). Painters whose names are known to the community of Orthodox patriots are mostly "political painters": their art works are very straightforward and do not permit a shade of doubt regarding the artists' political preferences.

Il'ia Glazunov is the most eminent person to consider with regard to political Orthodoxy and visual arts. As early as the Soviet period he was known for his articulated patriotism and "Orthodoxism." Currently the majority of the political Orthodox recognizes him as a "patriot" even in spite of his negative attitude towards the Soviet past and his status as a man of wealth and success (Glazunov is definitely not an "underground" painter).

Glazunov's pictures are characterized by stereotyped figures ("soldier," "mother," "monk," etc.) combined in various ways to achieve a desired political effect. Some figures appear to be borrowed from icons and others from Soviet and other propagandist posters. For example, his picture "Russia, awake!" portrays a young man (a soldier) with a machine-gun in one hand and the Gospel in the other hand. Behind him stands a girl in camouflage with a machine-gun holding Russian banner (a tricolor – which, by the way, is untypical for the political Orthodox). Here and there, behind and near the couple, one can see saints and heroes of the past (for example Minin and Pozharskii), soldiers of the 1940s, praying women and many other stereotyped and easily recognizable personages.

Along with most of the political paintings by Glasunov this one looks like a collage, a puzzle to be sorted out by an onlooker. Aleksandr Prokhanov was correct when he mentioned that Glazunov's last works "may not even be called pictures. They are even not panels. They are huge frescos for a temple to be built in the future."[148] There can be many interpretations regarding who

---

[148] See: Vladimir Bondarenko, *Plamennye reaktsionery: Tri lika russkogo patriotizma* (Moskva: Algoritm, 2003), 305.

symbolizes what, but in general Glazunov's enigmas may only be fully understood within the framework of political Orthodoxy.

Commenting on "Russia, Awake!" Prokhanov said the following: "Many people saw themselves on this picture. Men of Barkashov think that he has depicted them. Russian special forces battling in Chechnia take with them a copy of 'Russia, Awake!'. It is a mystical picture in which everyone who loves Russia may see himself."[149] Vladimir Bondarenko added that "a million copies of 'Russia, Awake!' should be printed and hung on every wall, until people actually awake."[150]

"The Market of Democracy" is another collage-like enigma where an onlooker becomes virtually lost in figures and items. It is hardly possible to describe this composition or to explain the meaning of each of its elements. What strikes the eye is a naked woman in the foreground wearing Russian traditional headwear. She holds a tray with a round loaf of bread, a traditional Russian sign of hospitality. A small Russian tricolor is stuck into the bread. This message seems understandable: Russia is being sold to enemies (more precisely: to foreign enemies).

More about the enemies may be inferred from the left upper corner of the canvas. Here one can see a pyramid consisting of numerous banners of various states; an eye is pictured on the summit of the pyramid. The pyramid reminds one, first, of the one-dollar banknote and, second, of Free Masonry. Near the pyramid there is the Statue of Liberty, around which several military planes ("NATO planes") are circling. "New world order forever" is written at the bottom of the pyramid.

Some of Glazunov's pictures are not so enigmatic, such as "The Black White House" depicting the burning parliamentary building in October 1993. The red background of the picture and black contour of the building (together with people idyllically walking in the foreground) create the desired impression: to bring to mind the "heroic siege of the White House" and to inflame feelings of hatred and revenge.

Another interesting feature of Glazunov's art is his portrayal of Russians as having blonde hair and blue eyes (with nearly no exceptions). Thus he contributes to the visualization of the ideal of the Russian race promoted by

---
[149] Ibid., 307.

nationalists. It is widely acknowledged among the political Orthodox that a Soviet painter Konstantin Vasil'ev (1942-1976) was the first one to present "the new Russian type" to the world. Vasil'ev created excessively high-spirited, severe, exaggeratedly "Germanized" generic images of Russians. Russians in Vasil'ev's pictures look "Nordic," meaning they have fair hair and blue eyes; they are tall and dolichocephalic.

His picture "Russian warrior" (1974) is very typical in this regard. Clouds behind this warrior are apparently shaped as an eagle. In the Soviet cultural discourse an eagle could have been associated either with imperial Russia or with Germany (in the Ancient Rus symbols such as the eagle were not in use). Moreover, this supposedly Russian warrior is wearing an ancient German helmet. His mail is decorated with images of the Sun, which is a symbol of manhood. Such details are not accidental because Vasil'ev was also known as an illustrator of Wagner's "The Ring of Nibelungs."

There is a cult of Vasil'ev's pictures in the contemporary Orthodox political community. In September 2003 *Partiia "Evraziia"* ("Eurasia" Party) held its regional conference in the Vasil'ev Museum in Kazan. Currently a virtual museum of Vasil'ev is being developed at http://vasilyev.evrazia.org/ (so far they have only the address of Vasil'ev's museum in Moscow). A virtual collection of Vasil'ev's pictures may also be found at a fundamentalist web-site "*Russkoe Nebo* (Russian Sky)" (www.rus-sky.com). Interestingly enough, the protagonist of Nesterov's novel *Skins* pays a visit to the Moscow Vasil'ev museum. In reality, Neo-Pagans often rent the museum hall for their meetings.

Sergei Bocharov is an artist whose pictures (or, to be precise, their copies) are often used to decorate walls during various patriotic events. His pictures are Glazunov-style collages but less populated and more understandable. Each of them is a politicized replica of some famous artistic work of the past known to virtually everyone in the former Soviet Union (these works have been repeatedly published in school textbooks). For example, "The Appearance of the People" is an imitation of Aleksandr Ivanov's epic picture "The Appearance of Christ to People." Instead of John the Baptist from Ivanov's canvas, one may see Metropolitan Ioann. Among people gathered under all sorts of banners (red, black-yellow-white, etc.) the onlooker recog-

---

[150] Ibid., 310.

nizes all major activists of political Orthodoxy, including General Makashov, Aleksandr Barkashov, Aleksandr Kharchikov and Aleksandr Prokhanov. Unlike Glazunov, Bocharov prefers to portray real people, rather than symbolic personages.

Bocharov's picture "Rooks Have Come" includes a fragment from a famous landscape by Aleksandr Savrasov but most of the canvas is occupied by a cloud consisting of faces of the 500 "lying journalists," i.e. journalists of liberal orientation. At the foreground one may see Metropolitan Ioann leading by the hand a girl dressed in red (the idea is that she symbolizes Russia). Some pictures by Bocharov are claimed to be blessed by the Metropolitan.

"Unequal match" (named after a famous picture by Vasilii Pukirev) depicts a beautiful Russian woman in a traditional costume (*saratan*) whose bridegroom is George Bush Sr. Yeltsin and the other supporters of liberal reforms celebrate the event on groaning boards. The leaders of the patriotic opposition of that period (1989) are portrayed in a cage, unable to prevent what is going to happen.

It is evident that political painting performs the limited function of visualizing the pantheon and the "anti-pantheon" of political Orthodoxy. The only requirement is that all personages should be recognizable and all symbols readable. Such pictures remind one of political cartoons painted in oils.

Speaking about cartoons, we should also mention the painter and drawer Gennadii Zhivotov, whose cartoons accompany every editorial appearing in *Zavtra* newspaper (he has drawn about 600 such cartoons, each of which is dedicated to some important political event of the current week). Zhivotov also paints canvas and makes water-drawings; the former are mostly non-political while the latter are highly politicized. His drawings are characterized by the demonization of political adversaries mostly depicted as small but ugly demons with black bat-like wings (for example, the 2000 drawing "Battlefield" features demonic images of Boris Yeltsin, Viktor Chernomyrdin and others). Tatiana D'iachenko, Yeltsin's daughter, has once been portrayed by Zhivotov as a witch flying on a broom. Such caricatures of the enemies are commonly used during oppositional demonstrations as posters. At the same time, Gennadii Zhivotov has painted several idealized portraits of the leading oppositionists, such as Aleksandr Prokhanov.

In his drawings Zhivotov, evidently reflecting the Orthodox Communist position of *Zavtra*, mixes Soviet and Orthodox symbols: crosses and five-ended stars, space rockets and the head of an ancient Russian warrior in a helmet as well as an Orthodox cross standing on a submarine. The submarine is supposed to be "Kursk" – a symbol of Soviet military strength in decay; in one of the cartoons "Kursk" beams as a sacral object thus illustrating Aleksandr Prokhanov's intention to portray its sailors as "saints." (To be precise, this idea may be found across the whole spectrum of political Orthodoxy. In January 2004 in Moscow several icons with the images of sailors were exhibited; they were depicted, however, not in the central part of icons, but at the margins.)

Apart from highly politicized painters like Glazunov or Bocharov there are painters whose art works from time to time reveal spiritual kinship to political Orthodoxy. For example, Father Mikhail Maleev is in no way a "political painter" but his picture "Kulikovo Battlefield. 21st century" portraying a monk-warrior with a naked sword could have become an illustration for any theoretical work on political Orthodoxy. Kulikovo Battlefield, the place of a decisive battle against Tatars in 1380, is often used by Orthodox ideologists as a symbol of the spiritual battle for Russia they claim to conduct (for example, one of the songs by Hieromonk Roman is called "All of Russia Has Become Kulikovo Battlefield").

It is hard to name a fiction movie that would be a product of the cultural underworld of political Orthodoxy. This is the result of financial restraints: it is much cheaper to publish a book or to record a CD than to make a fiction movie. Nikolai Burliaev, a film director supporting the ideas of political Orthodoxy, shot his last film in 1990, in the Soviet period.

There are, however, many documentaries inspired by political Orthodoxy. These may be purchased via Internet, during various patriotic events or at a church. Such films are normally not screened in movie theaters except in special cases, such as a festival of Orthodox films, TV- and radio-programs called "Radonezh," held each year since 1995. In 2004 the Moscow Committee of the KPRF initiated the All-Russian Contest of Patriotic Movies and Videoclips *"My ne slomleny"* (We are not broken down) where one can also see some documentaries with religiopolitical background.

Among documentaries available at stores and web-sites, one could name "Behind the Veil of Masonry," about the Masonic conspiracy against Russia, "The Advance of Satanism," "It's Me, Apocalypse" (prize-winner at "Radonezh" festival of 2003), "Hollywood Terrorism," and "Russian Cross," about anti-Russian activities of the West.

There is also a category of "resistance films," which may not be called "Orthodox" in the strictest sense. Nevertheless, most of them contain references to some ideas or symbols of political Orthodoxy. For example, a film by Nikolai Pchëlkin entitled "Betrayal," screened during the Second All-Russian Contest of Patriotic Movies and Videoclips (24 April 2005) included the chronicle of street-fighting in 1993 accompanied by a song about fighting Satan and Satanism, providing a religious dimension for the political event in question.

Let us have a closer look at the documentary "Russian Map" by Ivan Sidel'nikov[151]. The film consists of two parts: part one has nothing to do with political Orthodoxy, but is rather a nationalistic piece with emphasis on geopolitics and economy; part two is very much the same. However, in the end of part two the author (and narrator) suddenly jumps to a city fest at the ancient Russian city Belozersk. We see church domes and crosses; the narrator says that citizens of Belozersk are now recalling their ancestors' great deeds at Kulikovo Battlefield. The major of Belozersk explains that the most important thing is to return to our roots. "There are spots of awakening on the Russian map," Sidel'nikov states. In Russian history, he continues, periods of trouble always interchanged with great empires. Then the author informs us (also suddenly) that Russia is the old country of Aryans and that modern civilization has come to the dead-end. No direct conclusions are made; the general impression is, however, that Russia as an Orthodox and Aryan country has some great world mission.

A documentary "Russian Mystery" dedicated to the events of October 1993 is extremely popular with the political Orthodox (1996, director: Viacheslav Tikhonov, narrator: Nikolai Burliaev)[152]. This movie contributed a great deal to the understanding of the siege of the White House as a *religious* event. The means it utilizes are in no way rude or simplistic. The authors

---

[151] "Russkaia karta", "Russkaia karta II", a CD (producer unknown).

thoroughly create the impression that defenders of the building killed by the army are, in fact, saints. The father of a slain seventeen year-old boy Roman Verëvkin, for example, recalls that his son's girlfriend visited him "like we go to confess, to take communion, like we go to the church." Family stories of the victims acquire epic features: they turn into hagiography of holy warriors or martyrs. The mother of a fourty-one year-old victim recalls his words: "Mom, I need nothing... Russia is dying." She also insists that "they perished protecting Rus, the Holy Rus." In the end dozens of names of the victims are screened under the headline "Passional." We would like once again to stress that for political religions words like "martyrs" and "holiness" are not figurative expressions; their meaning is overt and direct.

The siege itself, as well as the rebel's unsuccessful attack upon the TV-centre are portrayed in the documentary as a cosmic battle between Good and Evil. The authors use slow-motion screening and religious music off-screen so that all movements of rebels with various flags (red and black-yellow-white) resemble religious processions – slow and solemn. An anonymous "protector of the Constitution" recalls that "the sky that day was clear," a manifestation of God's help to the rebels. As for the enemies, they appear virtually satanic: for example, Yeltsin's face suddenly becomes black-and-white and then red with goggle white eyes. One of the survivors, singer Tamara Kartintseva, recalls how one of the governmental armored cars pursued a priest with an icon and then "ran him over." We neither question such stories nor insist on their reliability; reliable or not they contribute to the vision of the 1993 uprising as a sacral event.

In the end of the film the narrator unravels the "Russian mystery": the Orthodox faith is able to save not only Russia but the whole world. Western civilization, on the contrary, is portrayed as a quintessence of Evil, as the main cause of Russian misfortunes. It is not accidental that a rotating street clock with an advertisement for cigarettes "West" constantly reappears in the frame, evoking the image of both a rotating cannon and some fantastical radiator of poisoning rays.

Some movies of this sort are distributed for free only. For example, a film called "Russian Tanks in Pristina" (2004, author: Aleksei Borzehko, cam-

---

[152] "Russkaia taina," a DVD (producer unknown).

era: Anton Peredel'skii) dedicated to the idea of Slavic brotherhood is available for downloading at "Russian Orthodox Television" web-site. Under the heading "To buy a videotape" one finds the following information: "Non-available; for free only. Such videotapes are not available commercially and will not be until our Victory comes." (http://russtv.ru/content2/patriot/patriot_war/patriot_war5.shtml).

The absence of fiction movies makes the political Orthodox accept some mainstream movies as "crypto-patriotic." A popular movie by Aleksei Balabanov "War" (*Voina*)* serves an example. According to some Orthodox nationalist observers, it educates Russian youth in the spirit of war heroism. The movie clearly demonstrates that Russians morally, intellectually and physically outmatch Europeans; it also contains a set of stereotypes about Chechens portraying them as either brutal gunmen, or cowardly traitors. It is a disputable question whether Balabanov is a conscious nationalist. Patriots, however, count him among "us."

---

* Shot in 2002. Director: Aleksei Balabanov; Starring: Aleksei Chadov, Jan Kelly, Sergei Bodrov, et.al.

III. 3 Mass Media

In the Orthodox political subculture, the mass media performs several important functions. First, they inform members of the community about events taking place within the subculture (conferences, demonstrations, contests, etc.). Second, they interpret, in the spirit of political Orthodoxy, the events taking place in the outside world. Third, they provide communication within the subculture. And fourth, they translate the opinions produced by the subculture to the outside world.

With all these various functions, there is one thing they don't do, which is to inform people about the events in the outside world. The religiopolitical mass media is thereby useless for those not belonging to that community; to be one of their consumers is to testify to one's membership in this community. The first question for the uninitiated is: "Do you read our newspapers, patriotic newspapers?" The political Orthodox, of course, must utilize the "alien" mass media just to know what is going on. But people outside the community (apart from researchers and human rights advocates) become familiarized with religiopolitical mass media only by accident.

Some religiopolitical media publish private ads clearly demonstrating their community-building function. In the newspaper *Radonezh* one may find an ad such as: "Housework assistant (Orthodox) needed," or "An Orthodox artist seeks job in a publishing house." *Russkaia Pravda* (Russian Truth) advertises "Russian massage" promising "discounts for Russian nationalists;" it also needs a "driver-patriot with his own car." We suggest that nothing demonstrates the existence of religiopolitical subcultures better than such ads.

Television and Radio
Unlike the publishing of newsletters, the making of TV-shows requires significant monetary inflows and official consent. Due to this fact, there have been only two nation-wide TV-programs expressing Orthodox political ideas: *Russkii dom* (Russian Home) and its successor *Russkii vzgliad* (Russian Vision).

Russkii dom was initiated by the "Moskoviia" channel in 1992. Journalist Aleksandr N. Krutov, then the general manager and the editor-in-chief of "Moskoviia," became its regular host until in October 2003. *Russkii dom* was suddenly terminated and replaced with the new program *Russkii vzgliad*, hosted by Ivan Demidov. The official explanation for this change was that Krutov had been elected to the parliament and could no longer host the program.

There are obvious differences between *Russkii dom* and *Russkii vzgliad*. Krutov (born 1947) is older than Demidov (born 1963) and has milder appearance and voice. Dressed in a light-colored suit, a white shirt and a tie he sat against a modest background of an icon of St.Sergii of Radonezh. Demidov sits against a futuristic red-colored background resembling a panorama of New York. He wears suits and shirts of dark colors and no tie (see in the end of the chapter for more about ties) and his general manner of speaking is more aggressive. (It should be mentioned that both Krutov and Demidov are recent Orthodox converts.)

Differences in style are less important than changes in the program's agenda. *Russkii dom* was a peculiar combination of political fundamentalism, Russian nationalism and Orthodox Communism. The latter was represented by a political analyst, former intelligence officer General-Lieutenant (Ret.) Nikolai Leonov. *Russkii dom* was tightly connected not only with "Orthodox patriots" as such but with the national patriotic opposition as a whole. As a result, its position was pronouncedly anti-governmental regardless of who was in the office: Yeltsin or Putin. "The loss of national awareness is a tragedy of the Russian people nowadays. The country is dismembered and oppressed by foreigners and by pseudo-Russians who speak and write Russian but think and behave like enemies of Russia," Krutov said on the air on 31 August 2003.

Russkii vzgliad evidently distances its self from the "old" national patriots and often invites people who never appeared on *Russkii dom*: for example, Aleksandr Dugin is presented as a "philosopher" or "political analyst." In spite of its more modern and aggressive external appearance, the position of *Russkii vzgliad* is closer to that of the official nation-building project.

A TV-analyst Mikhail Leont'ev, one of the propagandists of "official nationalism," has defined *Russkii vzgliad*'s ideology as "calm, normal, civilized, Orthodox etatism." (Leont'ev, who never appeared in *Russkii dom*, is often invited to *Russkii vzgliad* as a commentator). Commenting on the previous program he mentioned: "As for '*Russkii dom*,' they professed the ideology of a besieged castle: we die, but we don't give up. The authors of '*Russkii dom*' felt themselves permanent losers, martyrs... Orthodox, imperial nationalism does not need the ideology of a besieged fortress and does not need cheap xenophobia."[153] In fact, *Russkii vzgliad* is no less xenophobic than *Russkii dom*; it is just pro-presidential. In spite of the fact that *Russkii vzgliad* remains a politicized Orthodox program, it is much closer to the official position of the ROC than *Russkii dom* which automatically makes it more loyal to the authorities.

Even when criticizing the policy of the government the program never attacks Putin. On 8 March 2005 *Russkii vzgliad* presented a report about liberal reforms in the sphere of housing. Being highly critical of the governmental proposals, the program assigned responsibility for them to the government exclusively (more precisely, to minister Mikhail Zurabov), without even mentioning Putin's position. The same approach was taken on 3 April 2005, when the new governmental concept of health service was repeatedly referred to as "Zurabov's concept."

It is no surprise that a significant percentage of the political Orthodox considers *Russkii vzgliad* to be a "pseudo-Orthodox" and "pseudo-patriotic" program. A participant in the *Russkii dom* web-forum has reacted to the change in the following way: "Instead of Aleksandr Nikolaevich [Krutov] we have *Russkii vzgliad* with some idiotic aliens. Instead of a wonderful Orthodox program they have started Zionist propaganda..." (19 October 2003).[154]

As recently as the end of 2004 the number of Orthodox political programs on TV has grown to include a mysterious program entitled *Nasha strategiia* (Our Strategy). While it does not appear in TV-guides, it has been aired on Saturdays at approximately 6:40 p.m. on channel TV-3. Its host is Mikhail Shiriaev and its symbol is a two-headed eagle in flames. Apparently, the program is aired on a commercial basis; in fact it seems to be nothing but a lengthy commercial. Most likely the project has been initiated by *Rodina* because the members of this parliamentary faction (Aleksandr Krutov, Nataliia Narochnitskaia) constantly appear in the program. The purpose of the program was articulated as "an attempt to work out a Russian vision in order to

---

[153] Mikhail Leont'ev, "Otnosheniia Putina s ierarkhiei: dolzhnaia distantsiia pri polnom uvazhenii," http://www.religare.ru/print7637.htm (as of 16 December 2003).

[154] Quoted in: Ol'ga Chapnina, "Obzor SMI. Reaktsiia na zakrytie 'Russkogo Doma'," http://www.religare.ru/print7637.htm/print7126.htm (as of 29 October 2003).

maintain Russians as a state-constitutive people" (*Nasha strategiia*, 5 March 2005).

Nasha strategiia is not anti-presidential; it is, nevertheless, much more radically "patriotic" than *Russkii vzgliad*. For example, on 9 April 2005 the program was dedicated to "anti-Russian sentiments" among Jews. Mikhail Shiriaev made several "anti-Russian" quotations from the book *Kitsur Shulkhan Arukh*, an ancient Hebrew code of behaviour published by the Congress of Jewish Religious Organizations and Unions in Russia. Then he suggested that Russians should borrow from the Jewish experience of struggle against "hostile states" and initiate an Anti-Defamation League for Russians, who lost their state in 1917. This, the host stressed, would contribute to anti-xenophobic activities of president Putin and prevent further "anti-Russian and anti-governmental" attacks.

It is interesting to note that in spite of their closeness to the ROC, both *Nasha strategiia* and *Russkii vzgliad* are highly esteemed by extreme nationalists professing Neo-Paganism. This position has been articulated, for instance, by co-chair of the NDPR Aleksandr Sevast'ianov during the Second Congress of Slavic Communities (Moscow, 30 April 2005).

As a spectacle, *Nasha strategiia* so far falls behind *Russkii vzgliad* or *Russkii dom*: it has no live programs, only "talking heads" and screened texts. However, it has apparently been successful in utilizing many symbols and stereotypes of national patriotism: for example, it claims to rely on consultation from a "retired counter-intelligence officer," as the participation of such a person is obligatory for an Orthodox patriotic event. At the moment we shall not attempt to predict the future of this TV-program or to trace its actual financial and ideological sources.

The situation regarding radio programs does not differ much from that of television. Broadcasting is expensive and requires special permits. One may name three middle-wave radio stations disseminating some ideas of political Orthodoxy. These are radio *Radonezh*, *Narodnoe radio* (People's Radio) and *Rezonans* (Resonance), though the latter have been defunct since the fall of 2004. Only *Narodnoe radio* broadcasts from 7:00 a.m. to 7:00 p.m.; *Radonezh* is on the air from 8:00 p.m. to 11:00 p.m., while *Rezonans* broadcasted from Monday to Saturday, 5:00 p.m to 9:00 p.m.). *Radonezh* and *Narodnoe radio* are also available via Internet.

None of the above-mentioned stations is a "voice" of political Orthodoxy in the full sense. *Narodnoe radio* is much more a communist and socialist station. It has, however, noticeable religiopolitical dimension. The logo of the station – a ringing bell – is also a wide-spread symbol of political Orthodoxy: it reminds of *nabat* (a church alarm bell) used to warn people about coming threats. *Narodnoe radio* emphasizes that it started broadcasting on 14 October 1997, which is the Orthodox holiday of the Veil of Our Lady.

Narodnoe radio features a special program entitled "Preacher," moderated by Father Pavel Burov. This program is characterized by extreme Orthodox nationalism and fundamentalism with constant attacks against globalization, "Judeo-Masonry," "Jewish extremism," and so forth. The program hosted such people as Mikhail Nazarov (a former émigré and extreme Orthodox nationalist), Boris Mironov (the author of "Jewish Yoke"), Il'ia Chislov (chairman of the Society of Russo-Serbian Friendship) and other prominent Orthodox nationalists and Pan-Slavists. Besides "Preacher" the station has also broadcasted a weekly program *Russkii dom* (related to the TV-namesake), though it has been terminated for unclear reasons.

Many other programs also incorporate some elements of political Orthodoxy. The station is focused on such issues as threats from the side of NATO and the West in general, the union between Russia and Belarus, and "patriotic education," just to name a few recurrent themes.

On 7 April 2005, for instance, *Narodnoe radio* informed the audience about an Orthodox secondary school in Moscow where children study Serbian culture and language. Its director Igor' Buzin explained why his school has chosen this path:

> It is not a secret that nowadays all schools teach, first of all, Western languages. But when studying a language a person has to dip into the culture of the people who speak that language... We would not want our children to dip into Western ideology, to learn it deeply and to accept it into their hearts. We wanted them to be accurately educated on the basis of Eastern Christianity.

This quotation demonstrates how political Orthodoxy infiltrates information provided by this supposedly secular station.

Radio *Radonezh*, initiated by the Orthodox society (brotherhood) "Radonezh" is more an "Orthodox" station than narrowly "political Orthodox." Most of its broadcasting time is occupied by non-political topics (the Scripture, church holydays, church music, etc.). Nevertheless, when *Radonezh* talks about politics, it advocates fundamentalist and Orthodox nationalist positions. Anti-liberal and anti-Western rhetoric is accompanied by anti-migrant sentiments. Russia is portrayed as a country occupied by some hostile forces (although fundamentalists rarely use the term "anti-people regime," popular among the rest of Orthodox patriots).

For example, on 19 February 2004 radio *Radonezh* organized a roundtable discussion of an explosion in a Moscow subway, understood to be a terrorist act. It was claimed that "Russian" (i.e. ethnically Russian) people have died once again and that this problem has become the central issue for "Russian" (again, ethnic Russian) society. Then it was said that inside the country there is an "anti-Russian, anti-Orthodox fifth column" directing the activities of the Muslims "against the Slavic and ethnic Russian" population of the country. One of the participants of the discussion, Vladimir Semenko, said that this community (the "fifth column") is totally hostile to Russians at the spiritual level, thus lending both an ethnic as well as religious dimension to the issue of terrorism.

Having made some remarks about the above-mentioned topics, another participant, Mikhail Smolin, put forward the idea that Islamic terrorists, in fact, serve that very "big Satan" (America) whom they pretend to confront. We have already mentioned that most of the political Orthodox don't see "Caucasians" and Muslims as a sovereign adversary, considering them agents of the West. This permitted the participants of the roundtable discussion to avoid blaming Islam as a whole: they came to the conclusion that real, "traditional" Islam is not to be held culpable.

Radio *Rezonans* was, like *Narodnoe radio* a communist station. It was notorious for a program called "Resistance Songs," which was the only broadcasting program where one could listen to radical oppositional songs, sometimes with an Orthodox and/or nationalist flavor.

Newspapers and Journals

Most of the printed media disseminating Orthodox political ideas are organs of various political organizations. Even the smallest ones often have their own newspapers/newsletters. Such printed production does not perform community-building functions; instead, these micro-newspapers build tiny networks within the Orthodox political subculture. They rarely (or never) provide space for discussions or publish authors who are not members of this particular grouping within political Orthodoxy.

An Orthodox survey *Radonezh* is what immediately comes to mind with regard to political Orthodoxy. However, unlike its radio-namesake, this newspaper is characterized by a mild political fundamentalism which is only slightly more radical than the official position of the Church. Due to this fact *Radonezh* is less prone to establish contacts with the other versions of political Orthodoxy and never allows them to disseminate their ideas in its pages. It is very much a "partisan" newspaper more useful for the fundamentalist "subculture within subculture" than for the Orthodox political movement as a whole. The moderate position of the survey is explained by the relative rigidity of printed media in comparison with radio and the Internet. It is much easier to control what is printed than what has been said; besides, it is easier to file a suit based upon something what has appeared in print.

A self-proclaimed independent patriotic Orthodox newspaper called *Rus' Pravoslavnaia*, edited by Konstantin Dushenov, fulfills, in a way, the role of a community-builder. In 1993 this publication, blessed by Metropolitan Ioann, first appeared as an insert in the paper *Sovetskaia Rossiia* and only as late as in 1997 was transformed into a separate newspaper. Being radically anti-ROC, Dushenov is not bound by loyalty to the church. *Rus' Pravoslavnaia* features discussions among columnists (for example, in Summer-Fall 2004 a discussion about "the red idea" between M. Fedorov and Vladimir Neviarovich was printed), interviews people who may not be genuine fundamentalists (like Iurii Savel'ev, an Orthodox Communist with nationalist inclinations) and raises a voice in support of neo-Pagan "Russian patriots" (like Roman Perin). Nevertheless *Rus' Pravoslavnaia* has too limited a circulation to even consider offering free access to its Internet-version.

Zavtra – a legendary weekly of the patriotic movement – is the only political Orthodox printed organ with national circulation. It is also one of two oppositional newspapers (together with *Sovetskaia Rossiia*, the "independent people's newspaper") that may be bought at "normal" news-stands. Initiated as *Den'* (Day), it was banned in 1993 and reborn as *Zavtra* (Tomorrow). First, it was sold as "a newspaper of spiritual opposition" and since 1996 as "a newspaper of the State of Russia," meaning, most likely, the Russia of "tomorrow." Aleksandr Prokhanov is its editor-in-chief.

Zavtra serves as a source of information about all patriotic events, as a reviewer and advertiser of books and as a forum for the Orthodox patriots. It posts information from all sources, even from those furthest from its own ideological position (which is Orthodox Communism with a nationalist flavor). For example, sometimes *Zavtra* advertises anti-Orthodox books by extreme nationalists. The spectrum of people to whom *Zavtra* have ever provided the floor is very broad, ranging from secular Communists to real Nazis.

Zavtra serves as a nursery for the emerging leaders of political Orthodoxy, giving them an opportunity to reach nation-wide audience. This was the case of Aleksandr Dugin. He was known to a tiny circle of Moscow counter-culture intellectuals and acquired nation-wide popularity thanks to his publications in *Zavtra* where he edited an inset "Invasion: The National Bolshevik Territory" and then "Eurasian Invasion." Due to Prokhanov's pro-imperial, essentially Eurasianist position *Zavtra* often hosts authors who are ethnically non-Russian (a rare thing among Orthodox patriots). An Israeli anti-Zionist author Israel Shamir is a regular author in the weekly.

In many aspects, *Zavtra* is an "anti-newspaper." It publishes no fresh or exclusive information: only interpretations and explanations of current events. It does not publish many advertisements (apart from patriotic advertisements). Sometimes it devotes entire pages to verses, short stories or fragments of novels. This only proves that in the underworld of political Orthodoxy, the mass media exist not to inform but to indoctrinate and to consolidate.

Apart from newspapers, there are the literary journals *Moskva* (editor-in-chief: Leonid Borodin) and *Nash sovremennik* (Our Contemporary, editor-in-chief: Stanislav Kuniaev). *Moskva* is closer to political fundamentalism; it has a supplement "Domestic Church." At the same time, the journal does not reject the "imperial" (Eurasianist-cum-Communist) approach. *Nash sovremennik* is an organ of *Soiuz Pisatelei Rossii* (see above) and gravitates to a more general "patriotic" position often publishing Gennadii Ziuganov, Sergei Glaz'ev, Sergei Kara-Murza and other people for whom socialism seems to outweigh Orthodoxy. Nevertheless, the journal has published Metropolitan Ioann's "Triumph of Orthodoxy" and other purely fundamentalist pieces.

Molodaia gvardiia (Young Guard, editor-in-chief: Evgenii Iushin) is a literary journal that became notorious for its articulated anti-Semitism as early as in the beginning of the 1990s (in fact, the journal was seen as "patriotic" already in the 1960s). Above-mentioned poet Valerii Khatiushin is its deputy editor-in-chief. One could also name an illustrated monthly *Russkii dom* (editor-in-chief: Aleksandr Krutov), published with the subhead "A magazine for those who love Russia." Interestingly enough, in the 1990s it was advertised as "A magazine for those who *still* love Russia."

Internet

The Internet is the most important media for the political Orthodox. Supporting web-sites does not require large monetary expenses and, at the same time, permits access the most geographically remote audiences. Since political Orthodoxy is insufficiently represented on national TV, the slogan "Internet against TV-screen" gains more and more popularity.

Some Orthodox political web-sites have been initiated especially as alternatives to television. One of them is the so-called "Internet TV-channel" *Radonezh* (www.radonezh.ru/telekanal/). In fact it is not an Internet-channel but an archive of Orthodox TV-programs (including *Russkii vzgliad*) previously broadcast by various channels. It also offers viewings of various documentaries. Another prominent resource of this kind is "Russian Orthodox Television on the Internet" (http://russtv.ru/) disseminating mostly "resistance films." The purpose of this web-resource is formulated as "witness to Christ; propaganda of Russian patriotism; rebirth of Russia; informational confrontation to lies."

Apart from collections of video films and songs, there are web-libraries of "patriotic" orientation where one may find Orthodox and nationalist literature. These are, for example, www.patriotica.ru; lindex.narod.ru; www.arcto.ru; www.zaistinu.ru; www.libereya.ru/biblus/. It is worth mentioning that most of the above-mentioned libraries and collections are supported by private citizens at their own expense.

Several sites claim to be alternative sources of the news, providing an alternative to the mainstream mass-media, which is dominated, as they insist, by anti-Russian and anti-Orthodox information. Among the best known are *Agentstvo Russkoi Informatsii* (The Agency of Russian Information, www.ari.ru) and *Russkaia liniia* (Russian Line. The Orthodox Information Agency, www.rusk.ru). However, both of them follow the pattern of printed Orthodox media in that they are not so much alternative sources of information as commentators and interpreters of information available through other sources. "Ari.ru" (it has also English version) is characterized by extreme nationalism, not as much Orthodox as semi-Pagan. "Rusk.ru" sometimes provides information related to Orthodox political activism which is not available via the mainstream media. It also hosts an "Orthodox patriotic calendar" informing about various events that happened in the past on a given day which may be interesting for an Orthodox patriot.

Nearly all Orthodox patriotic organizations and some prominent public figures have their own web-sites. Such websites (most of those mentioned in this chapter) are united into a "Web-ring of Patriotic Resources" (www.patriot.rossija.info). So far it has about 143 participating sites. Another joint resource where one may find links to many Orthodox political organizations is Nationalism.org. Normally Orthodox political web-sites place banners of the other like sites under the subtitle "links," or "friends." The presence of some links may seem peculiar; for example, "Evrazia.org" web-site accommodates a banner of the KPRF in spite of their unfriendly terms. Fundamentalist organizations often host links to Serbian Orthodox nationalist sites (and vice versa), of which many have Russian versions (for example, www.srpska.ru; www.pogledi.co.yu/ruski/index.php).

Aleksandr Dugin has initiated two huge web-resources: one is *Arktogeia*, dedicated to philosophy and culture (www.arcto.ru), the other one is *Evraziia*, (www.evrazia.org) dedicated to current political issues. Here one may find everything said or written by Dugin or his comrades-in-arms and everything said or written about them. "Evrazia.org" offers versions in English, French, German, Italian, Spanish and Turkish although they are not so informative and frequently updated as the Russian one (still, the majority of Orthodox political sites exist only in the Russian version). *Arktogeia* has two forums: one to discuss "philosophy of the sacral," the other to discuss politics and geopolitics.

Evraziia accommodates many links to organizations and web-resources that would be hard to find otherwise, for example, a Transdniestrian web-magazine *Russkii Rubezh* (Russian Frontier), an Australian esoteric magazine *New Dawn*, a Serbian Eurasianist resource "Endkampf.net" and so on. Interestingly enough, some of these web-recourses are available in local languages only (for example, in Turkish, Serbian, etc.), apparently in order to stress the universality of Eurasianism.

There are a number of websites which are not "religiopolitical" in the strict sense yet periodically post materials professing some ideas of political Orthodoxy. These are, for example, www.portal-credo.ru; www.pravoslavie.ru; www.pravaya.ru. "Credo.ru" is a site which collects Orthodoxy-related information and conducts mass media monitoring; it often republishes fundamentalist materials or interviews leaders of political Orthodoxy. "Pravoslavie.ru" (English version available) is close to the official position of the ROC. However, many materials this site hosts (especially those marked as "Analytics") disseminate fundamentalist and nationalist ideas. The banner of "Pravaya.ru" designates it as an "Orthodox political site," but this is not strictly true, at least, according to our understanding of political Orthodoxy. Nevertheless, the recourse reproduces articles on political Orthodoxy that appear somewhere else; it also offers sort of "alternative news" meaning mostly news interpreted in the spirit of moderate fundamentalism.

Internet forums and mailing lists are extremely important for building networks between groups and individuals related to political Orthodoxy. Most of these people are not wealthy; it is often problematic for them to attend a meeting or congress (for organizations it is equally problematic to hold a meeting or congress). Forums are used not even so much for discussing topics but for placing information about events and organizations, exchanging addresses, sharing methods of political struggle, and so on.

Mailing lists perform similar functions. Some organizations create databases of people interested in their ideology (i.e., mailing lists subscribers) and assist them in networking, thus building local organizations from a scratch. Nationalists are particularly good at this, due to the fact that they are wary of legal prosecution and try to be as invisible as possible. Large organizations often finance purchasing computers for their local units.

III.4 Hangouts and Dress Code

Extreme fundamentalists sometimes settle in secluded compounds such as a self-described "city Cossack community" named *"Spas"* (Savior) that emerged in the town of Obninsk near Moscow.[155] Members of the community bought a former *sovkhos* and transformed it into an agricultural cooperative. The community produces all of its own food, dishes and even clothes (women knit and sew). Prayer accompanies every activity and rules of behavior imitate monastic ones. The members of the community also learn martial arts. However, not many people agree to encapsulate themselves in such compounds. The subculture of political Orthodoxy is therefore a non-territorial network.

This subculture nevertheless exhibits some physical dimension. Mikhail Polikarpov, the author of an autobiographic book *Sacrifice*, about Russian volunteers in Serbia, has coined a phrase "patriotic hangouts" (*patrioticheskie tusovki*). Hangouts may be spatial (where such people may be found hourly) or temporal (in cases where one must be informed where and when to come).

In Moscow there is a spot (at the entrance to "Ploshchad' Revoliutsii" subway station) where one can always buy various newspapers and books on political Orthodoxy. Films, CDs and audiotapes are available on Saturdays only; one may, however, ask for a specific production and the distributor will be contacted. One of the stands sells Nazi books and movies; when customers look through them with interest, the seller whispers: "Would you like *Mein Kampf*?" (The sale of this book is prohibited in Russia).

So far there have been no bookstores in Moscow that would sell this sort of literature exclusively (except for party offices or publishing houses). However, some bookstores are considered by religiopolitical organizations as their bases, where they hold meetings with authors and which they recommend as sources for books. Historical and religious association *Arktogeia* and *Mezhdunarodnoe Evraziiskoe Dvizhenie* have adopted the "Transylvania" bookstore, which also sells horror movies and other similar products. The NDPR and *Soiuz Slavianskikh Obshchin* consider the store "*Belye Oblaka*" (White Clouds) as their base, always stressing that it is a "respectable" bookstore. A kiosk at the Konstantin Vasil'ev's Museum also sells mostly Neo-

Pagan and nationalist literature. (We have already mentioned that this museum and the one in Kazan are often venues of religiopolitical events). One may also name a bookstore of *Soiuz Pisatelei Rossii* in Moscow selling patriotic literary works.

A store that may serve a model of a fixed patriotic hangout is located in Minsk (Belarus). Named *"Pravoslavnaia kniga"* (Orthodox Book), it sells not only books and films, but also icons and canonicals. Moreover, it is the headquarters of a fundamentalist political organization called ZAO *"Pravoslavnaia initsiativa"* where various meetings and lectures are conducted. The store is located in a common concrete apartment house, but its interior resembles a church (we have already mentioned the slogan "The Orthodox of the world, unite!").

These are, so to say, spatial hangouts. As for temporal ones, one may mention All-Russian Contests "Songs of Resistance" held once a year since 1997 to commemorate the siege of the parliament in 1993. The Contests are sponsored by the KPRF and *Duel* newspaper, though the latter is not a religiopolitical publication. Nevertheless, the Contests are dominated by political Orthodox and nationalist songs; there are few leftist songs without references to religion or nation.

An anonymous reviewer at the web-site of the left anarchist organization *"Avtonomnoe deistvie"* (Autonomous Action) had the following impression of the 2004 Contest: "I myself expected the participants to sing exclusively anti-capitalist songs... I was shocked to discover that, upon having heard several songs, I had been attending a "red-brown" concert (well, hardly even red)."[156] When Aleksandr Kharchikov sang his "Kill the Yid Inside Yourself" (in the Contest program, by the way, it was designated as "Kill the Slave Inside Yourself") a group of leftists began shouting "Down with Fascism", but the majority of the audience, as we have already mentioned, did not support them. Anatolii Beliaev, a singer, whose turn was next, "pacified" anarchists with the following phrase: "Of course, down with Judeo-Fascism!" Such exchanges, we suggest, essentially convey the Contests' atmosphere.

---

[155] See: Nikolai Piniasov, "Zhit' – Bogu sluzhit'," *Pravoporiadok*, July 2002, http://www.sv-rus.ru/st/obninsk.html (as of 20 November 2004).

[156] "Moskva: anarkhisty vzorvali 'Pesni Soprotivleniia'," http://avtonom.org/img/pesni/ (as of 1 December 2004).

Winners of the Contests are expected to be named by the audience. Together with the ticket each onlooker gets a ballot with numbers assigned to the participants and has to nominate three of them as prospective winners. Than a commission collects the bulletins and announces three prize-winning songs/authors. Besides, various organizations and private citizens are allowed to award participants upon their choice. This system seems democratic enough; however, in 2004 Aleksandr Kharchikov, first time since 1997, was awarded none of the prizes. He suggested that since "Kill the Yid Inside Yourself" did not become the winning song, fraud must have been involved in the vote.[157] There are, thus, internal conflicts even in the community of patriots.

The 2004 Contest was the first one to be (partly) televised by a country-wide TV-channel NTV (on 30 November 2004, on the "*Strana i mir*" program). It was presented as a marginal cultural event, having the flavor of counterculture. It should be mentioned that such temporal hangouts mostly take place in remote and shabby concert halls. Information about them may be found on the Internet but even there it is hard to trace. Information flyers are also distributed from hand to hand during various events. As a result, they mostly attract people who already belong to the subculture of political Orthodoxy.

Some events of this sort are open to the broader public; however, events held by "subcultures within the subculture" are often difficult to even learn about. Such was the case with the Second Congress of Slavic Communities, where only people who were issued personal invitations knew where it took place, moreover, besides, members of the NDPR youth section guarded the event and turned back people with "non-Slavic" appearance.

Annual *Vsemirnyi Russkii Narodnyi Sobor* held since 1997 under the patronage of the Patriarch had been designed as an event uniting all Orthodox patriots and providing them with a space for exchanging opinions. It is, indeed, attended by most of the leaders of political Orthodoxy representing all of its ideological variations (Aleksandr Panarin, Aleksandr Dugin, Boleslav Tejkovsky, Leonid Shershnev – all these people had a chance to address the *Sobors*). Gennadii Ziuganov is traditionally invited as a quest; the 2005 *Sobor* has also been attended by Viktor Ianukovich seen, based upon his would-be "pro-Russian" position as one of "us."

---

[157] Personal conversation with Aleksandr Kharchikov, 4 May 2005.

However, *Sobors*, due to their closeness to the ROC and semi-official status (in 2005 this organization will most likely be granted the ECOSOC consultative status), fail to completely perform their purported tasks. *Sobors* are attended by the president and the hierarchs of the ROC; as a result, the most radical opinions may be heard not at plenary sessions but only during panels. The fact that the state seems to encourage these events reveals its implicit function of a valve letting off the steam accumulated within Orthodox radicalism. *Sobors* still serve a useful forum and a meeting place for the political Orthodox, but the majority does not take them too seriously.

Dress-code is an important characteristic of youth subcultures, for instance, everyone knows about the dress-code of skinheads. The issue is of less importance when one focuses on adult people. Of all the partisans of political Orthodoxy only fundamentalists have something resembling a dress-code, though not every fundamentalist follows it and not everyone who follows it is a political fundamentalist. Fundamentalists as a political community are very close to what we have previously described as a subculture of parishioners. Nevertheless, if someone is consistently (not only inside a church) dressed in accordance to the rules prescribed by the Church one should assume that he or she is a fundamentalist (though perhaps, non-political).

Fundamentalist women wear long skirts (or *sarafans*), blouses with long sleeves and scarves (special white scarves, sometimes with lace decorations, are available at church stores). Men wear blouses (often black) with stand-up collars (*kosovorotka*) or coats without lapels and in most cases have beards. Fundamentalists don't wear ties. Vladimir Osipov, the head of *Soiuz "Khristianskoe Vozrozhdenie,"* commented on those attending the Church of St.Nicolas at Bersenevka: "Most parishioners prefer to dress like our pious ancestors – men wear *kosovorotkas* with belts, women wear *sarafans* and scarves pinned to hair."[158] Fundamentalists, dressed in this manner, are very noticeable in public places, such as libraries or stores.

Some radical neo-Pagans insist that a true Pagan (*rodnover*) must wear specific clothes – a Slavic shirt and a headband. Neo-Pagan web-sites provide recommendations about sewing Slavic shirts. The majority, however, wears "Pagan" cloths only during religious events. Vladimir Avdeev has once said in an interview: "I have Pagan initiation; I have a sacral Pagan name. I have everything. But I don't play these games; I don't run around with a headband. I wear suit and tie as a normal European man... There are many ways to please gods."[159] The more politicized neo-Pagans become, then, the less they exhibit concern about being "properly" dressed.

With regards to the remainder of the political Orthodox, one should simply note that the majority of such people lack the financial resources necessary to be choosy about clothes (even Russian skinheads often don't follow the dress-code because they can not afford it). Many people just don't care about congruence between their religiopolitical position and external appearance. That is why our further observations about dress-code concern only people who deliberately make their clothes express their ideological preferences.

Most of these people wear dark clothes; for example, men prefer dark shirts. (As strange as it may sound, women are generally much less concerned about demonstrating their religiopolitical preferences through their choice of clothes). Very often men are dressed in camouflage, with or without emblems designating their membership in an organization. Some people wear *kosovorotkas*. Above all, however, it is important to notice that the political Orthodox rarely wear ties.

The issue of ties has been discussed specifically by Aleksandr Dugin in his essay "All about ties." He points out that the Old Believers (the "real" Orthodox) never wore ties, calling them "Judas loops." "In Rus a man with a tie had always been equated with the apostate Judas Iscariot," Dugin writes.[160] Then he provides a religious explanation regarding why one should wear belts and not ties (both divide the human body into bottom and summit, though one who wears a tie makes his heart "a bottom").

It is hardly possible that the political Orthodox follow Dugin's advise thoroughly (although the essay, published by *Zavtra*, became known nationwide). The issue of ties, however, constantly reappears among the Orthodox

---

[158] Vladimir Osipov, "Bersenëvskuiu obshchinu khotiat izgnat' ne tol'ko za antiglobalizm," http://portal-credo.ru/site/?act=news&id=32621 (as of 5 April 2005).
[159] Vladimir Avdeev, "Rossiia nikogda ne byla pravoslavnoi stranoi," http://portal-credo.ru/site/?act=news&id=29897 (as of 11 January 2005).
[160] Aleksandr Dugin, "Vsë o galstuke," *Zavtra*, 25 May 1999.

patriots. Well before Dugin, General Makashov indicated that "in Rus people rarely wore ties; mostly, they wore shirts undone to show everyone whether or not you wear a cross."[161] Once again, we don't insist that patriots always do as Makashov says. The fact is that they rarely wear ties. Most likely, ties are associated with the (corrupt) officials, considered to be servants of the "anti-people regime."

Ties and white shirts are worn by those leaders of religiopolitical and nationalist movements who want to look "respectable." Aleksandr Sevast'ianov in the NDPR's program brochure found it necessary to justify his bowtie: "The practice shows that our common adversaries are not so much afraid of nationalists in boots and black blouses... A nationalist with a bowtie – a scholar, a writer, a banker, a top-administrator, a lawyer – horrifies them."[162] Still, those who wear ties must be willing to offer an explanation.

In conclusion, we would like to refer to an interview with a famous Russian clothing designer Viacheslav Zaitsev, published in 2000 by *Vtorzhenie*, a supplement to *Zavtra* (he is known in the West thanks to "Maroussia" perfume). Zaitsev regrets that in contemporary Russia one is not able to find traditional Russian clothes (linen *sarafans* and *kosovorotkas*). This fact he explains by a "conspiracy against Russian clothes": "Someone tries at any price to distract us from the traditional costume, to make us wear alien clothes – clothes programming us for anti-national, anti-patriotic reactions and which make us an easy prey for evil forces reigning contemporary world..."[163] Apparently, the issue of clothes has religious connotations for the political Orthodox, even in the absence of a strict dress-code.

---

[161] "'Vsem pavshim – tsarstvo nebesnoe'".
[162] *NDPR – partiia russkogo naroda* (Moskva: Natsional'naia gazeta, 2005), 63.
[163] "Zagovor protiv russkoi odezhdy," *Vtorzhenie* no. 6 (2000), http://arcto.ru/modules. php?name=News&file=article&sid=815 (as of 19 February 2005).

IV The Political Orthodox as Believers

IV.1 Ideological Religiosity vs. Traditional Religiosity

The issue of religiosity is of crucial importance since religiosity makes political religion the most likely choice in the absence of ideological alternatives. Obviously, people must first be religious before a religion can become politicized. It is not, however, quite clear what sort of religiosity engenders political religion. As paradoxical as it may seem, politicization is most likely to occur under circumstances where people have just returned to their semi-forgotten religious beliefs and where the majority of population does not observe the rituals and does not know the fundamentals of their religion. The lack of knowledge and devotion to rituals may well be accompanied by the most fervent nominal religiosity.

This situation has been thoroughly studied with regard to the Russian North Caucasus (Chechnia and Dagestan) by scholars trying to explain a "sudden" outburst of political Islam. Ol'ga Bibikova points out that political neo-Wahhabism emerges where traditional Islam is weak: for example, in the areas dominated by Sufism ("popular Islam") or state-imposed atheism.[164] Anatolii Savvateev indicates that Chechens, prior to the advent of Wahhabism, were not religious in the traditional sense (i.e., they were not theologically literate and did not observe rituals).[165] Likewise, in the beginning of 1990s most of Soviet Muslims consumed alcohol and did not observe food bans.[166]

The rise of political Islam in the North Caucasus is, as Vladimir Maksimenko puts it, an instance of a "second Islamization" appearing in the do-

---

[164] Ol'ga Bibikova, "'Vakhkhabizm' v SNG", in *Islam i politika* (Moskva: IV RAN; Kraft+, 2001), 87-88.
[165] Anatolii Savvateev, "Islam i politika v Chechenskoi Respublike," *Obshchestvennye nauki i sovremennost'* no. 2 (2000): 87.
[166] Aleksei Malashenko, *Islamskie orientiry Severnogo Kavkaza* (Moskva: Gendalf, 2001), 83-84.

main of ideology rather than in the domain of faith.[167] Restoration is the key word. Two factors contribute into growing influence of political religions: on the one hand, people are not able to identify differences between a religious ideology and the official version of a religion; on the other hand, they are not accustomed to communicating with traditional religious leaders. These leaders, in their turn, after having been isolated within their subculture for an extended period of time, have become unable to communicate with ordinary people and to speak their language.

Prior to being indoctrinated with political religions by the religious-minded intelligentsia, most people adhere to so-called "popular" religions. While popular religious practice often significantly differs from the official form of a religion, it does not become politicized. Popular religions in most cases don't tackle the deepest layers of human consciousness. Adherence to them implies observing rituals which are often meaningless for participants themselves. Popular versions of universal religions are mostly ethnicized and incorporate elements of previous (for example, Pagan) beliefs that existed before the dogmas of the official religion had been formulated. The practice of popular religion does not require significant efforts and easily turns into religious indifference when religion becomes an element of "our culture."

Popular religions have their own spiritual leaders distinct from the leaders of an official, institutionalized religion. Religious politicization, thus, engenders a collision of three social groups: (1) religiously oriented lay intellectuals supporting politicization and their followers; (2) the religious establishment (clergymen and educated lay theologians, or religious professionals) and (3) the followers of popular religion and their unofficial leaders.

The second group is a constant and educated opponent of politicization. Its members understand the heretical nature of political religions and often "unmask" it with the help of mass media. The third group is determined to lose its supporters, who spontaneously respond to calls for "returning to foundations of our religion." At the same time, however, they are often unable to distinguish these "foundations" from innovations. Most people don't even understand exactly what transformation of social life on the basis of "traditional

---

[167] Vladimir Maksimenko, "Fundamentalizm i ekstremizm v islame. Predislovie," in *Islam i islamizm* (Moskva: RISI, 1999), 9.

values" means. Intellectuals – supporters of political religions – make use of this lack of understanding.

In the Russian North Caucasus one may see a collision of "three Islams": (1) the official Sunni Islam, (2) the unofficial popular Sufi Islam, and (3) the new Wahhabist "pure" Islam introduced by intellectuals. Political religions undermine the authority of the establishment by making it consolidate to protect itself.[168] In Chechnya, for example, both the officials from the Spiritual Departments of Muslims and the unofficial leaders of the local Sufi orders accuse Islamists of betraying genuine, traditional Islam. The point is that both are concerned about preserving the status quo, while the leaders of "pure Islam" aim at destroying the existing system. In Christian countries churches often consider popular religion to a lesser evil in comparison to political religion, because popular religion never confronts the hierarchy and demonstrates nominal respect for the religious establishment.

The situation with religiosity in the "Orthodox" (populated by ethnic Russians) regions of Russia is slightly more complicated. Most people practice neither the canonical version nor the popular one; although many have some fragmented knowledge of popular Orthodoxy this does not seem to influence their everyday behaviour. The same situation is typical for the other two Slavic republics of the former Soviet Union (Belarus and the Ukraine).

Many Russian scholars think that the politicization of Russian Orthodoxy is unlikely because the majority of the population is rather indifferent to religion and is not religious in any meaningful sense.[169] The same position has been expressed by Ukrainian sociologists suggesting, who hold that the mispractice of "their" religion by the majority of Orthodox believers (e.g., they don't know how to hold candles properly) indicates that "religious parties" would not be popular with such people.[170]

These arguments seem valid. As previously mentioned, mass religiosity is one of the factors contributing to religious politicization (including neophyte religiosity). Many authors measure Orthodox religiosity by attempting to de-

---

[168] Malashenko, *Islamskie orientiry Severnogo Kavkaza*, 62-63.
[169] Fedor Ovsienko, N.A.Trofimchuk, "Konfessional'nyi faktor v rossiiskom politicheskom protsesse: sushchnost' i mesto (obzor)" in *Religiia i kul'tura. Referativnyi sbornik* (Moskva: INION RAN, 2000), 107.

termine to what extent a believer practices his/her religion.[171] The data is rather disappointing.

Sociological surveys conducted in Russia, the Ukraine and Belarus demonstrate that many more people consider themselves "Orthodox" than "believers." In 1999, according to a Russo-Finnish study of religiosity "Old churches, new believers," 82% of all Russian respondents called themselves adherents of Orthodoxy.[172] Thus, the number of the Orthodox has significantly exceeded the number of believers (42% of respondents). 98% of Russian believers, 90% of those who hesitated, 50% non-believers and even 42% of atheists called themselves Orthodox. They evidently thought that one may be an Orthodox while not being a believer.

The authors of the above-cited research, based on polls conducted in 1991, 1993, 1996 and 1999, agree that a "pro-religious" and "pro-Orthodox" consensus exists in Russian society: 94 % of respondents have shown a "very good" or "good" attitude towards Orthodoxy, significantly exceeding the number of believers; 84% of atheists have a "good" attitude and 24% of them have a "very good" attitude toward Orthodoxy.[173] The authors conclude that for the majority of Russians Orthodoxy is not a religion but a symbol of Russian specificity and the spiritual value of this specificity; they define this phenomenon as "ideological Orthodoxy." Similar terms have been appearing in recent writings, such as "the new Orthodox," or "the new believers".

The ideological Orthodox can be distinguished from the "real" Orthodox, first of all, because they don't practice Orthodoxy. The new Orthodox rarely attend churches. According to VTsIOM (the All-Russian Centre for Studying Public Opinion) 1996 data, 55% and in 1997, 57% of respondents calling themselves Orthodox nearly never attended church services; 31 and 34% attended them 2-4 times a year. Two-thirds (1996) and 68 % (1997) never took communion, which means that 82-85% of the Orthodox were not practicing

---

[170] M. Ribachuk, M. Kiriushko, S. Smirnov, "Na perekhresti politiki i religii," *Viche* no. 9 (1998): 93.
[171] Kseniia Tsekhanovskaia, "Rossiia: tendentsii pravoslavnoi religioznosti v XX veke," *Etnograficheskoe obozrenie* no. 5 (1999): 60.
[172] Kimmo Kääriäinen, Dmitrii Furman, "Religioznost' v Rossii v 1990-e gody," in *Starye tserkvi, novye veruiushchie: religiia v massovom soznanii postsovetskoi Rossii* (Sankt-Peterburg; Moskva: Letnii sad, 2000), 16.
[173] Ibid., 11-12.

religion according to the church rules. Only about 4-5% of the Orthodox took communion once a month, which is a minimal frequency.[174] The same data was obtained by the authors of the "Old churches, new believers" research (Table 1).[175] Table 2 provides comparative data for Belarus.[176] It demonstrates that more Catholics attend church more often than the Orthodox and that fewer Catholics "never attend" church. This does not mean that Catholics are more religious but that two different kinds of religiosity (traditional and ideological) are being represented here.

Table 1. Church attendance in Russia, the Orthodox, 1991-1999 (%)

	1991	1993	1996	1999
At least once a month	6	7	6	7
Several times a year	8	10	20	19
Once a year or less often	27	21	25	29
Never	59	62	48	45

Table 2. Church attendance in Belarus, 1997 (%, survey conducted by the Byelorussian State University)

	Regularly attend	Sometimes	Never
Believers	18,5	62,2	19,3
The Orthodox	14,9	65,9	19,2
Catholics	43,0	47,2	9,8

Interestingly enough, the data obtained in the Orthodox countries shows that relatively low church attendance does not prevent religious politicization. The situation in the Orthodox regions of the former Yugoslavia resembles the one in Russia. In spite of the fact that the Russian Orthodox media constantly compares the religious indifferentism of Russians with the supposedly ubiquitous religiosity of the Serbs, sociologists are of a different opinion. According

---

[174] Fedor Ovsienko, N.A.Trofimchuk, "Pravoslavie v kontekste rasvitiia federativnykh i etnopoliticheskykh otnoshenii v Rossiiskoi Federatsii" in *Religia i kul'tura. Referativnyi sbornik* (Moskva: INION RAN, 2000), 99.
[175] Kääriäinen, Furman, "Religioznost' v Rossii v 1990-e gody," 21.
[176] Lidia Novikova, "Osnovnye kharakteristiki dinamiki religioznosti naseleniia," *Sotsis* no. 3 (1998): 96.

to World Values Survey (1990-1993)[177] only 7% of adults attended church at least once a week in Serbia (as opposed to 22 % in Slovenia and Croatia). The same index in Slovakia was 47%, in Bulgaria, 10%, and in Russia, 2%.

Considering that in Russia and Serbia religion is noticeably politicised, that in Bulgaria, Slovenia and Croatia it is politicised insignificantly and that in Slovakia it seems to be not politicised at all, one may conclude that religious politicization and church attendance are interdependent in a reverse manner.

Apart from church attendance there are some other indicators of religious devotion (i.e., knowledge of prayers and the Bible, fasting, frequency of praying, confession, communion, etc.). Only 4% of the Orthodox believers fasted in 1996 and 1999; 69% in 1996 "practically never" read the Bible, 44% in 1999 "never opened" it.[178] Communion was taken (April 1998) by the Orthodox with the following frequency: 0.6 % - once a week, 2.2% - once a month, 12 % - several times a year and 16.6% - once a year or less.[179]

Greek scholar George Mavrogordatos suggests that an Orthodox revival in the end of the 20th century is not a revival of religion as such, but rather of nationalism identified with Orthodoxy.[180] According to the European Values Survey in 1999, when politicization of Orthodoxy in Greece was at its peak, 53.9% of Greek respondents attended churches on special occasions, 20.9%, once a month and 22.3%, once a week[181] These numbers are, of course, higher than in Russia and Belarus, but they are not impressive for a country where Orthodoxy is a state religion. This Orthodoxy, then, must be the very "ideological Orthodoxy" we have already mentioned. Mavrogordatos suggests that "secularization in Greece, which is comparable with that in

---

[177] Vjekoslav Perica, *Balkan Idols: Religion and Nationalism in Yugoslav States* (New York: Oxford University Press, 2002), 305 (footnote).
[178] Kääriäinen, Furman, "Religioznost' v Rossii v 1990-e gody", 22.
[179] Mikhail Tul'skii, "Rol' tserkvi v zhizni rossiiskogo obshchestva," *NG-religii*, 9 August 2000.
[180] George Mavrogordatos, "Church-State Relations in the Greek Orthodox Case" (Paper presented to the workshop «Church and State in Europe», ECPR Joint Sessions, Copenhagen, 14-19 April 2000).
[181] Lina Molokotos-Liederman, "The Religious Factor in the Construction of Europe: Greece, Orthodoxy and the European Union" (Paper presented at the 1st London School of Economics Ph.D. Symposium on Modern Greece: "Current Social Science Research on Greece", London, 21 June 2003).

Western countries, appears quite irrelevant in this context."[182] Secularization results in diminishing religious practices, but people still stick to Orthodoxy as ideology.

The new Orthodox are not just bad parishioners, they are also theologically "illiterate." Most of them have eclectic religious beliefs sometimes contradicting the Church doctrine and often taken from "popular Orthodoxy." For example, according to the data obtained by the Center for Sociological Research (1996) 47% of all the Orthodox respondents believed in witchcraft and evil eye, 42%, in soul immortality and resurrection of Christ, 40%, in the Last Judgment, 39%, in salvation, 32%, in the devil, 31 %, in life after death, 21%, in the Antichrist and 18 % in the Doomsday.[183] According to a poll conducted in the Republic of Tuva in 1999, 40% of people calling themselves "Orthodox" (of whom, by the way, 36.36% never go to church) believe in "auras" and 21.82% in "karma."[184]

Both anthropologists and local clergymen register numerous superstitions and even false religious concepts as widely held among Orthodox believers (even among church-goers). Hieromonk Tikhon (Polianskii) observes that ethnofolkloric relics of Paganism, such as the making a funeral rice dish, are perceived by their bearers not as something non-Orthodox but as Orthodox traditions.[185] A belief that each saint has his/her own specialization, widespread throughout "the Orthodox world," is also a fragment of Pagan beliefs.[186] Nevertheless, in most Russian churches one may see a variety of small icons offered with detailed explanations regarding to whom to pray in a specific cases.

Even a brief analysis of the above-listed data provokes a question: Do true Orthodox believers exist in Russia? It is not surprising that the authors of the "Old churches, new believers" research reach the pessimistic conclusion

---

[182] Mavrogordatos, "Church-State Relations in the Greek Orthodox Case".
[183] Valentina Mikhaliuk, "Religioznye orientatsii naseleniia: sotsiologicheskii srez," *Politiia* no. 4 (1997-1998): 42.
[184] See: Ol'ga Khomushku, "Vliianie religii na etnokul'turnye i etnopoliticheskie protsessy v Respublike Tyva" (Paper presented at the international conference "Chelovek – kul'tura – obshchestvo", Moscow, 13-15 February 2002).
[185] Hieromonk Tikhon (Polianskii), "Proiavleniia iazychestva i ikh preodolenie v prikhodskoi praktike," *Missionerskoe obozrenie* no. 9 (2002): 11.
[186] Slavka Grebenarova, "The Bulgarian in Crisis: A Pagan, a Christian or an Atheist," *Ethnologia Bulgarica* no. 2 (2001): 44.

that the idea of a "religious revival" as it pertains to Russia should only be understood figuratively. They suggest that "this revival is very superficial and 'ideological' not affecting deeper layers of consciousness."[187]

We suggest, however, that instead of distinguishing "genuine" from "false" Orthodox religiosity, one should simply acknowledge the existence of two types of religiosity, i.e., "traditional" and "new." Traditional religiosity involves performing rituals, knowledge of the catechism and an unconditional trust in the church hierarchy. New religiosity entails a free approach to rituals and dogmas and does not consider the clergy as a primary source of knowledge about religion. Thus, we question the position that practicing a religion and knowing its foundations are the only possible indicators of religiosity.

It is evident that the religiosity of the majority of the Russian population is not church-oriented and is non-dogmatic. Neither does it imply the observance of rituals: although some new believers observe some rituals, they prefer to choose for themselves which rituals to observe. Many people, for example, don't want to confess because in Russian churches confession mostly takes place in the presence of other people, who are able to hear what a confessant says.

A description of the feelings of such a believer was given by a liberal Christian magazine *Istina i zhizn* (Truth and living):

> ...Tatiana... has been regularly attending a church for two years but she has never confessed or taken communion. She thinks that the clergymen she knows are unable to sort out her spiritual problems and, most likely, will not even listen to her. Along with many other believers among the humanitarian intelligentsia, Tatiana was previously interested in... occultism and Oriental religions. Having come to a belief in Christ, she does not indiscriminately reject the knowledge obtained prior to her conversion. On the contrary, she became firmer in her opinion that evaluations given by clergymen regarding non-Christian spiritualities are baselessly negative and often disputable.[188]

---

[187] Kääriäinen, Furman, "Religioznost' v Rossii v 1990-e gody," 38.
[188] Vasilii Kandalintsev, "Novye pravoslavnye," *Istina i zhizn'* no. 2 (2000): 12.

Although a description of an individual person, this is, in fact, the story of an entire generation of "the new Orthodox" that emerged after the collapse of socialism, not only in Russia but everywhere in the "Orthodox countries." For a significant part of the contemporary Orthodox intelligentsia religiosity does not necessarily entail "practicing" religion, or at least, practicing it in the forms prescribed by the church.

It is worth mentioning that a free approach to rituals and dogmas in no way determines political preferences of these new believers. Such preferences depend on many social, economic and psychological factors not related to religion. Some of them conclude that the Church is too restrictive and become Orthodox liberals; some decide that the Church is too liberal and become fundamentalists. All the new believers are highly critical of the church hierarchy and of the clergy in general, for various reasons (e.g., "they are obscurantist," "there are too many Jewish clerics," "they don't know foundations of Orthodoxy," "they serve Mammon, not God" – all these objections are, in fact, equally valid).

Mutual dislike and distrust characterize relations between the Orthodox intelligentsia (both "practicing" and "non-practicing," liberal and conservative) and the Orthodox clergy. The clergy does not meet the excessively high expectations of the new believers. These expectations have been plainly described by deacon Andrei Kuraev (he himself begun his ecclesiastical career as a student at the chair of scientific atheism of the Department of Philosophy at the Moscow State University): "I myself remember my own idealized vision of religious people in the period when I was at the verge of faith... I thought that all monks are ascetics; they eat one little host a day and drink a spoonful of holy water..."[189] This description is, of course, facetious, but it reflects the idealized vision of the clergy by neophytes. In their opinion, the clergy should have only spiritual interests and should talk only about faith and morality. It is also important to note that the clergy did not approve of "enriching" Orthodoxy with Aryan, Vedic, Islamic and other traditions. Most of the new Orthodox, even those rejecting ecumenism, mix Orthodoxy with which ever fragments of religious and ideological traditions best answer to their spiritual and political needs.

Religious revival in Russia (and in the most "Orthodox" countries) has replaced decades-long religious indifference, when contacts between the clergy and the majority of the population remained minimal. The intelligentsia (unlike, for example, peasants) tried, in many ways, to be involved in decision making, thus rendering communication with the Church even more difficult. Most intellectuals voluntarily distanced them selves from the clergy – with the exception of a fringe of "religious dissidents." As a result the Church and its faithful laymen became a subculture with its own behavioral patterns, communication rules, language and even dress code.[190] This subculture is alien and hostile to religious intellectuals and often annoys them.

Popular Orthodoxy in the USSR was embodied in rituals, such as attending churches on important holydays or celebrating Christmas and Easter. Even state-supported atheist propaganda was unable to eliminate this ritualistic Orthodoxy completely. Intellectuals were the most alienated from popular Orthodoxy and encountering it was an unpleasant surprise for them. They did not consider the consecration of Easter cakes and willow, religious processions or Easter kisses as "religion." Moreover, intellectuals were able to notice Pagan relics within popular Orthodoxy which were invisible to its devotees.

Religiously minded intellectuals wanted the Church to answer the most pressing social, political and even economic questions of modernity. They wanted it to become their spiritual leader. Instead they found a closed subculture that wanted them to observe rituals they never knew and never understood. This subculture implied established ties, unknown to them, and it was not really friendly to them. An intellectual comes into a church to learn how to live, and is told that he/she takes a candle with the wrong hand, stands in the wrong place and should get out because he/she is wearing the wrong clothes.

As a result, in Russia there is a stratum of "Orthodox believers" who are completely alienated from any religious organizations or established religious practices ("ideological religiosity.") These are socially active and educated people whose spiritual needs are not being satisfied. While they have the

---

[189] Deacon Andrei Kuraev, "V poiskakh 'zolotogo' veka," http://www.kuraev.ru/zoloto.html (as of 1 August 2002).

[190] On parishioners as subculture see: Konstantin Kostiuk, "Pravoslavnyi fundamentalizm," *Politicheskie issledovaniia* no. 5 (2000): 140-142; Nikolai Mitrokhin, "Iavliaetsia

greatest respect for Orthodoxy, they do not know exactly what to expect from this religion. They simultaneously represent both the milieu where Orthodox political ideologies are developed and the target group for religiopolitical propaganda.

A society characterized by high degree of religiosity (that very "pro-Orthodox consensus" registered by sociologists) and accompanied by lack of knowledge about "our" religion becomes extremely vulnerable to religopolitical propaganda. Any version of Orthodoxy invented by ideologists of political religion will be met enthusiastically. It is evident that to prevent religious politicization people should obtain a better knowledge of canonical Orthodoxy (as well as other religions), but it is unclear who would provide such knowledge. The clergy is not ready to communicate with people outside the subculture of parishioners. So far only the backers of political Orthodoxy have been eager to disseminate their ideas.

---

li tserkovnyi prikhod iacheikoi grazhdanskogo obshchestva?", http://www.inp.ru/main.html?code=73 (as of 20 November 2004).

IV. 2 Religiosity of the Political Orthodox

The ideological religiosity of the new believers does not prevent them from being active participants of religiopolitical movements. Quite the opposite: on 17 April 2005 *Russkii vzgliad* informed the public about Moscow dwellers protesting against building a "Russian-American Christian Institute" in their neighbourhood. Activists suggested that building a Protestant facility in close proximity of the World War II beds of honour is a sacrilege. One of the protesters, a young woman, said: "I am personally not a believer myself, but it is our Orthodox culture, we should respect it." This seeming contradiction ("not a believer" – "*our* Orthodox culture") appears to be a normal way of thinking for the Orthodox political activists.

Most of the current leaders of political Orthodoxy have converted to Orthodoxy just recently and often suddenly. Some have passed through prolonged religious quests (Oriental religions, occultism, etc.). Nearly none of them received religious education from their parents. As a result, they always have been and partly still remain alienated from rituals and the other forms of communication with the Church.

Some of the political Orthodox (the majority of political fundamentalists) are church-goers but they attend specific churches where priests share their political preferences. A church of St. Nicolas at Bersenevskaia embankment in Moscow (Bersenevka) is an example of such ecclesiastic-cum-political symbiosis. For many years the prior of this church, Father Kirill (Sakharov) headed *Soiuz Pravoslavnykh Bratstv*. In 1999 he declined this position but remains the secretary of this organization. The headquarters of *Soiuz Pravoslavnykh Bratstv* is located within the church complex. The Church of St. Nicolas in Pizhi is another example. Its prior, Father Aleksandr Shargunov, is one of the leading fundamentalist authors. People who destroyed the "Beware, religion!" exhibition in 2003 belong to the community of this church.

The community of Bersenevka belongs to one of the branches of Old Believers, recognized by the ROC (*edinoverie*). *Edinoverie* is characterized by a more austere rituals and code of behavior than official Orthodoxy. According to Father Kirill (Sakharov) none of the parishioners descend from a family professing *edinoverie*.[191] This peculiar community of newly converted Old Believers is a clear demonstration that the political Orthodox are at odd terms with rituals. Some of them (fundamentalists) suggest that rituals of canonical Orthodoxy are unsatisfactory in terms of austerity and rigor and form Bersenevka-like communities – dissident but still related to the official Church. Some reject the ROC's mode of practicing Orthodoxy altogether.

Professor Yurii Saveliev, former President of the St.Petersburg Baltic State Technical University and now a parliamentarian (*Rodina* faction), said in an interview to *Rus' Pravoslavnaia* that "not being a person really practicing Orthodoxy", he is, nevertheless, an "Orthodox fundamentalist."[192] The notion of a non-practicing Orthodox fundamentalist is, of course, nonsense – from the canonical viewpoint but not from the position of political Orthodoxy. It is this very ideological Orthodoxy that allows people to call themselves Orthodox without believing in dogmas or following the rites.

Aleksandr Lukashenko is credited with coining the phrase "I am an atheist, but I am an Orthodox atheist." So far the author has failed to identify where (and whether) the president of Belarus said this. Nevertheless, this phrase is commonly referred to by both scholars (to identify religious beliefs of many leaders of political Orthodoxy) and the new Orthodox intellectuals themselves.[193] The latter see no contradiction in combining these terms. For example, General Leonid Shershenev wrote, that "I relegate myself to atheists, meaning to Orthodox non-believers, to the Orthodox civilization."[194]

Such non-practicing Orthodox believers often stop by churches and perform some rituals upon their choice. Aleksandr Sevast'ianov, who is in fact a

---

[191] Father Kirill (Sakharov), "S tochki zreniia Soiuza Pravoslavnykh Grazhdan, my – radikal'nye fundamentalisty," http://portal-credo.ru/site/print.php?act=news&id=18452 (as of 20 February 2004).

[192] Iurii Savel'ev, "Ia – russkii imperialist i pravoslavnyi kommunist," *Rus' Pravoslavnaia*, September–October 2002.

[193] This would-be quotation from Lukashenko may be found (without references) in: Lev Mitrokhin, "O religii, ateizme i pravoslavii," http://www.religare.ru/analytics1062.htm (as of 1 October 2002); Andrei Kishtymov, "Uniatstvo i belorusskaia natsional'naia ideia: ot Kastusia Kalinovskogo do nashikh dnei," *Adkrytae Gramadstva* no. 2 (2002), http://www.data.minsk.by/opensociety/2.02/5.html (as of 3 May 2005); A.A. Krasikov, "Religiia v massovom soznanii rossiian," http://www.ieras.ru/journal/journal4.2001/15.htm (as of 3 May 2005).

[194] Leonid Schershnev, "Osobennosti sovremennogo liberalizma," http://www.fnimb.org/doc_rik_2.htm (as of May 3, 2005).

neo-Pagan, admits that "sometimes I come to the church, perform some rituals which I consider true, effective. I worship many saints, especially my patron Aleksandr Nevskii... I light candles to commemorate my dead relatives, everyone whom I know and remember."[195] To understand what such people feel, let us quote from the author's interview with one of the activists of political Orthodoxy (the original style preserved):

> I feel myself an Orthodox Soviet person and I think that a genuine Orthodox is the one who rejects the Old Testament, and lives according to the New Testament. As for contemporary pseudo-Orthodox church, in 70% of its sermons it mentions personages of Judaic origins from the Old Testament... I go to church but irregularly. One woman has written to me that she will never enter a church where president VVP [Putin] worshiped (to Jehovah, I suggest). Today, unlike in the so-called godless time, Our Orthodox Russian God does not live in most churches any more, because these "churches" have been turned into houses of Mammon... God – He should be not in bricks, but in ribs, not in logs, but in soul.[196]

Answering the author's direct question about whether he confesses and takes communion, the same person answered: "No. I have no time."[197]

Apart from people simply not practicing Orthodoxy in any meaningful form, there is a strata of the political Orthodox who have invented their own quasi-Orthodox rituals. Radical fundamentalists, for example, have developed cults of Ivan the Terrible, of Evgenii Rodionov, an 18-year-old conscript killed in Chechnia supposedly for refusing to convert into Islam and of Grigorii Rasputin. They paint icons depicting them as saints and disseminate texts of prayers to them. Members of some brotherhoods that seceded from the ROC (for example, the brotherhood founded by Andrei Shchedrin – *Oprichnoe Bratstvo*) are reported to practice initiation rituals and to confess to the head of the brotherhood (such reports are questionable, however, due to lack of re-

---

[195] *NDPR – partiia russkogo naroda* (Moskva: Natsional'naia gazeta, 2005), 10.
[196] Interview, 23 April 2005 (So far this person has not authorized publicizing his name).
[197] Interview, 4 May 2005.

liability).[198] *Oprichnoe Bratstvo* also positively evaluates Stalin as a "crypto-Orthodox," although it is not reported that they worship him.[199]

It is natural that neo-Pagans should invent their own rituals. While some of them claim to possess clandestine knowledge about real ancient Pagan rituals, the others openly admit that most of rituals have to be reinvented anew. The latter also point out that Russian "native religion" (*rodnaia vera*) included esoteric components now mostly lost and in need of reconstruction. Some of the rituals of Neo-Pagans seem politicized: for example, the members of the Union of Slavic Communities glorify their gods by raising hands in a Nazi salute and saying "Glory to gods!"

We think that the political Orthodox are earnest and in their own way religious people, but their beliefs differ from what the church doctrine teaches. The "Orthodoxy" they profess is in many aspects their own invention. Many leaders of contemporary political Orthodoxy recall their long journey towards this religion, their interest in mysticism, their visions, etc.

For example, Aleksandr Prokhanov (at the moment of interview the editor-in-chief of *Den*) revealed the following about himself:

> I read a lot, although without system. At 25, being possessed by pride, I even thought that I had known nearly all schools of thought, that I was nearly "an initiate." I studied Oriental philosophy, meditation practices, sank into native Orthodoxy, was devoted to folklore; I was always interested in Paganism. Moreover, at that moment I had individual mystical experience, relatively strong and intense...: mystical insights, visions, even epiphanies.[200]

---

[198] On *Oprichnoe Bratstvo* see, for example: Aleksandr Dvorkin, "Psevdopravoslavnaia sekta 'Oprichnoe bratstvo' i eë rukovoditel' N. Kozlov (A.A. Shchedrin)", http://iriney.vinchi.ru/sects/001.htm (as of 25 February 2004); Boris Knorre, "Oprichnyi mistitsizm v religioznykh praktikakh tsarebozhnikov" (Paper presented at the Second French-Russian Colloquium "Religioznye praktiki v sovremennoi Rossii," Moscow, 17-18 January 2005).

[199] Knorre, "Oprichnyi mistitsizm v religioznykh praktikakh tsarebozhnikov".

[200] "Russkii khaos. Interv'iu s A.Prokhanovym," *Elementy* no. 1 (1992): 9.

A sudden insight or an inner personal transformation is nearly commonplace for biographies of new Orthodox intellectuals, although not everyone would admit having such a mystical experience.

Let us recite the story of conversion of singer Zhanna Bichevskaia (narrated by Father Andrei Kuraev):

> Everything started as usual: occult literature, Blavatsky, Roerichs, Vivekananda, Ramakrishna... And one night I was reading one more occult book and came upon a very common occult statement: 'Way up and way down is the same... What is up, is down... good and evil are the same...' And suddenly I was so terror-struck – it was equating God and the devil; it was, in point of fact, Satanism![201]

As a result Bichevskaia became not just an Orthodox (with Christian name Anna), but a fundamentalist. Her relationship with the ROC, however, remains dubious. An article about Bichevskaia with a distinctive headline "From Zhanna to Anna" (an allusion to a Russian proverb "from Savl to Pavel" hinting at people who, like Apostle Paul, have radically changed their beliefs) appeared at the web-site on an anti-cult Center of St. Irinei of Lion under subhead "Distortions of Orthodoxy and Para-Orthodox Sects."[202] The article was highly critical of Bichevskaia's political Orthodox songs and preaching activities and questioned her being a "true" Orthodox.

There is also an interesting testimony related to personal mystical insights from Yugoslavian experience of religious politicization, found by Paul Moijes. Radovan Karadzic has once mentioned in an interview that he believes that the Holy Spirit speaks through him:

> God... was the one to teach us what should be done, and the Holy Spirit whispered into our ears what we should say, of which I am particularly convinced, because often I went to meetings without a prepared concept – actually, it was always like that... – and I have always followed the Gospel: Don not

---

[201] Deacon Andrei Kuraev, *O nashem porazhenii* (Sankt-Peterburg: Svetloiar; Fond 'Blagovest', 1999), 390.
[202] Natal'ia Volkova, "Ot Zhanny – k Anne," http://iriney.vinchi.ru/sects/004.htm (as of 21 March 2005).

worry about what you are going to say. The Spirit itself will tell you what you have to say.[203]

Insufficient devotion of the political Orthodox to the Church, their pragmatic approach to religion (the way they pick up rituals and beliefs suitable for them) provokes negative feelings of both clergymen and scholars who study the phenomenon in question. They often suggest that new intellectuals are not sincere, that they are not "true believers" because true faith should be non-political.[204] This position seems questionable to us. We do not wish to theorize on the nature of genuine religious faith. The backers of political religions believe as much as they are able and in what they are able to believe. We should, however, admit that what the political Orthodox believe in contravenes the position of the Church.

Leaders of Orthodox religiopolitical movements don't consider their disagreements with the Church a problem and never insist that their followers should become good parishioners. For example, Aleksandr Dugin said in his interview to "*Religiia i SMI*" Internet-portal: "I do not support a strict division of Orthodox Christians into church-goers and non-goers. I think that everyone who identifies himself with Orthodoxy is an Orthodox. As for myself, I am a practicing Orthodox Christian and wish everyone to be like this."[205] (To be precise, he is a practicing Old Believer).

Il'ia Chislov also admits that both Serbs and Russians are not practicing enough. He, however, forgives them asking a rhetorical question: "Well, is General Ratko Mladic (not mentioning Radovan Karadzic) less Christian than the church-going Moscow Jews...?"[206] Chislov quotes from a Serbian author Zelko Poznanovic: "Being reproached that these people do not practice Orthodoxy in the full sense, we answer that if they did – they would be even better warriors, even more dangerous for the enemies of Serbdom and Ortho-

---

[203] Quoted in: Paul Mojzes, "The Camouflaged Role of Religion in the War in Bosnia and Herzegovina" in Paul Mojzes, ed. *Religion and the War in Bosnia* (Atlanta: Scholars Press, 1998), 88.

[204] Vjekoslav Perica, *Balkan Idols: Religion and Nationalism in Yugoslav States* (New York: Oxford University Press, 2002), 218.

[205] "Ob otvetstvennosti Putina pered Khristom i smene rossiiskikh elit," http://evrazia.org/modules.php?name=News&file=article&sid=1542 (as of 18 November 2003).

[206] Il'ia Chislov, "Na strazhe Evropy," *Nash sovremennik* no. 6 (1999): 178.

doxy."²⁰⁷ In simple words, if the political Orthodox had been practicing their religion, it would have been great. If not – OK.

Generally speaking, the leaders of political Orthodoxy tend to see all Russians as "natural" (nearly "genetic") Orthodox Christians. For example, on 3 April 2005 Mikhail Kuznetsov, a lawyer who supported fundamentalists in their legal case against the organizers of "Beware, Religion!" exhibition, said on *Russkii vzgliad* that the fact that these people had been fined was "the victory of all Orthodox Russia – both believers and non-believers." The same idea was expressed by a leading national patriotic author Vadim Kozhinov in his interview to the authors of "Russian Mystery" film. He said, that "our country... it is fully Orthodox. And it is in no way necessarily connected with some religious notions or even with believing in God. It is already in flesh and blood."²⁰⁸ Thus we once again return to the notion of "Orthodox non-believers" or "Orthodox atheists."

The same vision of the relationship between ethnic groups and Orthodoxy also characterizes the Balcans. Radovan Karadzic, whose opinion is highly esteemed by Russian political Orthodox, openly admitted that "The Serbian Orthodox Church is not merely a religious organization, it is a cultural institution and part of national leadership; the Church is highly important for all Serbs, and it is irrelevant whether one believes in God or not."²⁰⁹ The issue of church-going becomes, thus, not even of second but of third significance. According to ideologists of political Orthodoxy, to be a "proper" Orthodox one need not attend church or even believe in God.

Even political fundamentalists are rather tolerant of insufficient religious devotion among their backers. For example, Konstantin Dushenov does not blame those who, unlike 5% of real church parishioners, are "just believers," merely considering themselves Orthodox or simply sympathizing with the church. Among laymen Dushenov envisions three groups: liberal church-going intelligentsia (which, according to him, is heretic and possesses too much money but is "insignificant" in terms of numbers), people who are not

---

[207] Ibidem.
[208] "Russkaia taina," a DVD (producer unknown).
[209] Quoted in: Perica, *Balkan Idols*, 162.

yet true practicing Christians but who gravitate towards Orthodox patriotism and the Orthodox patriotic movement as such.[210]

It is worth mentioning that Dushenov clearly sees the difference between the liberal *church-going* intelligentsia and non-church-going (so far) patriots. We have already quoted from an article by Il'ia Chislov, where he also opposes "*church-going* Moscow Jews" to the Mladic and Karadzic, who are genuine Orthodox Christians although not practicing. One may conclude that practicing religion is as such not so much a virtue for the leaders of political Orthodoxy even when they understand its importance. Practicing "too much" may even provoke suspicions about one's political preferences and ethnic origins.

Political organizations created by supporters of politicization may well be called "paraecclesiastical": on one hand, the church hierarchy does not approve of them, on the other hand, each necessarily includes a priest (or priests) providing a sort of obligatory religious sanction. All Orthodox political organizations have their ghostly fathers, for example, Father Dmitrii Dudko (died in 2004) was a ghostly father of the *Zavtra* newspaper. There are even clergymen participating in semi-Pagan organizations. From the viewpoint of political Orthodoxy this, however, is no surprise. Clergymen, nevertheless, are normally not leaders of Orthodox political movements; neither do they prevail among their members.

Some clergymen and even highly-positioned hierarchs (such as Metropolitan Ioann) may support this or that Orthodox political ideology. However, the opinion of the church as an institution is not just a *sum total* of all opinions of its separate representatives; there is a common church position reflected in official documents and in presentations of the leaders having formal right to speak out in behalf of the church as a whole. This position, as a rule, demands depoliticization of paraecclesiastical activities, calling for peace and reconciliation.

So far no one has conducted comprehensive sociological surveys among the participants of Orthodox political organizations. Nevertheless, it seems that the majority of their members are professionals having higher education (including the former military). Interesting (and seemingly reliable)

---

[210] Konstantin Dushenov, *Molchaniem predaetsia Bog* (Sankt-Peterburg: Tsarskoe de-

information about the social background of the members of an extremely nationalist St. Petersburg's *Slavianskaia obshchina* may be found in an interview with its leader Roman Perin. According to him, 70% of the Community members have higher education, of them 40% have been educated in technology and 30% in humanities; about 5% are students, 10% are pensioners and 15 % are former army and navy officers.[211] Fundamentalist activists who destroyed the "Beware, religion!" art exhibition seem to belong to the same social group: according to *Izvestia* newspaper, Mikhail Liukshin is a programmer, Nikolai Smakhtin a legal advisor and Grigorii Garbuzov has technological and musical education.[212]

We still lack research exploring why this social group has become particularly sensitive to religiopolitical indoctrination. We suggest that relative economic deprivation is a crucial factor contributing to the popularity of political Orthodoxy. Relative deprivation does not mean exceptional poverty, but rather a sharp contrast between the previous (expected) socio-economic status of a person and his/her current status. The new status may mean a higher monetary income but a lower socioeconomic position (for example, a retired officer becomes a guard, or a driver).

Some insights may be provided by Aleksandr Tarasov's seminal research on social background of Moscow skinheads. Tarasov demonstrates that before the reforms families of most skinheads belonged to what he calls "Soviet middle class."

> Skinheads are not children of chronic alcoholics and criminals; they are children of the former highly-paid workers, engineers, employees of research institutes and constructing bureaus... These people have survived psychological dramas and moral humiliation... Adolescents from these families have transformed their deep disappointment in social reality into nihilism, racism and nationalism.

---

[211] lo, 2000), 95-96.
"Beseda s Romanom Perinym", *Za russkoe delo* no. 1 (2005).
[212] Dmitrii Sokolov-Mitrich, "Ubit' postmodernista," http://www.izvestia.ru/person/article 30906 (as of 5 March 2003).

Tarasov writes.[213] Most parents of skinheads, after the economic reforms, had to change their social status abruptly and to become, instead of intelligentsia members, retail dealers or petite entrepreneurs. 58% of skinheads known to the Moscow police have parents working in trade or catering, of whom 22% have their own businesses. There are nearly no skinheads born in the families of intelligentsia or workers,[214] groups whose socioeconomic status has not changed in the last decades. We suggest that the same abrupt downshift in status is responsible for the fact that middle-aged people with higher education tend to be involved into Orthodox political activism.

---

[213] Aleksandr Tarasov, "Goriuchaia smes' s zamedlitelem," *Novaia gazeta*, 1-4 August 2002.
[214] Ibid.

V The Political Orthodox as Intellectual Community

V.1 New Orthodox Intellectuals and their Style of Writing

Such concepts as "new intellectuals" and even "lumpen-intelligentsia" have been introduced by Olivier Roy, a leading French scholar of political Islam, to describe intellectuals producing Islamist political concepts.[215] We think the notion of "new intellectuals," although mostly applied to the world of Islam, is relevant to our analysis of political Orthodoxy as well. These are people conducting para-academic activities (writing books and articles, presenting papers) that contribute to the formation of political religions. Most of them are also active in religiopolitical movements.

Roy makes a distinction between new intellectuals and the traditional clergy, on the one hand, and between new intellectuals and traditional intellectuals, on the other hand. The clergy and traditional intellectuals have one point in common: "their social status is guaranteed by processes of investiture and authorization that distinguish them from the masses."[216] To become a member of the clergy one should obtain the approval of the other members of this corporation. In Christian countries this means ordination, which is even harder to get. To be accepted by the traditional intellectuals, one needs a recognized diploma, a degree certificate and a university position. For the most part, the new intellectuals have none of the above-listed qualifications.

Most new intellectuals have no theological education and no firm theological knowledge. Daniel Pipes, director of the Middle East Forum, pointed out that traditional Islamic theologians went through a lengthy course of learning and studied a huge corpus of information including debates among scholars, jurists and theologians. Islamists, by contrast, "tend to be well educated in the sciences but not in Islam; in their early adulthood, they confront problems for which their modern learning has failed to prepare them, so they turn

---

[215] Olivier Roy, *The Failure of Political Islam* (Cambridge, Mass.: Harvard University Press, 2001), 51.
[216] Ibid., 92.

to Islam. In doing so they ignore nearly the entire corpus of Islamic learning and interpret the Koran as they see fit."[217]

Sometimes new intellectuals have no higher education at all; in most cases their education is not related to the humanities or social sciences. They are not professional scholars or lecturers at any officially recognized educational facility (ecclesiastical or secular). For this reason, new intellectuals often initiate their own research or educational institutions not recognized by the established epistemic community. Olivier Roy mentions that

> The state has no means by which it can control the new Islamist intellectual in his social function. His thought does not correspond to his social position, he does not live from his profession, the networks of his activities are on the fringe of institutions, when they are not entirely clandestine.[218]

Based upon our own experience, we would like to add that the fact that new intellectuals have no theological education (and often no humanitarian education at all) heavily influences their attitude toward religion. On the one hand, they approach religious dogmas freely, adding or excluding various elements. On the other hand, they often have no understanding of possible alternative interpretations of the dogma (known, most likely, to every student specializing in philosophy or theology).

The new Orthodox intellectuals in Russia, as well as in the Islamic countries, are alienated from the established community of scholars. Most of them have higher education, but normally not in the sphere of humanities. There are many former army and navy officers (retired or in reserve) among new Orthodox intellectuals in Russia (Konstantin Dushenov, Leonid Shershnev, Valerii Demin and others). The other primary group may be identified as "writers and journalists." It should be mentioned that most of these writers have never gained popularity for their literary works (for example, Boris Mironov).

The education of most ideologists has been practically oriented and highly specialized (engineer, translator, chemist, physicist, and so on). Some

---

[217] David Pipes, "Islam and Islamism. Faith and Ideology," *The National Interest* (Spring 2000): 91.
[218] Ibid., 95.

have research degrees – in Chemistry or Mathematics – which does not help much. New Orthodox intellectuals obtain their knowledge of religion, philosophy and political theory not at universities but through self-education and extensive reading. Since they have no exposure to schooling at humanities departments, they don't speak the language of the official science and are not acquainted with recognized research methods. As a result, even having accumulated extended information they are unable to express themselves in the form acceptable for the established academic community.

Most new intellectuals never use foot/endnotes or (at best) make footnotes without paginal references. Students at departments of humanities learn how and why one should make references to the publications one cites within their first year at a university; they gather this information from their professors or simply when reading scholarly monographs by senior scholars. New intellectuals extract their knowledge either from popular books or from classical works of the past, which often contain no references as well. For example, Vladimir Boiarintsev (Dr.habilitat in Mathematics and Physics) in his anti-Semite "study" *Russian and Non-Russian Scholars: Myths and Reality*[219] often quotes from a popular book *100 Great Scholars* (without paginal references) never questioning the reliability of this source.

The prevalence of "technicians" (including former military) is responsible for the fact that most of the new Orthodox intellectuals read none of the foreign or ancient languages needed for a substantial historical/philosophical research. This limits their sources to those available in Russian translation: as a result, they are acquainted neither with non-translated sources, nor with alternative translations. People like Aleksandr Dugin, who claims to speak nine languages, or Nataliia Narochnitskaia, who speaks four languages, are rare. Of them Dugin is self-educated person, while Narochnitskaia is a graduate of MGIMO (Moscow State Institute of International Relations) which provides highly specialized education with more emphasis on foreign languages and consular work than on humanities as such (thus resembling "technological education").

The majority of new intellectuals are unable to conceive of the volume of literature on their subjects of discourse. When encountering knowledge which is new for them (for example, when a former officer first time learns about apocrypha), they assume that this knowledge is equally new for everyone. As a result, they have difficulty acquiring basic knowledge available to an average student of humanities. For example, many politicised Orthodox intellectuals are enthusiastic about the ideas of the French New Right theorist Alain de Benoit and tend to present him as their own "discovery." However, the author of this book, as a 1994 graduate of the Department of Philosophy of the Moscow State University, may confirm that Benoit's theories were being analysed by professional philosophers as early as in the end of the 1980s and presented to students during various courses in contemporary French thought. (Of course, for the traditional philosophical community Benoit has never been a mainstream figure.)

New intellectuals read a lot but without any system. Vladimir Shnirel'man provides the following comprehensive description of books written by new intellectuals:

> unprepared people read a lot of academic literature, pick out what they like so as to create a concept which they like. This approach distorts facts because they have been taken out of the context and makes them look totally mythical... At the same time they refer to authorities: 'that professor has said, this academician has said...[220]

One may add that new intellectuals always try to present their intellectual production as "scientific knowledge" stressing its "objectivity" and methodological infallibility. They thereby never acknowledge ideological (or even mythological) nature of their works.

New intellectuals try to make their works appear to be as "academic" as possible. For example, a book entitled *The Great Civil War*, which is in fact an apology for German National Socialism, was published with a sub-title "academic edition" (although it contains nothing specifically academic, including foot/endnotes). Its annotation says that "this book is a teaching and methodological aid for teachers of history at secondary schools, students and teachers

---

[219] Vladimir Boiarintsev, *Russkie i nerusskie uchenye: mify i realnost'* (Moskva: Russkaia pravda, 2005).

[220] See: *Rasizm v iazyke sotsialnykh nauk* (Sankt-Peterburg: Aleteia, 2002), 149.

of respective subjects and for everyone interested in their own destiny."[221]
Conspirology by Aleksandr Dugin was prefaced by a similar annotation: "this publication is of a strictly scientific, research-oriented nature."[222]

---

[221] *Velikaia grazhdanskaia voina 1941-1945* (Moskva, no publisher, 2002), 2.
[222] Aleksandr Dugin, *Konspirologiia* (Moskva: Arktogeia, 1993), 2.

V. 2 Political Religion and Para-Science

Some traditional scholars refer to the knowledge produced by the new Orthodox intellectuals as "pseudo-science" or "false science;" however, in many of these fields of study, the difference between pseudo-science and real science remains subject to debate. We prefer designating this knowledge as "para-science" characterized, first of all, by its indiscriminative choice of sources and, second, by its references to authority or to intuition instead of valid rational arguments. Generally speaking, the books written by new intellectuals resemble academic treatises of the Middle Ages and the Renaissance, thus signalling an archaisation of knowledge, of its return to the past forms. The purpose of such books is not critical investigation, but furnishing apologetics for what is already seen as the absolute truth.

Indiscriminative choice of sources leads to combination of reliable and non-reliable information, of the rational and the irrational in the books by new intellectuals. This sometimes happens due to lack of the above-mentioned research skills (some authors seem unable to distinguish between reliable and non-reliable sources). However, in most cases combining the rational and the irrational is a conscious choice.

For example, public lectures on so-called "Reasonably General Theory of Management" (Russian abbreviation: DOTU) given by *Edinenie* included some seemingly reliable and rational information related to general systemic theory (about open and closed systems), management theory (about management by exception), general psychology and so on. This rational information alternated with fully irrational assertions, for example, that prophesies are information provided by the supreme reality, from "the level of egregors [an occult term] up to God."[223] This is an obvious case; in some cases only a specialist is able to distinguish between reliable and non-reliable information. People, attracted by what seems reliable and rational (and, thus, useful), simultaneously learn the irrational doctrines of political religion.

In general, the new Orthodox intellectuals pick up sources randomly and appropriate them in order to convey the impression the author wants. Often unequal or incompatible sources are recited concurrently, thus supporting

---

[223] Public lecture given at the Moscow Polytechnic Museum, 16 April 2005.

the illusion of equal validity. An illustrated magazine *Elementy – Evraziiskoe Obozrenie* (Elements – Eurasian Review), previously published by Aleksandr Dugin, exemplified this indiscriminate approach to sources. Under one cover one might find quotations from books by respectable scholars and fragments of comics, as well as portraits of Bismark and Ezra Pound.

Elementy was especially noticeable for its sophisticated use of illustrations with accompanying inscriptions. Very often illustrations seemed fully irrelevant to the articles published and selected on a random basis; however, their inscriptions filled all possible interpretation gaps. For example an article on Western anti-Russian geostrategic plans (No.4, 1993, page 26) was illustrated by several photos of military planes that could have well been taken from an airplane-building company booklet. The inscription, however, was: "The Atlantic monsters of American 'aerocracy' threaten Eurasia." In the same issue one could see a photo of a US missile; the inscription informed: "It is aimed at you!" (page 30). Strangely enough, such methods, which would contribute greatly to the effectiveness of propaganda, are currently not utilized by the other illustrated Orthodox mass media.

New intellectuals are not afraid of eclecticism. Sergei Kurekhin (1954-1996), a musician and a shining example of a new intellectual once said in an interview to *Elementy* that "Postmodernism… is based on connecting things you love. And love is inseparable. Things you love are for you, in principle, the same… A man may, speaking about his personal tradition, unite, say, Bataille and Evola – people who are not compatible."[224] A traditional intellectual can not help panicking when observing this attitude toward sources. Kurekhin's expression "personal tradition" is, or course, a contradiction in terms, but it perfectly conveys the thinking of new intellectuals.

References to authority or to intuition, rather than reliance on valid arguments, once again, results both from new intellectuals' ignorance about the nature of academic research and from their ultimate desire to validate what they consider the absolute truth at any cost.

Reference to authority is the main tactic of Evgenii Troitskii (Dr. habilitat in Philosophy) when he tries to establish his idea of "the Slavic-Orthodox civilization." Having brought numerous quotations from various writers and philosophers who postulated the existence of such civilization (it should be mentioned that Troitskii, being a member of the traditional academic community, never forgets about paginal references), this author pays no attention to comparing these theoretical ruminations with reality - either modern or past.

Some new intellectuals simply state that they "intuitively" know that their conclusions are true. This was the idea expressed by Nikolai Bogdanov, the author of a book *The Role of Doctors in Killing Csars*, where he insists that many Russian csars have been deliberately put to death by their doctors belonging to "international Masonry."[225] The author of this book had a chance to talk with Bogdanov during the Book Exhibition and Fair in Moscow on 13 March 2005. Bogdanov admitted that "official historical science" would most likely want him to offer some evidence of this Masonic conspiracy, but in his opinion, where conspiracy is concerned there can be no evidence. He just knows that there had been a conspiracy.

A specific niche within the intellectual community of the political Orthodox is occupied by Sergei G. Kara-Murza (although he is not a pronouncedly Orthodox thinker, as his position is closer to that of secular Communism). To be precise, he is a "new intellectual": even though he is currently presented as "political scientist" he is, in fact, a chemist (Dr. habilitat in Chemistry) who up to the end of the 1980s was known for his popular articles on chemistry. Having begun publishing his political works in the late 1980s and early 1990s, Kara-Murza assumed the position of a "traditional" rationalist scholar who deconstructs the liberal mythology dominating the consciousness of post-Soviet Russians.

Using rationalist instruments, such as comparing various statistical data or indicating logical fallacies, Sergei Kara-Murza deconstructs such myths as "the myth of the economic crisis in the USSR," "the myth of Stolipin," "the myth of Stalin's repressions" and the other like myths. It is evident that by doing this he creates new myths, or anti-myths in reaction to what he calls "liberal mythology"; nevertheless, he firmly sticks to a position of a rationalist scholar in revealing the logical incapacity of his opponents. It should be mentioned that Kara-Murza sometimes makes paginal references and sometimes

---

[224] "'Esli vy romantik, vy – fashist': Interv'iu s Sergeem Kurekhinym", *Elementy* no. 8 (1996\1997): 82-83.

[225] Nikolai Bogdanov, *Rol' vrachei v ubiistve tsarei* (Moskva: Russkaia pravda, 2004).

refers to enigmatic sources like "a message from American press" without any indication of where exactly the information was taken from[226].

Generally speaking, the idea of "deconstruction of liberal myths" or "dezombifying" is popular with the new intellectuals (one of Kara-Murza's early articles was called "Pull the electrodes out of our brains"). The whole enterprise of songs/films of "resistance" contains undertones of a mission to "awaken" people, liberating their minds from the chains imposed by liberals. However only Sergei Kara-Murza has tried to perform this task by means of an appeal to rationality and analysis, rather than through emotional appeals.

Sometimes "traditional intellectuals" (i.e., professionals in the human sciences) join the new ones in producing publications of a para-scientific nature. In such cases they abruptly change the style of their publications. Aleksandr Panarin, full-time professor of the Moscow State University (who died in 2003) is one of the most evident examples. Panarin has always been one of the most respected political theorists in Russia. In the beginning of the 1990s he initiated from scratch the chair of political science at the MSU Department of Philosophy. In that period he was known for his research in French and American neo-conservatism; as early as in 1989 he presented the New Right French thinkers, now praised by many theorists of political Orthodoxy, to the Russian scholarly community. Of course, Panarin's book about these issues was unequivocally academic, with all the necessary trimmings like footnotes.[227] The author of this book, as a student at the MSU Department of Philosophy, attended Panarin's lectures and may positively assert that in that period (the beginning of the 1990s) he supported liberal democracy and a market economy (i.e., he was an "Atlanticist," to use the terminology of the political Orthodox).

Panarin's political orientation had changed by the end of the 1990s and he started to define his position as "late Eurasianism." In fact, his radical vision of the mission of the Orthodox civilization has gained him popularity far beyond Eurasianist circles. Panarin's work was highly esteemed by representatives of the whole spectrum of political Orthodoxy, from fundamentalists to

---

[226] See, for example: Sergei Kara-Murza, *Poteriannyi razum* (Moskva: Algoritm, 2005), 388-389.

[227] Aleksandr Panarin, *Stil' 'retro' v ideologii i politike* (Moskva: Mysl', 1989).

Neo-Pagans. (On 28 September 2003 *Russkii dom* conveyed the information about his death to the whole community of the political Orthodox).

Panarin's reputation among the academics was by that time so firm that even the publication of evidently "ideological" books was not able to shatter it. One can not help observing, however, that Panarin's later books acquired features typical of the works of new intellectuals, such as no paginal references and the confusing mixture of reliable and unreliable information. For example, in his book *Orthodox Civilization in the Global World* Panarin sympathetically quoted from a fundamentalist brochure *Electronic cards and the Seal of Antichrist* (translated from Greek) and concluded that "the new natural selection of the liberals of globalism threatens with a new bestialization of mankind. It smells the Beast already."[228] The brochure was quoted by him as a fully reliable source.

Unlike Panarin, most of traditional intellectuals who break with academic formalities are determined to conflict with their own environment. Their radical opinions (not academically moderate and balanced) and political activism are not accepted by those loyal to more traditional approaches.

The escapees from the traditional academic circles have brought to the discourse of the new intellectuals some features characteristic of the late period of Soviet social sciences and humanities. These are:

1) Constant references to "Western scholars" often used as *ultima ratio*. In the late Soviet period quoting from Western sources signified the author's access to a sort of clandestine knowledge because such books were only available to those admitted to the West or those having allowance to work in classified library departments (*spetskhran*). In the case of political Orthodoxy, of course, the list of Western authors has radically changed. It now includes above-mentioned Alain de Benoit, Western revisionist historians and Holocaust deniers, American right-wing politician Patrick Buchanan (portrayed by the political Orthodox as an influential political figure and world-known political scientist) and the anti-globalist American economist Lyndon H. LaRouche. The political Orthodox are proud to invite foreign guests to their events and always emphasize their participation. The ideological closeness of these guests seems to play no significant role.

Among the most often cited foreign authors one may find Samuel Huntington, whose idea of the clash of civilizations evidently plays into the hands of political Orthodoxy. Orthodox ideologists, however, prefer to speak on behalf of the "rest" united against the West. Paradoxically, Huntington has become one of the authorities new intellectuals refer to when they lack rational arguments. When discussing geopolitical issues they also like quoting from Zbignev Brzhezinsky and other Western "hawks" who apparently confirm their worst suspicions about the West.

2) Scientism, or the utilization of an "overly scientific" style with diagrams, graphs, technological terminology (like "field" or "feedback") and so on, accompanied with constant references to the data of science. The "science" to which the new intellectuals refer is typically cited in the form of vague statements such as: "modern linguistics demonstrates," "modern medical science proves" or "the latest achievements of science testify." These authors, for the most part, do not designate the specific scientific sources they lean upon. (This seems natural, because, as far as we have been able to determine, this "evidence" is not taken from original scientific publications but rather from references to scientific studies found in popular newspapers).

With regard to scientism it is worth while to mention the "Tesla electric generator" (named after US engineer Nikola Tesla) that is expected to generate free electric energy from "ether" (meaning electromagnetic medium in the 19th century believed to fill the atmosphere and the outer space). When we first time came across with the idea of such device in Iuliia Voskresenskaia's books, we attributed it to the imagination of the author. However, the Tesla generator has proven to be a popular concept in the Orthodox political community. Eventually we were able to obtain a brochure by engineer Vladimir Atsiukovskii where he explains how one can make one's own Tesla generator.[229] However, the majority of the Orthodox intellectuals don't explore technology very seriously.

3) The utilization of some notions that used to be popular in Soviet humanities but remained mostly unknown in the West (or, at least, marginal).

---

[228] Aleksandr Panarin, *Pravoslavnaia tsivilizatsiia v global'nom mire* (Moskva: Algoritm, 2002), 486.
[229] Vladimir Atsiukovskii, *Generator Tesla: energiia iz efira* (Zhukovskii, 2004).

The most widely discussed of such notions is that of "noosphere"[230] introduced by a Russian geologist and philosopher Vladimir Vernandskii (noosphere is defined as "a hypothetical future state of human society and its interaction with nature, when mind would occupy the place of priority"[231]). This concept became extremely popular in the late Soviet years because at that time it seemed to be a valid alternative to Marxist-Leninist vision of human future. It is hardly possible that the new intellectuals referring to "noosphere" understand that this concept is in no way widely accepted (even within Russia) as being indisputably "scientific." On the contrary, they seemingly use it to make their own publications appear to be more academic.

Such constructions as "post-industrial society" or "scientific and technological progress" have also been frequently used by mainstream Soviet philosophers, who are primarily focused, unlike their Western colleagues, not on semantics and psychoanalysis, but on the issues of historical progress and the role of "science" (i.e., natural and exact sciences) in this progress. The above-mentioned notions, of course, are not unknown in the West (actually, some of them *originate* from the West) but they have never been in the focus of philosophising there, not to mention that they have never been seen as something which adds "academism" and "scientific flavour" to a publication. When, for example, Evgenii Troitskii writes that the emergence of the Slavic civilization will provide "the most painless transition of the Slavic world to the technologies of postindustrial society," he unmistakably reveals his Soviet philosophical background.[232] People having no such background and who are not interested in imitating Soviet patterns of philosophizing (for example, Aleksandr Dugin or Geidar Dzhemal') never use the above mentioned phrases. Moreover, the concept of noosphere has once been described by

---

[230] As an example, see a para-anthropological publication: Oleg Gusev, "Neandertalets: zagadka ischeznoveniia" in *Rasovyi smysl russkoi idei. Tom 1* (Moskva: Belye Al'vy, 2000), 162-181.

[231] Arkadii Ursul, "Noosphere," in *Global Studies Encyclopedia* (Moscow: Dialog; Raduga Publishers, 2003), 363.

[232] Evgenii Troitskii, "Kontseptsiia russko-slavianskoi tsivilizatsii," in Evgenii Troitskii, ed., *Russko-slavianskaia tsivilizatsiia: istoricheskie istoki, sovremennye geopoliticheskie problemy, perspektivy slavianskoi vzaimnosti* (Moskva, 1998), 27.

Elementy as an example of "pretentious banality of pseudo-mystical Soviet consciousness of the 1970s-1980s, typical of intelligentsia and engineers."[233]

4) Sometimes the new intellectuals appropriate Marxist-Leninist concepts and terminology. Most likely, they do so unconsciously. Along with all students of "non-ideological" (technology, philology, medicine and so one) disciplines in the Soviet Union they participated in the compulsory learning of dialectic materialism and scientific communism – for the majority it was the first encounter with the humanities. It is not surprising, then, that Aleksandr Sevast'ianov (a graduate of the MSU Department of Philology) writes that "the other world, soul and God are fully material because they are objective, real and given to us in our perceptions."[234] The author most likely did not notice that his phrase contains a hidden quotation from Lenin's major philosophical work *Materialism and Empiriocriticism* (namely, that "matter is objective reality given to us in our perceptions"). The very use of the word "objective" in the sense "independent to us, people" is a feature of Marxism-Leninism that may hardly be found anywhere else. Once again, people who never underwent schooling in the spirit of Marxism-Leninism are the least likely to unwittingly refer to communist sources; when they quote from Marx or Lenin, they do it deliberately.

---

[233] "Monstruositas," *Elementy* no. 4 (1993): 64.
[234] *NDPR – partiia russkogo naroda* (Moskva: Natsional'naia gazeta, 2005), 10.

V. 3 New Intellectuals and the Established Academic Community

Contradictions between the new Orthodox intellectuals and the "traditional intellectuals" are in no way less profound than the differences between lay activists and the church leadership. In most cases the traditional intellectuals ignore publications of the new ones. They collide when new intellectuals try to penetrate the domain of traditional intellectuals without documents affirming their qualification, such as diplomas awarded for higher education in the humanities, research degrees, etc.

This has been done by Aleksandr Dugin, who in 2000 submitted a Ph.D. (Philosophy) dissertation on "Evolution of Paradigmal Foundations of Science. Philosophical and Methodological Analysis" at the Rostov State University. It should be mentioned that Dugin, unlike the majority of the new intellectuals, was always concerned about not having appropriate education and about not being accepted by the traditional academics. On 5 November 1997, during Dugin's meeting with the students of the Moscow State University (he was invited by a discussion club "Dialog" as a politician, but tried his best to look like an academic, expecting to give a lecture) he simply refused to answer a question about his educational background; at that moment he had no higher education at all.

Nevertheless, by 2000 Dugin had acquired a diploma and submitted his Ph.D. dissertation. This fact was met with hostility by most of the traditional academics. Their position has been summarized in an article by Boris Rezhabek (Dr. habilitat in Philosophy, the Rostov State University) dedicated more to Dugin's biography than to his positions, including biographic data evidently borrowed from a web-tabloid Compromat.ru. Let us quote from this article considering that *Vestnik rossiiskogo filosofskogo obshchestva* (The Bulletin of the Russian Philosophical Society), the journal which published this piece, is not widely circulated:

> Aleksandr Dugin is a domestic self-taught thinker, enjoying broad popularity in the narrow circles of National Bolsheviks and their sympathizers, as he is an extremely exuberant writer. Having flunked out of the Moscow Institute of Aviation (although he likes to say that he was expelled for anti-Soviet

activities), Dugin embarked upon a quest into the occult and sexual experience. This was not so good for his future – after he had adopted the role of an Orthodox and became a member of the Central Council of the National Patriotic Front *"Pamiat'*," they found what he is and kicked him away...[235]

Therefore, the main problem with Dugin and the other new intellectuals is not that their ideas are "weird" or "pseudo-scientific." Many people having legitimate higher educations and research degrees often articulate even stranger notions. However, if one is to speak out about philosophy, religion or politics, one should first secure the approval of the respective institution. Otherwise, an effort to enter academic establishment provokes the annoyance and scorn of traditional intellectuals. "...Not being satisfied with his position of a Gnostic geopolitician he decided to enter the academic community as a Ph.D. in Philosophy... the ideologist of the 'conservative revolution' demonstrated to the Academic Board... a diploma from extra-mural department of the Novocherkassk Institute of Melioration Engineering!", Rezhabek continues.[236] Since this does not necessarily sound like an illegitimate act, the article hints that Dugin "managed to get" this diploma (supposedly not in the legal way).

Still, in 2004 Aleksandr Dugin "managed to submit" at that very Rostov State University his Dr. habilitat dissertation in Political Science ("The Transformation of Political Structures and Institutes in the Process of Modernization of a Traditional Society"). Now he wishes to be called "doctor Dugin" which is normally not done in the Russian academic community (in Russia calling researchers "doctor Petrov" or "doctor Ivanov" betrays a foreigner because such titles are reserved exclusively for physicians). This overemphasis on status seems to result from Dugin's long-time struggle for being accepted by the traditional academic community.

In 2004 he continued this struggle in Belarus. In fall 2004 representatives of *Mezhdunarodnoe Evraziiskoe Dvizhenie* visited two leading Byealrussian academic units: the Presidential Academy of Management and the Center for International Studies at the Byelorussian State University. They offered

---
[235] Boris Rezhabek, "Noosfera ili Arktogeia?," *Vestnik Rossiiskogo filosofskogo obshchestva* no. 3 (2001): 79.
[236] Ibid., 81.

cooperation plans, including conferences, and even promised to finance them. Nevertheless, both institutions declined this offer. The head of the international cooperation department of the Academy of Management explained to the author of this book that "we should be very careful about whom to cooperate with."[237] Russian academic institutions continue to ignore Dugin as a colleague; instead they consider him a subject to study.

Most of the other new Orthodox intellectuals are not so concerned about being acknowledged by the established academic community. They simply don't believe that expertise and specialized education are needed for conducting a historical, philosophical or theological research. Valerii Demin, for example, wrote his book *From Aryans to Rusichs* covering millennia of world history within the period from 1996 to 1997. Viktor Shnirel'man, the Leading Research Fellow of the Institute of Ethnology and Anthropology of the Russian Academy of Science reviewed this book and pointed out that the author is not aquatinted with methods of historical analysis. Responding Shnirelman, Demin wrote that the art of historians is similar to martial arts, and that being a lieutenant colonel in reserve, he has good command of all methods.[238] This seems to be a common position among new intellectuals.

However, they sometimes attempt to feign academic respectability. On 20 February 2005 (Sunday) the NDPR rented the conference hall of the Institute of Philosophy of the Russian Academy of Science for its conference "Genocide of the Russian people in 20th – 21st centuries" promoted as "the first scientific conference" on this topic. As a result, the event was portrayed by the media as held "at" (if not "by") the Institute of Philosophy. The plenary report of Stanislav Terekhov stressed that genocide of the Russian people "is a scientific fact that should be described, studied and acknowledged by the world community."[239] The presenters spoke before a background bearing the slogan "Stop the genocide of the Russian people and the politics of Judeo-Fascism!" Soon the representatives of the Institute came to the hall and asked the participants to leave by 3 p.m. in spite of the fact that the hall was

---

[237] Personal conversation with Aleksandr Kopot', 3 January 2005.
[238] Valerii Demin, "Otvet na retsenziiu moei knigi 'Ot Ariev k rusicham' V. Shnirel'mana" (2003), http://www.ruspravda.org/news/otvet.htm (as of 1 March 2005).
[239] "Konferentsiia 'Genotsid Russkogo naroda v XX-XXI veke'. Press-reliz", http://www.ndpr.ru/messages/?mid=123 (as of 11 March 2005).

rented till 6 p.m. Interestingly enough, so far no one at the administration of the Institute has admitted that he or she leased the hall for this notorious conference.

The fact that *Edinenie* rents for its public lectures a lecture hall at the Moscow Polytechnic Museum, in our opinion, also signifies their wish to look as "academic" and "respectable" as possible. This lecture hall is mostly used for giving public lectures on the latest discoveries in natural sciences and is associated with the highest level of scientific reliability.

Not all traditional intellectuals are hostile to the new ones. Nevertheless, the two groups fail to understand one another. Traditional intellectuals try to approach the new ones from the positions adopted by academic community. They find, of course, many grounds for criticism. New intellectuals often treat "classical" ideas out of the context; they do not hesitate to add their own ideas to the classical ones, a practice which the traditional intellectuals are literally unable to bear. Traditional intellectuals mostly consider a set of ideas (Eurasianism, for example) as a "research subject," or something complete, which should be studied thoroughly but to which one may not add even a line. As for the new intellectuals, they approach the same set of ideas as a material for building their own theories. This is not acceptable for a traditional researcher.

What provokes even more criticism is their free interpretation of sacral texts. One article, that used to be broadly cited, has even accused the backers of political Orthodoxy of "entrenching the Text," or re-interpreting the closed corpus of sacral texts.[240] Nevertheless, neither this article, nor any of the others disparaging this "transgression" have explained exactly why this corpus should be considered closed. As we have already mentioned, political religions are more often criticized for contradicting dogmas than for promoting xenophobia and intolerance.

It is no surprise that new Orthodox intellectuals attempt to establish independence from the mainstream academic community, which has been so hostile to them. They initiate their own research organizations and educational facilities needed not so much for collective research activities as for their leaders' self-presentation. Most "para-academic" organizations created by new intellectuals have no physical dimension: at best, these are small rooms with a phone and one person to take calls. Nevertheless, they allow their leaders to introduce themselves as "presidents of foundations," "academicians" or "chairs of associations." Such organizations also allow them to publish books with seemingly respectable logos.

The function of self-presentation is also achieved through various academies. Generally speaking, the status of these academies in the eyes of the established academic community is close to the status of some "Academy of Astrology" or "Academy of Witchcraft." *Mezhdunarodnaia Slavianskaia Akademiia* and *Russkaia Akademiia* (the Russian Academy) are the most well known. We don't wish to imply that there are no respected scholars among the members of these academies; however, generally both unite prominent ideologists and activists of political Orthodoxy regardless of their academic merits. For example, Vladimir Chertovich, the leader of *ZAO "Pravoslavnaia initsiativa"* typically signs his publications as "academician of the Russian Academy"; we, however, have been unable to ascertain his actual contribution into any sort of research.

Some para-academic facilities also aim at raising money through the organization of various paid trainings and seminars for officials from governmental and commercial organizations. Apart from providing financial benefits such activities serve to help indoctrinate the elite of the society. The author lacks information regarding how successfully these facilities fulfill both tasks (though we know that, thus far, many of them have not been commercially beneficial).

Their activity is organized in the form of short-term seminars (workshops), disallowing the appointment of permanent lecturers. Instead, like-minded intellectuals are temporarily hired to fulfil a specific task. Some provide participants with certificates indicating that they have completed an "executive course" with some neutral name; this often attracts corporations or local municipalities wishing their employees to acquire new skills. Lectures are mostly given in temporarily rented conference halls and classrooms.

Among related organizations we would mention the Fund of National and International Security "NIMB," headed and created (in 1990) by Leonid

---

[240] Zoia Krakhmal'nikova, "Ideologiia raskola. Opasnost' politicheskikh igr vlastei s pra-

Shershnev. The Fund publishes a bimonthly *Bezopasnost'* bulletin. It also hosts a regular workshop "Youth and National Security of Russia in the Period of Transition" headed by Leonid Shershnev's son Il'ia Shershnev. The purpose of the workshop, intended for students, is, in spite of its seemingly neutral title, to educate the youth in the spirit of ideas promoted by the Fund (a mixture of Eurasianism, Orthodox Communism, nationalism, etc.). Among the lecturers of this workshop one may find prominent ideologists and activists of political Orthodoxy and national patriotic opposition such as Sergei Kara-Murza (an expert of "NIMB"), Tat'iana Shishova (a prominent fundamentalist author, also a "NIMB" employee), Andrei Parshev (the author of a patriotic bestseller *Why Russia is not America*) and others. The workshop also includes trainings in personal security and survival in extraordinary situations.

"NIMB" is characterized by combining peaceful (one would say "overly peaceful") official rhetoric with unofficial adherence to radical religiopolitical ideology. The language of its official documents is dominated by such terms as "peace," "human security," "world community," "survival of humankind" and so on. At the same time, the articles published by *Bezopasnost'* bulletin or presentations by General Shershnev are militantly anti-liberal and focused on the idea of the "World War Four," or "civil war" waged by the West against Russia. Addressing the 2005 *Vsemirnyi Russkii Narodnyi Sobor*, Shershenev, for example, said: "Finally, you should get rid of horror at war, not to be afraid of war... This war is for us morally justified, just and holy. Wars end not with peace, but with victory."[241] Such ideas hardly seem compatible with the official creed of "NIMB" – *Ad Vitam* (For Life) and its idyllic logo with two human hands on a globe. It seems that the fund deliberately utilizes liberal rhetoric in order to avoid unnecessary attention to its activities.

Apart from "NIMB" we would like to mention a few other para-academic organizations initiated by the military/intelligence officers and ideologically based on political Orthodoxy. First of all, there is *Akademiia geopoliticheskikh problem* (first vice-president: General Leonid Ivashev) and its associate Center for Ethnopolitical and Islamic Studies (headed by Den'ga Khalidov). These organizations cooperate with so-called Analytical Center "NAMAKON" (Rus-

---

[241] voslaviem", *Izvestiia*, 19 April 1994.
Leonid Shershnev, "Molodoe pokolenie Rossii v tekushchei grazhdanskoi i Chetvertoi mirovoi voine," http://www.fnimb.org/doc_mosgu.htm (as of 1 May 2005).

sian abbreviation for Independent Agency, Marketing and Consulting) initiated by former intelligence officers. "NAMAKON" is noticeably connected with national patriotic opposition cooperating with *Zavtra* and *Nash Sovremennik*. It has published some books that help and encourage religiopolitical activities, including *Small-scale War. Guerrilla and Sabotage* by M. Drozdov which seems to be a useful textbook for paramilitaries. The logo of "NAMAKON" depicts a ship with cross-shaped mast; its creed states "Fight, Love, Disdain." At the web-site of this organization one may find a database of publications headlined as "Confessional Aspects" (http://www.namakon.ru/). All publications are infiltrated by the spirit of militant political Orthodoxy.

Aleksandr Dugin at the dawn of his political carrier has founded a historical and religious association *Arktogeia* accompanied by the Center for Special Metastrategic Studies. In 1998 an *Arktogeia*-based "New University" was founded which sought to be "an educational facility of a new type, needed to fill the gap in Russian science and higher education system."[242] The function of the university is to teach such disciplines as traditionalism, theology, history of religions, metaphysics, hermetism, geopolitics, sociology, philology, history, ethnology, psychology, political science and conspirology. The New University does not aim at educating the public; it is rather a facility attracting people interested in mysticism and occultism. The purpose of indoctrinating officials (and bringing monetary benefits) seems to be performed by the "Center for Geopolitical Expertise" also initiated by Dugin.

Kontseptual'naia Partiia "Edinenie" has initiated the Academy of Management where teaching methods are based on the above-mentioned DOTU (Reasonably General Theory of Management). So far (as of May 2005) this Academy has completed one "executive course" that took place in the town of Kirov at Novosibirsk *oblast* (a region where General Petrov gained a record percentage of the vote). According to *Edinenie* the course was attended by small and medium-scale businessmen, regional officials and students.[243] We suggest that these people had been attracted by the opportunity to obtain some knowledge related to management and decision-making theory; in addition they were indoctrinated by General Petrov's religiopolitical ideas.

---

[242] http://universitet.virtualave.net/str1.html (as of 29 October 2003).
[243] V.P. Goncharov, "Pervyi vypusk Akademii upravleniia", http://www.kpe.ru/rating/events/world/1142/ (as of 1 April 2005).

One may also mention a scientific community called AKIRN (*Assotsiatsia po rompleksnomu izucheniu russkoi natsii*, Association for Complex Studies of the Russian Nation) founded and headed by Evgenii Troitskii. Troitskii has also organized a workshop "Philosophical Problems of the Russian Nation and Slavdom" under the aegis of the Russian Philosophical Society. Club "Catechon" is another example of a para-academic organization. This Club began as a seminar at the Institute of Philosophy and not only new but traditional intellectuals group around it. Nevertheless, the chair of the Club Arkadii Maler definitely belongs to the new intellectuals.[244] The main activity of "Catechon," now renamed as "Byzantist Club," is the organization of meetings with various people that may be regarded as Orthodox political activists. Meetings are held, once again, at the Institute of Philosophy, thus making it an increasingly "patriotic hangout."

---

[244] "Biografiia Arkadiia Malera," http://www.katehon.narod.ru/biografy.html (as of 1 October 2003).

VI The Politicization of Orthodoxy, the Church and the State

VI.1 The Russian Orthodox Church and Politicization of Orthodoxy

One of the most common trends in the analysis of religious politicization involves presenting this process as a result of the activity of clergymen or other religious professionals. This approach is understandable: it seems evident that the participants of a religiopolitical movement would trust religious professionals and that these professionals would advocate the idea of an ideocratic state. The reality of the situation, however, is not as simple. Certainly, some religious professionals support religious politicization and develop religious ideologies. These people, however, should not be equated with so-called religious establishment.

The religious establishment consists of those religious professionals who have been fully integrated into the ruling elite, thus providing leaders with moral and religious legitimacy. Normally it enjoys all of the privileges and benefits enjoyed by the elite in a given society (in post-Soviet state this may mean better health service, better housing, state-sponsored vehicle, etc.). For the religious establishment, privilege takes precedence over dogma, since it constantly re-interprets dogmas in order to adjust them to the demands of the elite.

The religious establishment is not fundamentalistic. Its pragmatism and flexibility resemble that of political religions. Both are prone to neglect dogmas in order to achieve their goals or introduce new dogmas to better accommodate changes in society. Neither of these deviations from Orthodoxy are possible for fundamentalists (at least, within the limits they have set for themselves). There is, however, a radical difference between the religious establishment and supporters of political religions. The establishment changes dogmas to preserve the current situation and to legitimize it; political religions endeavor to usurp the current situation. This is why they often become the most vicious of political enemies.

The religious establishment is considered by supporters of political religions one of the most formidable obstacles to ideocratic government (not counting, of course, pro-Western liberals). Thus, the ideologues of political religions constantly criticize the establishment. The establishment, in turn, considers such critics to be dangerously radical, urging the clergy and laymen "not to be politically engaged," thus refraining from political activities hostile to the ruling elite. This demand for "depoliticization," for the most part, results in the formation of a subculture which unites the religious establishment and faithful believers. Although this subculture may dislike some contemporary developments, it does not attempt to influence the rest of society.

According to John Esposito, the Islamic revolution in Iran (1979) was instigated not by the traditional *ulama* (official spiritual leaders) but by "a religiously minded lay intelligentsia."[245] Khomeini himself has acknowledged the role of radical intelligentsia in the revolution, declaring that the clergy had remained "asleep" until "awakened" by protesting university students.[246] This religiously minded intelligentsia inevitably conflicts with both the religious establishment and the conservative clergy and believers. The conflict with the loyal establishment is caused by intelligentsia's intention to displace the ruling elite, while the conflict with the conservatives is determined by the fact that the intelligentsia does not aim at returning to the traditional society of the past.

A struggle between the "depoliticized" (meaning: loyal to the ruling elite) religious establishment and the supporters of political Catholicism (liberation theology) took place in Latin America of the 1970s-1980s as well. This example is especially relevant because of the structural similarities between the Catholic Church and the Orthodox Church: unlike Islam, both are characterized by separation of the clergy and the laity. Liberation theology and its grassroots organizations (i.e., CEBs or *communidades eclesiales de base*) were initiated not by the clergy but by the lay Catholic intelligentsia.[247] That is

---

[245] John L. Esposito, *The Islamic Threat: Myth or Reality?* (New York; Oxford: Oxford University Press, 1992),108.

[246] Ervand Abrahamian, *Khomeinism: Essays on the Islamic Republic* (Berkeley: University of California Press, 1993), 23.

[247] See: Milagros Pena, "Liberation Theology in Peru: an Analysis of the Role of Intellectuals in Social Movements," *Journal for the Scientific Study of Religion* 33:1 (1994). Taken from EBSCO database Academic Search Premier. Item 00218294; Thomas Bruneau, "Brazil: The Catholic Church and Basic Christian Communities" in

why CEBs are most often seen as "paraecclesiastical" organizations.[248] Meanwhile, the Catholic establishment ("bishops") and the conservatives in Latin America rejected radical ideas of liberation theology, and the Vatican constantly urged its supporters (especially among the grassroots-level clergy) to "depoliticize."[249]

While many authors understood the politicization of Islam as a result of a "conspiracy of imams," just as many regard the politicization of Orthodoxy to be a result of activities of the Orthodox clergy (meaning, first of all, the Russian Orthodox Church). Within this framework, the study of the politicization of Orthodoxy entails the examination of the role of the Church in political affairs. Many scholars agree that the ROC not only engages in very little political activity, but also discourages activism on the part of laymen and individual clergymen.[250]

The manner in which the ROC approached the issue of so-called individual tax-payer's numbers (ITNs) may serve as an example of the ROC's attitude toward grassroots political activity. Since 2000, ITNs have been obligatory for all citizens of Russia and from the very beginning the issue of accepting or rejecting a number became quite controversial. A significant number of radical Orthodox believers supported by certain priests have claimed that ITNs are nothing but that Seal of Antichrist, which, as mentioned in the Book of Revelation, would be necessary to sell and buy anything. Protest actions against obligatory ITNs, including demonstrations and protest letters began, indeed, a great many of these letters were sent to the Patriarch and the other Church hierarchs.

This campaign was in no way specifically Russian. Having started in Greece in 1993 (after liberal government had declared that religion should not be mentioned in people's identity cards) it spread throughout the whole "Or-

---

Daniel H. Levine, ed., *Religion and Political Conflict in Latin America* (Chapel Hill & London: The University of North Carolina Press, 1986), 107.

[248] Charles A. Reilly, "Latin America's Religious Populism" in *Religion and Political Conflict in Latin America*, 49.

[249] Daniel H. Levine, David Stoll, "Bridging the Gap Between Empowerment and Power in Latin America" in Rudolf S., Piskatori, ed., *Transnational Religion and Fading States* (Boulder, Colo.: Westview, 1997), 81.

[250] See, for example: Jeff Haynes, *Religion in Global Politics* (London, New York: Longman, 1998), 14; Konstantin Kostiuk, "Pravoslavnyi fundamentalizm", *Politicheskie issledovaniia* no. 5 (2000): 152.

thodox world" (i.e., the transnational network or religiopolitical Orthodox movements). Radical believers protested against electronic identity cards, databases, bar-codes, smart-cards, taxpayer's numbers, etc. The idea that bar-codes include the Number of the Beast, or 666, gained enormous popularity among the protesters.

It is no surprise that political fundamentalists have lead these protests against ITNs. For them this development indicated that Russia had entered global civilization, a fact that they would rather not admit. Representatives of other ideologies of political Orthodoxy remained rather calm about the issue. They, however, never denied that the ITN is a symbol of the Seal of Antichrist, or that bar-codes include the digits 666. The issue of bar-codes, individual codes and ITNs became so widely discussed in Russian society that even respectable scholars (like Aleksandr Panarin) took part in the controversy. Nevertheless, only political fundamentalists organized mass protest actions against ITNs. Thus a political movement very close to the Church came into collision with the leadership of the ROC.

These mass political activities forced the leadership of the ROC to pay attention to this issue, which it had previously tried to ignore. On 19-20 February 2001 the 7th extended plenary session of the Synodal Theological Commission was held in the Moscow Ecclesiastic Academy to discuss the ITN issue. The problem of accepting the number was linked to the problem of globalisation, which was seen as a process hostile to Orthodoxy.

After a lengthy discussion, the Commission came to the conclusion that the ITN issue is of no religious significance and that the acceptance or rejection of an ITN should be regarded as the private choice of each individual believer.[251] The final decision of the session also referred to the tradition of the Holy Fathers, who have clearly stated that the Seal of Antichrist would be something that at a person would freely accept, thus voluntarily rejecting Christ. This, for instance, was the position of Archimandrite Ioann (Krestiankin), who was quoted in the final decision.[252] His position may be seen as a manifestation of traditionalism or conservatism (or, alternatively, non-

---

[251] "Itogovyi dokument zasedaniia rasshirennogo plenuma Sinodal'noi Bogoslovskoi komissii," *Moskovskii zhurnal* no. 4 (2001): 31.
[252] Ibid., 29.

political fundamentalism), which views religious issues independently, without reference to politics.

As stated above, while traditionalists may choose to either join or distance themselves from the religious establishment, for the most part, they don not openly confront officials even when they disapprove of their actions. In fact, traditionalists pay no attention to contemporary issues, remaining isolated from the modern world within their own subculture. The traditionalist position was expressed by Andrei Zubov (Professor at the Orthodox University of St. John the Theologian):

> The Church should return to the practice of the first centuries of its existence, when Christians yet lived in a non-Christianized state. Then they laboured not to change, to Christianize the laws of a state...but to ensure that Christians avoid all these phenomena, situations and temptations.[253]

Political fundamentalists, however, do not accept such a narrow, isolated stance; instead, they intend to influence the rest of society.

At the same plenary session, some ROC hierarchs backing moderate traditionalism (for example, Archimandrite Theognost) remarked that the ITN is a minor issue because people of Russia now face much more important social problems. Archimandrite Tikhon (Shevkunov) expressed the common position in the following way: "strengthening defence capabilities and the might of our Fatherland is the real struggle against globalization. But in no way does it means calling for destructive and disruptive measures and, of course, it does not require demonstrations."[254]

Both traditionalists and members of the establishment considered the problem of ITNs to be minor and secondary. While this is absolutely correct, every scholar of mass political movements would also assert that very often major uprisings have begun with protests concerning some minor issue. These "minor issues" are used by politically engaged people as catalysts to

---

[253] Andrei Zubov, "Esli by ot mira sego bylo Tsarstvo Moë..." *Znamia* no. 10 (1997): 182. Quoted in: Deacon Andrei Kuraev, *O nashem porazhenii* (Sankt-Peterburg: Svetloiar; Fond "Blagovest," 1999), 394.

[254] Archimandrite Tikhon (Shevkunov), "Bolevaia tochka Tserkvi," *NG-religii*, 28 March 2001.

accelerate mass protest. Even though such protests are ultimately the result of more significant issues, their causes remain ambiguous, since complicated social problems are difficult to formulate. It is much easier to mobilize people to fight a specific manifestation of globalisation (ITN) than "globalisation in general." The point is that the ROC *does not want* to accelerate protests.

Another example of the ROC's quietism and loyalty to the state is the Social Concept of the Russian Orthodox Church adopted by the Bishop's Council of the Russian Orthodox Church on 13-16 August 2000, though not so much the document per se, as its interpretation by the Church leadership. The Concept is supposed to express the position of the Church on the most controversial issues facing modern Russia and the rest of the world. The most important feature of this Concept concerns the fact that the Church, for the first time since the Revolution of 1917, has proclaimed the right of the Orthodox Christians to disobey the government in cases where the state would force believers to deny Christ and His Church or to commit sinful deeds (Article III.5).[255] This endorsement of possible civil disobedience has been evaluated by some scholars as a "revolution of ideas" in the Church doctrine.[256] In fact, the article has been formulated broadly enough to allow both literal and more open-ended interpretations. Had the Church so desired, this article could have been used to justify any mass protest actions against the state. Nevertheless, the interpretations given by the hierarchy dismiss the suggestion that the ROC envisions itself as the ideological centre of civil disobedience.

Discussing the Concept at a roundtable discussion (Russian Academy of State Service, 24 October 2000), Kirill, the Metropolitan of Smolensk and Kaliningrad said that "we have chosen the following path: we have clearly designated, on the one hand, our distance from the state power and, on the other hand, our full loyalty to the state..."[257] His subsequent argument clarifies this enigmatic statement. Answering a straightforward question regarding whether the "civil disobedience" mentioned in the Concept indicates the

---

[255] *Sotsial'naia kontseptsiia Russkoi Pravoslavnoi Tserkvi* (Moskva: Danilovskii blagovestnik, 2001), 54.

[256] "'Natsional'naia' tserkov': privelegiia ili otvetstvennost'? Kruglyi stol," *Otechestvennye zapiski* no. 1 (2001): 39.

ROC's authorization of mass protests against salary non-payments, Kirill stressed that

> no salary non-payments and no ideal of social justice may become a foundation for civil disobedience. There can be two reasons for civil disobedience. First: if state law completely breaks ties with moral law given by God... If, for example, tomorrow we have a law allowing children to throw parents from their homes...the Church will declare civil disobedience... The second reason for civil disobedience involves calls for direct sins or the denial of one's faith.[258]

One can compare these words with Article VI.6 of the Concept, containing several biblical quotations referring to non-payments and saying that "The Church teaches that refusing to pay a fair salary for labour is not just a crime against person but a sin against God."[259] Even on the sole basis of what is explicitly stated in the Social Concept, salary non-payment may well be determined to be a very sinful deed which should be answered by civil disobedience. Nevertheless, the ROC leadership resists such an interpretation. The final decision of the plenary session of the Synodal Theological Commission explains that the statement regarding the possibility of civil disobedience "pertains to the Church and not to individual clergymen or laymen daring without approval to speak on behalf of the Church."[260] The position of the Church with regard to anti-state political activity is thus crystal clear: no extraecclesiastical initiatives are supported; no ecclesiastical initiatives are considered acceptable (unless a law about "throwing parents from homes" is enacted).

Mass protests against replacing social benefits (i.e., free use of public transportation or rent discounts) with monetary payments in January 2005 have once again demonstrated how carefully the ROC distances its self from any anti-governmental activities. Some mass media reports revealed that Irinarkh, the Bishop of Perm and Solikamsk, expressed (from the viewpoint of religion) approval for the protest meeting on 17 January 2005 in Perm city

---

[257] "Osnovy sotsial'noi kontseptsii Russkoi Pravoslavnoi Tserkvi. Kruglyi stol. 24 octiabria 2000 g. RAGS, Moskva," *Gosudarstvo, religiia, tserkov'* no. 2 (2001): 40.
[258] Ibid., 41.
[259] *Sotsial'naia kontseptsia*, 88.
[260] Itogovyi dokument, 30.

and disapproval of the proposed social reform. Soon afterward, on 25 January upon having spoken with the Major of Perm, Irinarkh retracted these statements and firmly condemned mass activities.[261]

We, of course, don't mean that the Russian Orthodox Church as an institution supports liberal democracy and a market economy. The ROC Social Concept contains many ideas resembling the tenets of political and non-political fundamentalism (e.g., the Church does not approve globalisation, promotes social justice, opposes "new world order", etc.). The same concepts are constantly expressed by the highest ROC officials during annual *Vsemirnyi Russkii Narodnyi Sobor* held under the aegis of the Church. Once again, while ideological positions may be firmly established, they are held without a willingness to be involved in political confrontation with the state in order to implement these positions. Sometimes the ROC disapproves of state activities, but, unlike political fundamentalists, it does not consider the state its political enemy. Unlike traditionalists, it also does not intend to create its own isolated enclave, breaking all connections with the state.

Official churches distance them selves from the political activity of laymen and individual clergymen nearly everywhere in "Orthodox countries," even if they generally approve their ideological statements. For example, in Georgia the supporters of Vasilii Mkalavishvili, a former priest of the Georgian Orthodox Church, periodically conduct violent actions against non-Orthodox religious groups. In one instance, they burnt non-Orthodox books in March 1997, assaulted 120 members of a "Jehovah's Witnesses" organization in Tbilisi on 31 October 1999 and burnt Baptist books and battered a warehouse on 3 February 2002. Nevertheless, these activities should not be considered as having been approved by the official Georgian Orthodox Church, which has defrocked Vasilii Mkalavishvili for anti-Church activities (although theoretically the GOC has maintained a negative attitude toward Jehovah's Witnesses, Baptists, etc.).

Official, institutionalised religious organizations always oppose politicization, and official religious leaders almost always associate themselves with

---

[261] "Permskii episkop zaiavil, chto on ne podderzhival aktsii protesta protiv monetizatsii l'got," http://religare.ru/news13949.htm (as of 26 January 2005).

the ruling elite of a given society.[262] This is why the Soviet state always wanted to institutionalise even religions normally having no hierarchical structure: Muslims had been united into Spiritual Departments of Muslims, Protestants into the Union of Evangelical Christians – Baptists, etc. Officially recognized religious leaders become part of the national or ethnic elite and enjoy all of its privileges. For example, the Patriarch of the Russian Orthodox Church is considered equal to the highest state officials; since 2000 he has been guarded by the Federal Security Service (*Federalnaia Sluzhba Okhrany*).

All officially recognized leaders of the major "traditional" confessions in Russia – Patriarch Aleksii, Rabbi Berl Lazar, the leader of the Federation of Jewish Communities of Russia, Ravil' Gainutdin, the leader of the Union of Muslims of Russia and Damba Aiusheev, the head of the traditional Buddhist sangha of Russia – have privileges such as special licence plates and winkers guaranteeing preferential passage in Moscow. As one may notice, only one religious organization was selected to represent the entire Orthodox, Islamic, Hebrew or Buddhist community of Russia; the leaders of the other organizations enjoy no state-guaranteed privileges.

Most European Orthodox churches have signed or plan to sign special agreements with states (concordats) allowing them to influence state policy through traditional power structures. As a bonus they get receive perks from the principles of secularism. In this situation it becomes problematic for an official church to criticise the ruling elite or to disagree with it. Having noticed the smallest signs of a conflict, the Church leadership faces a difficult choice: it either should openly collide with the state power, or submit to state authority. As a rule, the officially recognised Church leadership choose the second option.

Every official or semi-official church (especially in the case of Orthodox churches) must choose between a neutral, apolitical position and the open support of the state regardless of circumstances. The first position, of course, seems much more acceptable from a moral standpoint. Moreover, it allows a church to appear as a mediator in case of a civil conflict. However, a church is

---

[262] See: Mir Z. Husain, *Global Islamic Politics* (New York: Harper & Collins College Publishers, 1995), 12; Jeff Haynes, *Religion in Global Politics* (London, New York: Longman, 1998), 49.

able to be such a mediator only in situations where its authority is equally recognized and respected by both sides. In most cases Orthodox churches have no other option but to cooperate with the most powerful side of a conflict – with a state.

When calling for peace and reconciliation, an official church tries to fulfill the first requirement of a loyal partner by not engaging in conflict with the state. The second requirement, however, can be understood to call for active support of the state. At this point, conflict between radical laymen and the hierarchy grows into political schism. The ITN problem remained within a specific ecclesiastical subculture, but political issues of national significance reveal irreconcilable contradictions between the establishment and ordinary believers. The presidential elections of 1996, when it was no longer possible for the Church to stay away from politics and to remain neutral, may serve as an example. On 22 May 1996 Patriarch Aleksii declared that "I am sure that the Muscovites will not make a mistake in electing the President of Russia, because they remember who is responsible for destroying our sanctities, and they will not let history reverse its self."[263] This statement was intended to be adequately understood by former Soviet newspaper-readers, experienced in Aesopian language, as a call to vote against the Communist party. Some other ROC hierarchs had openly spoken not just against communists, but plainly in support of Boris Yeltsin. At the same time ordinary clergymen and laymen sympathized with Gennadii Ziuganov.[264] This tradition of supporting the state continued into the following period as well (no matter who was leading the state at the moment). For example, at the ceremony of consecration of the Cathedral of Christ the Savior on 31 December 1999, Patriarch Aleksii promised "to support Vladimir Vladimirovich [Putin] in his labors and deeds."[265]

---

[263] Aleksandr Verkhovskii, Ekaterina Mikhailovskaia, Vladimir Pribylovskii, *Politicheskaia ksenofobiia: Radikalnye gruppy. Predstavleniia politikov. Rol' tserkvi* (Moskva: Panorama, 1999), 74-75.

[264] Fedor Ovsienko, N.A.Trofimchuk, "Konfessional'nyi faktor v rossiiskom politicheskom protsesse: sushchnost' i mesto (obzor)" in *Religiia i kul'tura. Referativnyi sbornik* (Moskva: INION RAN, 2000), 76.

[265] "Polugosudarstvennaia tserkov' v polutserkovnom gosudarstve?", *Russkaia mysl'*, 30 March – 5 April 2000.

The same position is typical for the leaders of the Russian Islamic establishment, i.e., for the people from the Spiritual Department of Muslims. The official Islamic leaders of Dagestan working at the Dagestan Spiritual Department of Muslims and the Union of Muslims of Russia openly urged people to vote for Yeltsin in 1996.[266] This story was repeated on 9 September 2003 when an extraordinary meeting of the Council of the Coordination Center of Muslims of the Northern Caucasus addressed Chechen people with a call to vote for Akhmad Kadyrov as the president of Chechnia.[267] This proves once again that in spite of its "depoliticization" rhetoric the establishment is easily co-opted as an active supporter of any ruling regime.

The formal closeness of church and state creates an illusion that religion has a significant impact on politics. Nevertheless, clericalism (i.e., the influence of clergymen on politics) does not necessarily engender the politicization of religion. No one objected to clericalism more than Ayatollah Khomeini, or even the contemporary supporters of political Orthodoxy. Even in the Soviet period clergymen conducted some political activities (namely, took part in the international peace movement) which in no way involved the politicization of Orthodoxy. Contrary to expectation, the presence of clergymen among state officials does not mean that a country becomes a theocracy. This may be illustrated by Albanian Orthodox bishop Theophan (Fan) Noli (1882-1965), the first prime minister and regent of independent Albania (June 1924). If we equate "religious" with "clerical," a state headed by bishop would inevitably become an Orthodox theocracy; nevertheless, Fan Noli supported separation of church and state, against the theology taught at schools.

For a state to become ideocratic, clergymen who support the idea of remaking society in accordance with religious principles must be involved in politics (rather than just any). Even so, it is not important whether these are clergymen, religiously minded laymen, or even people practicing no religion. Of course, Orthodoxy is canonically impossible without church sanction. We, however, are not speaking about Orthodoxy *per se*, but about political Orthodoxy.

---

[266] See: Anna Matveeva, "Ugroza islamizma v postsovetskoi Evrazii," *Tsentral'naia Aziia i Kavkaz* no. 4 (1999): 97-98.
[267] Oleg Nedumov, "Muftii podderzhivaiut Akhmada Kadyrova", *NG-religii*, 17 September 2003.

VI. 2 Civil and Uncivil Religion: Transformations of Official Nationalism

Contrary to our position, expressed above, some observers tend to exaggerate the influence of Orthodoxy on socio-political life in modern Russia. What they find particularly alarming is the ROC's "penetration" of the Army and state schools: institutions that must be non-confessional in a secular state. We suggest, however, that this alarmism regarding "total clericalization" (often mistakenly equated with "religious politicization") is in most cases irrelevant. Russia is definitely not a secular state in the full sense. However, the same could be said about many democratic states supporting their moral integrity with the help of civil religions. States with ethnically and confessionally heterogeneous populations (e.g., the U.S., Indonesia, Yugoslavia or Russia) may hardly survive without religion-based national ideologies. It seems, then, that Russian leadership has been attempting to form some kind of civil religion.

Unlike political religions, civil religions aim not at reaching religious goals using political means but at the sacralization of the state and its institutions. As early as the beginning of this century, Nikolas K. Gvosdev, a prominent scholar of church-state relations, put forward the idea that the Russian state wanted to utilize "nationalized" Orthodoxy in order to provide moral legitimacy for itself. Gvosdev suggested that for the post-Soviet Russian society Orthodoxy might become a civil religion, i.e., a set of beliefs, rituals and ceremonies serving secular as opposed to transcendent or otherworldly goals.[268] Civil religion aims at strengthening ties between citizens and their state. In this case it does not matter whether this state is "Orthodox" (ideocratic), or not. As a civil religion Russian Orthodoxy would be equal to Shinto, American civil religion or even Indonesian *pancha sila* (the five principles).

Orthodoxy is increasingly perceived as a kind of civil religion: all citizens of Russia are automatically considered "Orthodox," except for members of several legally recognized confessions who are seen as "the Orthodox *honoris causa*." Nevertheless, it seems too simplistic to insist that Orthodoxy is the only basis of the newly formed civil religion. This basis consists, apart from Orthodoxy, of the other "traditional confessions" – loyal to the state, not proselytising with regard to each other and co-existing peacefully under the "umbrella" of civil religion.

The idea of a union between the traditional religions of Russia, in which Orthodoxy is the leading component of an emerging civil religion, appears to have been borrowed from the doctrine of Eurasianism. Indeed, this influence seems natural since Eurasianist ideology permits the integration of different ethnic groups and confessions into a single nation. (We would like to remind to the reader that there are many versions of Eurasianism, and that the radical version of Dugin and Dzhemal' is only one of them). The Russian leadership, unwilling to invent something fully new and artificial (like *pancha sila*), most likely prefers to utilize Eurasinism, which has become in contemporary Russia a popular and respectable ideology.

These traditional confessions are, according to the Federal law on freedom of consciousness and religious communities (1997, amended in 2002), "Christianity," Islam, Buddhism, Judaism and "other religions." Orthodoxy, being the religion of the largest ethnic group, is positioned above the other confessions; while it does not encroach on their territory, it does not allow them to occupy its domain. Strangely enough, "Christianity" was designated as a specific religion, distinct from "Orthodoxy," honoured in the preamble as having special role in Russian history and in the formation of Russian spirituality and culture. Most likely this term refers to loyal Protestants united in the Union of Evangelical Christians – Baptists.

It is clear that this approach has established unbreakable connections between ethic groups and religious organizations. For example, all Tatars are automatically seen as potential Muslims (they may remain secular but the ROC is not allowed to proselytise among them). Moreover, only specific Muslim organizations (state-recognized Spiritual Departments) are allowed to provide religious services to these Tatars. All aliens (such as Wahhabists or Turkish missionaries) are expelled with the help of a state. Baptists and the other recognized Protestants are seen as quasi-ethnic groups: these are mostly Protestants in the third or fourth generation. In fact, this means applying a specifically Orthodox concept of a "canonical territory" (i.e. a territory of one

---

268 Nicolas K. Gvosdev, "The New Party Card? Orthodoxy and the Search for Post-Soviet Russian Identity," *Problems of Post-Communism* 40:6 (2000): 29.

Orthodox Church where the other Orthodox Churches are not allowed to operate) to the other religions.

In 2002 the relationship between the ROC and the Catholic Church suffered a severe breakdown. The visas of several Catholic priests and bishops (citizens of Poland) were terminated and they were deported from Russia. This response was prompted by the Pope's decision, on 11 February 2002 to establish four Catholic dioceses in Russia instead of temporary institutions called apostolic administrations. The ROC considered this move to be an encroachment upon its "canonical territory" and petitioned for assistance from the state, resulting in this termination of visas and several declarations of the Foreign Affairs Ministry directed against the Catholic Church.

The state is thereby ready to guard the interests of the loyal confessions which contribute to its moral legitimisation. Nevertheless, the question of how much they gain and lose because of this protection is still disputable. The ROC may feel secure in defending Catholics "attacks" upon its Russian flock. At the same time, as a loyal traditional religious organization it has sworn not to proselytise Tatars in Russia or Kazakhs in Kazakhstan. "Ethnic Muslims" interested in Orthodoxy and wishing to convert often find no response from the Church, which is not willing to spoil its relations, not even with Islam, but rather with the Spiritual Departments and the state.

Most likely, the process of the formation of a civil religion will result in the signing of concordats between the state and the religions in question. Each religion will be represented by a hierarchical institution recognized by the state (including religions normally having no hierarchical structures). The ROC will be the first to sign the concordat, then Muslims, then the others. This is the only possible choice because a civil religion in Russia must successfully solve the problem of integrating citizens belonging to various ethnic and confessional groups into a single nation. Too much emphasis on the Christian component of civil religion might make other groups feel alienated from the national body.

Many "Orthodox countries" have already declared Orthodoxy a "national" ("state") religion and/or have signed concordats. Bulgaria adopted a law declaring Orthodoxy a traditional religion in December 2002, Georgia, in October 2002 and Belarus in June 2003. In most cases this process is theoretically open to the other "traditional religions" as well, in exchange for their loyalty to the state and a non-proselytising policy with regard to each other.

At the first glance it may seem that as a result of such concordats, religions acquire enormous influence on social life. One should not, however, forget two things:

(1) Concordats are signed not by "religions" but by specific religious organizations. It is not "religion in general" that becomes national as a result of a concordat but the version of this religion supported by that very specific organization. Thus, it is more accurate to speak of the influence of an organization, as opposed to the influence of a religion. This issue, while unimportant for Orthodoxy, is highly significant for Islam, which has several competing denominations.

(2) Concordats strictly distinguish between the sphere where a religious organization is allowed to "assist" the state and other spheres where neither "religion," nor "church" is welcomed. For example, according to the concordat signed on 12 June 2003 by the state of Belarus and the Byelorussian Orthodox Church, the sphere of cooperation between state and church is limited to a narrow segment of social reality (education, cultural heritage protection, charity and so on).[269] Concordats thereby restrict the attempts of a church to break away from the state-imposed limits.

What is crucial is that in case of civil religions the state utilizes religion and not vice versa. Recognized religious organizations gain benefits from cooperation with a state; at the same time, they often have to sacrifice their religious mission to the needs of a state.

In our opinion, the teaching of "Foundations of Orthodox Culture" in Russian secondary schools indicates not so much the penetration of "religion" into schools, as the penetration of state ideology embodied in a civil religion. Teaching "Foundations of Orthodox (Islamic, Buddhist) Culture" does not entail the complete "Orthodoxization," Islamization or "Buddhization" of education.

A true penetration of religion into schools has been demonstrated by the Islamic reform of education in Iran that started on 5 June 1980 when all universities of the country were closed for three years. All school and university textbooks (even the ones in Math) have been Islamized: for example, all women and girls were depicted in scarves.[270] In Russia "Foundations of Orthodox Culture" are taught (not nationwide so far) as a discipline equal to the others and imply no parallel "Orthodoxization" of curricula in Literature or Mathematics (for example, depicting all women in scarves and long skirts).

Having analysed the relationship between the ROC and the Russian Army, we found nothing that would exceed the limits of a civil religion. It is true that something resembling mini-concordats on cooperation in the sphere of the spiritual education of the military are being signed between the ROC and specific Army (or Navy) areas of responsibility. Nevertheless, so-called "chaplains" are not even servicemen – they are sent by the ROC to serve at specific regiments. This is apparently normal interaction between the Army and the Church, operating as two equal social institutions and not involving the Army as an instrument for achieving religious goals. The Army cooperates not only with the ROC but with the other loyal religious organizations (such as the Council of Muftis of Russia). While such policies may fall short of the ideal of a secular state, there is no reason to worry about "total clericalization."

We suggest that in the long run the formation of a civil religion based on Orthodoxy and the other "traditional confessions" might have contributed to democratisation of Russian society. The initial period of the birth of this civil religion is characterized by alarming outbursts of hostility toward the "others," though these sentiments are apt to dissipate over time. The position of Catholics and "sects" in Russia is particularly insecure because their ruling centres are located abroad and their loyalty to the state is constantly questioned. (Even in the US a Catholic president – John Kennedy – provoked anxiety).

Another source of the Catholic's current disadvantage is their proselytising activity: membership in the pool of "traditional confessions" is granted only to those who promise not to proselytise ethnic groups which have "traditionally" been considered as the domain of another confession. If the Catholic Church agrees to become a Church of ethnic Poles, it will, most likely, have

---

[269] Oleg Nedumov, "Vlast' i tserkov' vospitaiut narod. Pravoslavie v Belorussii stanovitsia gosudarstvennoi religiei", *Nezavisimaia gazeta*, 2 July 2003.

[270] See: Vladimir Iurtaev, *Studenty v islamskoi revoliutsii* (Moskva: Nauka, 1993), 167

no problems in Russia. Even "sects" may manage to build quasi-ethnic groups if they are able to survive more than one generation of followers.

Civil religions necessarily presuppose a gradual elimination of confrontation between religions. A nation-building enterprise with the highest probability for success will most likely involve a gradual secularizaton of the civil religion and a diminishing of reference to the supernatural. As a result, more and more religions will be considered "harmless" for state integrity. In this scenario, the end product would be a democratic, rather than ideocratic, state. However, the emergence of such positive dynamics seems very unlikely.

We have already mentioned that the success of a civil religion depends upon the success of the nation as such. A nation enjoying a healthy state of affairs, including a stable economy, political democracy and social security, allows people to unite in a civil society based on shared positive achievements. In cases where such achievements are absent, citizens may be united only "against" someone or something. Then a civil religion becomes uncivil, resulting in a monoethnic and monoconfessional state.

We do not question the idea that in time, Russia may very well become a successful nation-state: economically advanced, democratic and socially balanced. The point is that Russia's current leadership does not have time to consider long-term national development programs. By approximately 2003 it became evident that the establishment of a new ideological foundation for nation-building requires urgent attention. Otherwise the very existence of the current economic-cum-political elite is threatened by activities called, after the peaceful displacement of the Kuchma regime in the Ukraine, "orange revolutions" (within Russia also known as "the orange plague").

The issue of nation-building has suddenly become pressing for Russia as well as for the other CIS countries for the following reasons. Immediately after the dissolution of the Soviet Union most of the newly independent states were founded upon a full rejection of the Soviet (also seen as imperial) past. Thus, the new national identity offered was dominated by the ethnic element. Even in the Russia of the early 1990s there were attempts to "erase" the Soviet period from the new Russian history (this was also the time of active discussions about the reintroduction of monarchy). At the same time, other ideologists were developing a second, marginal nation-building project involving

Russia's transformation into a state of ethnic Russians. (The fact that in 1993, Boris Mironov managed to become the Chairman of the State Committee on the Press reveals that it was not as marginal as some imagined it to be).

By the mid-1990s the newly independent states had to abandon their ethnonationalist projects as they discovered that they were in fact ethnically and linguistically heterogeneous. In that period all of them had transitional regimes which were unwilling to produce anything to replace the deserted ethnic projects. There was a backlash in the process of nation-building: after a short period of militant ethnonationalism the newly independent states became the amorphous "Former Soviet Union" (FSU). In a way the FSU became the most successful integrative force for the post-Soviet states.

The situation has radically changed in 2003-2004. Both the population and the leadership of the newly independent states "suddenly" discovered that "the FSU" could no longer function as an integrating force and that they must cease to be "former" so as to become something "present."

At that moment "revolutions of flowers and fruit" occurred in Georgia, the Ukraine and Kyrgyzstan (the case of the latter is slightly different). By that time the initial ethnonational enterprise had been marginalized and forgotten. It was replaced with the project of building European-style civil nations to join, eventually, the European structures (EU and NATO). This project is not "oppositional" in the strict sense because, for the most part, the previous regimes had declared the same goals. However, in reality they would never be able to realize these goals, since their authority and wealth were based upon the idea of a post-Soviet amorphous state. For them, integration with Europe would mean losing everything they had and maybe even legal prosecution. To actualize the European (or Western) enterprise, the opposition in Georgia and the Ukraine had to dismiss the post-Soviet regimes.

These developments, as well as not-so-peaceful revolution in Kyrgyzstan, have become a source of frustration for the other two European "members of the FSU" – Belarus and Russia. Preventing "orange revolutions" is the most urgent task for both Lukashenko and Putin. Lukashenko was the first one to realize that slowing down revolutionary developments would be only possible when a state initiated its own nation-building project imposed from above.

In Belarus the task of working out a Byelorussian national idea was set as early as in 2003; currently (in 2005) the propaganda of national ideology is conducted via mass media, education, ideological trade-unions and youth organizations. (It is not accidental that the above-mentioned concordat was signed in 2003.) In Russia urgent nation-building began not earlier than in 2004. It is symptomatic that in his TV-address on 4 September 2004 (after the terrorist act in Beslan) Putin, for the first time, used the word "nation" (*natzia*) previously employed only by marginal nationalist political groupings (in the official language the word "people" (*narod*) was commonly used).[271] This address set a task "to mobilize the nation," or, in other words, to build a nation of the USSR fragments presently composing the Russian Federation.

The task of nation-building is so urgent that there is virtually no time left for a democratic civil religion to mature as well as for fulfilling a successful national development program. In these circumstances, national unity it limited to efforts against some external and/or internal enemies. This prevents the emerging civil religion from growing into a democratic one, thereby becoming an "uncivil religion."

The position of the external enemy is, of course, reserved for the West. This enemy, however, is much less utilizable for the purpose of nation-building than the internal enemy, or "the fifth column."

"Terrorists", more specifically – "Islamic terrorists" have become the first choice to play the role of the internal enemy. This position characterizes the infamous interview with Vladislav Surkov, the Deputy Head of the Presidential Administration. The rhetoric of this interview has shocked Russian liberals: "All of us should understand: the enemy is at the gate. Every city, every street, every house is at the frontline. We need vigilance, solidarity, mutual support, united efforts of citizens and the state."[272] Naming some ethnic and religious groups as the enemy, of course, would strip the official nation-building enterprise from all Eurasianist influences. Orthodoxy once again would become "the Russian faith" while Russia would be transformed into the state of Russian people.

---

[271] "Obrashchenie Prezidenta Rossii Vladimira Putina k grazhdanam Rossii," http://vip.lenta.ru/doc/2004/09/04/address/ (as of 4 September 2004).

[272] Vladislav Surkov, "Putin ukrepliaet gosudarstvo, a ne sebia," *Komsomol'skaia pravda*, 29 September 2004.

This vision of the enemy perfectly coincides with mass anti-migrant sentiments in big cities, where people are prone to blame the "Caucasian" migrants for all social problems. Nationalist and Orthodox nationalist paramilitary organizations (such as, for example, the Movement Against Illegal Immigration) welcomed this political move. Analysts from the Centre for Information and Analysis "SOVA" warn that radical paramilitaries are ready to take part in the state-sponsored anti-migrant activities.[273] The idea of "people squads" is widely discussed in Orthodox extremist circles now. For example, a fundamentalist paramilitary organization "*Stiag*" (Banner), established in 2004, suggests that "the squads of the People's Guard" may become a useful instrument of anti-terrorist activity.[274] "*Stiag*" theorists think that these squads armed with carbines may assist the police in the course of patrolling and in anti-terrorist operations. This shows that radical nationalists and fundamentalists are ready to support not only moderate opposition but even the state, to the extent that it becomes more "national" (meaning, ethnonational) and Orthodox. So far radical nationalists continue to articulate their emblematic anti-Putinism, but if the ethnization of the official nationalism were to occur, they may become one of the pillars of the state.

However, after revolutions in the Ukraine and Kyrgyzstan the official ideologists seemingly reached the conclusion that migrants as an internal threat are less dangerous than political opponents.

In the winter of 2005 mass protests against the monetarisation of natural benefits demonstrated the end of social apathy. For the first time in post-Soviet history of Russia oppositional forces from the left (KPRF, National Bolsheviks and *Rodina*) and from the right (*Iabloko*) proceeded to coordinate their activities and organize joint protest actions. Protests against corrupt local authorities (sort of orange mini-revolutions) increased in the national republics of Russia. All these protests can hardly be related to activities of "Chechen terrorists."

For the above-mentioned Surkov, political opposition was a minor threat in comparison to terrorists. However, he clearly insisted that:

---

[273] "Natsionalisty vyrabatyvaiut strategiiu 'bor'by'," http://www.xeno.sova-center.ru/45 A29F2/4F30C82 (as of 10 February 2005).

[274] Sergei Pakhmutov, "Druzhiny narodnoi gvardii – perspektivnoe sredstvo bor'by s terrorom," http://druzhina.rustrana.ru/stat/stat2.html (as of 17 April 2005).

> The fifth column of left and right radicals has emerged in a country, which is, in fact, under siege. Lemons and some apples [word-play: "lemons" refer to National Bolsheviks and "apples" to *Iabloko*] now ripen at one tree. False liberals and true Nazis have more and more in common. They have common sponsors of foreign origins. Common hatred to what they call Putin's Russia. In reality – to Russia as such.[275]

The "fifth column" in the official nationalist discourse is increasingly referred to as "Fascists." This word, however, is used regardless of one's ideology. It seeks to stigmatize and demonize the political opposition.

On 16 April 2005, *"Idushchie vmeste"* (Walking together) a pro-presidential youth movement was transformed into *Molodezhnoe Demokraticheskoe Antifashistskoe Dvizhenie "Nashi"* (the Youth Democratic Anti-fascist Movement "Us"). The word "Anti-fascist" in its title refers not to "Fascism" in any meaningful sense but to everyone being suspected in non-loyalty to the state. Making the opposition, labelled as "Fascists," the main internal enemy protects Eurasianist fragments in the ideology of official nationalism. At the same time, this tactic maintains the same degree of hatred towards the enemy, regardless of who they are. The role of religion here, if any, is fully instrumental.

Whether directed against ethnic non-Russians or against political opponents, the emerging civil religion increasingly undermines the goal of democratic transformation. Instead, it is being transformed into an uncivil religion promoting xenophobia, garrison thinking and witch hunting.

---

[275] Vladislav Surkov, "Putin ukrepliaet gosudarstvo, a ne sebia".

VII Political Orthodoxy at the Micro- and Macropolitical Level

Finally we would like determine the extent to which the ongoing process of politicization of Orthodoxy affects political developments in modern Russia. The impact of Orthodox political movements on Russian society may seem insignificant if judged by their electoral success (considering that many of them never participated in elections). Most of Orthodox political organizations have "activists" but have no "sympathizers" who would, for example, vote for them. For this reason, Orthodox political organizations prefer to pursue strategies other than traditional party policy.

Most nation-wide electoral coalitions uniting political Orthodox fundamentalists have never been able to get even as much as 1% of the vote (mostly less than 0.5%). In 1999 *"Za russkoe delo"* (For the Russian cause) coalition got only 0.17%[276]; in 2003 *"Za Rus' sviatuii"* (For the Holy Russia) got 0.49 %.[277] Archaic symbols and ideas discourage votes from the majority of the population. Tight connections with the church, which is an alien institution for the social majority, distract would-be supporters as well. Fundamentalism attracts only active church-goers or, at least, those who intend to become practicing Orthodox Christians.

Insufficient public support did not prevent fundamentalists from carrying out several political actions involving violence. In January 2003 an art exhibition entitled "Beware, religion!" opened in the Sakharov Center and Museum in Moscow. The exhibition included many controversial items, such as, for example, an image of Christ against the background of a Coca-Cola logo with an inscription "This is my blood." On 18 January (4 days after the exhibition was opened) six members of the fundamentalist organization *Obshchestvennyi komitet "Za nravstvennoe vozrozhdenie Otechestva"* entered the museum and destroyed the exhibits. Initially they were charged with vandalism

---

[276] Aleksandr Verkhovskii, *Politicheskoe pravoslavie: Russkie pravoslavnye fundamentalisty i natsionalisty. 1995-2001 g.* (Moskva: Tsentr "SOVA", 2003), 30.

but this charge was dismissed (instead, the initiators of the exhibition were charged with inciting religious hatred and found guilty in March 2005).

A similar event happened in February 2004 in St. Petersburg, where a group of radical fundamentalists smashed an exhibition of "interactive icons." In March 2005 fundamentalists sued the originators of another exhibition ("Russia-2"), which, they claim, provoked religious hatred and political extremism. They have also organized a series of non-violent political actions against various art events (for example, on 30 March 2005 fundamentalists picketed the Estrada Theatre protesting against a ballet entitled "Rasputin," where Nicolas II appears dancing). On 15 February 2005 people claiming to be members of an Orthodox brotherhood attacked the so-called "Russian Spirituality Center" belonging to the Center of God's Mother (*Bogoridichnyi Tsentr*), a religious organization considered by the ROC to be a "destructive sect."

Fundamentalists have thus managed to attract highly motivated people capable of direct political action. As early as ten years ago the events just described would have been impossible. It seems that fundamentalist organizations gradually build up their strength and social influence. This, most likely, results from social activities initiated by many fundamentalist organizations.

In fact, fundamentalists are in charge of all charity and catechization programs related to the ROC. Orthodox brotherhoods and sisterhoods existing at various churches collect and distribute second-hand clothes, organize summer camps for children and youth and provide catechization. Their non-political activities often become politicized or are politicized from the very beginning.

For example, the Orthodox brotherhood of Saint Apostles Peter and Paul (Novokuznetsk) initially dealt with catechization exclusively. The first meetings of the brotherhood were only attended by parishioners of the Savior-Transfiguration Cathedral. They read the gospels, watched Orthodox documentaries and studied the foundations of Orthodoxy. However, the scope of discussions eventually widened to include the contemporary social

---

[277] "TsIK oglasil ofitsial'nye rezul'taty vyborov v Gosdumu," http://www.vibori.info/news/article.php?id=398 (as of 19 December 2003).

situation.[278] The brotherhood overgrew the limits of a parish and now works with 22 organizations (schools, universities, social institutions, military regiments, etc.) and sets such goals as "to consolidate the sound social forces for a moral resurrection of Russia," "to oppose the forces of destruction and decay," and "to inspire patriotism, respect for the Russian army and a willingness to defend the Motherland if needed."[279]

Some brotherhoods, apart from charity projects, establish paramilitary organizations such as, for example, the Squad (*druzhina*) of Aleksandr Nevskii at the brotherhood of the Cathedral of Aleksandr Nevskii (Novosibirsk), combining propagandist activity with the "guarding" of churches and religious events and "anti-sect" activities.

Organization of various Orthodox "military-patriotic" activities for children and youth (e.g., summer camps, hand-to-hand combat clubs, etc.) is one of the most useful methods of winning public support. Let us name only a few of Orthodox summer camps for youth held in recent years (most of them are held regularly each year or several times a year): 2005, Serpukhov: Orthodox military-patriotic camp "*Ratnaia zastava*" (Fortress); 2004, Taiga: Aleksandr Nevskii's Orthodox patriotic camp; 2004, Ramenskoe (Moscow *oblast*): Orthodox military-patriotic camp for children and youth "*Bereg*" (Waterside); 2003, Zav'ialovo (Novosibirsk *oblast*): Orthodox military-patriotic camp, etc.

Military-patriotic clubs represent another branch of fundamentalist social activity. These include the Orthodox military-patriotic club for children "*Margelovets*" in Moscow, the Orthodox military-patriotic club "*Peresvet-M*" in Moscow, the Orthodox military-patriotic club "*Signal*" in Novosibirsk, the Military-sport club "*Stratilat*" at Danilovskii Monastery in Moscow and others.

In most of such camps and clubs children and adolescents learn, for example, Orthodox rites, Church history, Russian military history, hand-to-hand combat (in most cases it is stressed that this combat is "Russian" and not "Oriental"), shooting and survival. The youngsters are dressed in camou-

---

[278] Father Sergei Pukhkoi, "Pravoslavnoe bratstvo imeni Svv.Pervv. Apostolov Petra i Pavla v stanovlenii molodëzhnogo dvizheniia," in *Problemy sotsial'nogo sluzheniia i obrazovatel'noi deiatel'nosti Russkoi pravoslavnoi tserkvi* (Kemerovo: Kuzbassvuzizdat, 2001), 105-106.

[279] Ibid., 107, 108-109.

flage. Orthodox camps are supported by local authorities because they are seen as a means of preventing juvenile delinquency. They are often financed from local budgets and from the funds of the ROC.

It would be wrong to say that camps and clubs educate the next generation in the spirit of Orthodoxy; it would be more accurate to say that these children are being schooled in the spirit of the fundamentalist and nationalist version of political Orthodoxy. Formal documentation of these organizations includes no fundamentalist or nationalist ideas. In reality, though, all ideological tasks are typically performed by fundamentalists or other Orthodox nationalists, either clerical or lay. This, however, may be learned only in the course of communication with the executives of these organizations. An anonymous participant of a fundamentalist Internet-forum *Russkii dom* has briefly summarized the policy of these clubs in the following way: "From their childhood boys must understand two main things: 1) that they are warriors of Christ [and] 2) that they are patriots."[280] The very use of the word "patriotic" is a marker revealing the presence of political Orthodoxy.

The process of teaching and learning in the Orthodox military-patriotic camp *"Bogatyrskaia zastava,"* regularly conducted in Karelia (Prionezhskii *raion*), has been described in detail by one of its teaching staff. She tells how a priest who taught shooting showed children a photo of Evgenii Rodionov. The teacher narrates:

> We ask again: "who is this guy in camouflage? What has he done? "He may have killed many enemies in Chechnya," the kids suggest. We answer: "No. He did not have time to kill anyone. This good Russian guy was martyred by gunmen, but he did not take his cross off." We have many things to tell kids about their coeval who did not betray Christ and Fatherland.[281]

Even charity activities conducted by fundamentalists concurrently serve religiopolitical purposes. For example, a sisterhood that operates at the Ca-

---

[280] See: http://forumrussdom.russtv.ru, topic "Detskie pravoslavnye voenno-patrioticheskie ob"edineniia," posted on 14 February 2005.

[281] Elena Mazaeva, "Mozhet li igra v voinu stat' propoved'iu o Khriste?" *Belgorodskaia pravoslavnaia dukhovnaia seminariia. Missionerskoe obozrenie* no. 8 (2004), http://seminaria.bel.ru/pages/mo/2004/mo8_st_4.htm (as of 1 March 2005).

thedral of Aleksandr Nevskii in Novosibirsk exists to care for the patients of the state clinical hospital of Novosibirsk *oblast*. In addition to providing medical services, it spreads anti-abortion, anti-cult and other political propaganda among the patients.

Unlike fundamentalists, most of Pan-Slavist organizations limit their activities to cultural projects. They pay more attention to establishing ties with Pan-Slavists from the other countries than to attracting mass support within Russia. In spring 1999 thousands of Russians took part in spontaneous demonstrations and other mass protest actions against the military campaign in Kosovo. Even a May Day demonstration organized by loyal trade unions was held under slogans such as "No war" and "Down with NATO" (it is worth mentioning that local units of trade unions used Soviet posters portraying a dove of peace cracking a missile).

Pan-Slavists may have gained mass support if they had provoked spontaneous outbursts of pro-Serb sentiments and channeled them into an organized political movement. They, however, failed to initiate a lasting pressure campaign that would urge the government to "help" Serbia. They also proved unable to organize any significant support for Serbia in terms of money or humanitarian aid (not mentioning volunteers). It is worth mentioning that most fundamentalists and nationalists indoctrinate people with Pan-Slavist ideas as well; thus, there is no need for Pan-Slavists to initiate their own social projects.

Most neo-Eurasianists also limit their activity to propaganda. Aleksandr Dugin, who is a dominant figure of cultural Eurasianism, has thus far not gained any political success. In January 2004 he was expelled from his own *Partiia "Evraziia"* by his deputy Pëtr Suslov. *Obshchestvenno-politicheskoe dvizhenie "Evraziia"* (now *Mezhdunarodnoe Evraziiskoe Dvizhenie*), which has existed since 2001, has implemented virtually no political activity, having done nothing that would differentiate *Evraziia* as a *political* movement from *Arktogeia* as a *cultural* association. Organizing exhibitions of books by Aleksandr Dugin in various cities and countries seems to be the central preoccupation of *Mezhdunarodnoe Evraziiskoe Dvizhenie*. It also observed elections in Belarus and Kazakhstan, arriving at the conclusion that there had been no infringements upon voting rights.

Andreas Umland suggests that this lack of attention to political activity as such is a conscious tactic aimed at winning intellectual domination over society before proceeding to gain political power.[282] Nevertheless, at the moment nothing indicates that such a transition will transpire in the foreseeable future.

Dugin's political aspirations have apparently been weakened by his vocal endorsement of Vladimir Putin and his policies. *Evraziia,* since its inception, was presented as an unequivocally "pro-presidential" force aiming to join other "pro-presidential" political actors. Its task, according to Dugin, was "not to become the state authority but to struggle to influence it," which has meant offering various suggestions to the current president, who has been considered to be a crypto-Eurasianist.[283] The constitutive congress of *Mezhdunarodnoe Evraziiskoe Dvizhenie* has even addressed the presidents of Russia and Kazakhstan (Vladimir Putin and Nursultan Nazarbaev) with an offer to head the Supreme Council of this movement as co-chairs.[284] Speaking to the Political Council of *Evraziia* in 2001 Dugin insisted that "true Eurasianism can only be achieved via Putin. What stands against Putin is pseudo-Eurasianism."[285]

Dugin has formulated the task of restructuring the elite's consciousness, stating that the "xenomorphous" (i.e., non-Russian) elite should be impelled to give an oath of allegiance to the Russian nation.[286] This ambition seems hardly realizable. The elite can be moved to a more pro-Russian stance, as Dugin suggests, only by sacrificing Russia's position in the global economy. The wealth of the ruling elite in Russia depends not so much on the domestic situation but on the situation within the world market. The only elite group

---

[282] Andreas Umland, "Toward an Uncivil Society? Contextualizing the Recent Decline of Extremely Right-Wing Parties in Russia," http://www.wcfia.harvard.edu/papers/ (as of 10 October 2003).

[283] Quoted in: Nikolai Zimin, "Novoe politicheskoe dvizhenie poluchilo podderzhku traditsionnykh konfessii," http://www.sobor.ru/randp.asp?id=1810 (as of 22 April 2001); Maksim Shevchenko, "Podderzhivaet li patriarkhiia radikal'nykh sionistov?" *NG-religii,* 25 April 2001.

[284] "Sozdano mezhdunarodnoe evraziiskoe dvizhenie," http://www.evrazia.org/modules.php?name=News&file=article&sid=1545 (as of 21 November 2003).

[285] Aleksandr Dugin, "My boremsia za vliianie na vlast'," http://www.evrazia.org/modules.php?name=News&file=article&sid=88 (as of 11 October 2001).

likely to adopt "Eurasian consciousness" are the directors of large heavy industry and defense industry plants who depend on state orders (such as the "nationally-minded" industrialists used to support Hitler). But they don't possess the economic resources of those who control oil and gas supplies and whom Dugin defines as the "xenomorphous elite."

Nevertheless, Dugin's adherence to the idea of "unequivocal support" of Putin has not diminished with time (although this stance does not seem to bring him any political dividends). In fact, while addressing a conference entitled "National-Bolshevism: Lessons for the 21st century" on 18 March 2005, he repeated his previous position that today National-Bolshevism (or Eurasianism) entails supporting Putin in spite of his liberalism and other shortcomings.[287] Only the latest (as of April 2005) publications by Dugin show any misgivings regarding Putin's would-be "Eurasianism."[288] This "Putinism" endorsed by *Mezhdunarodnoe Evraziiskoe Dvizhenie* prohibits it from joining the united opposition in the event that it may at last arrive at a position which begins to question the current president's right to govern.

One may suggest that Dugin is not interested in political activism as such. However, a youth branch of *Mezhdunarodnoe Evraziiskoe Dvizhenie*, *Evraziiskii Soiuz Molodëzhi*, was initiated precisely in order to carry out political actions: namely, to oppose attempts to export revolutions from the CIS countries to Russia. The first meeting of the new Eurasian organization was held on 26 February 2005 in the town of Aleksandrov where Ivan the Terrible used to gather his own religiopolitical guard (*oprichnina*). The event was accompanied by Dugin's lecture, a visit to the Museum of Tortures and a lunch (all for 150-200 rubles; tickets were available at the "Transylvania" bookstore). *Evraziiskii Soiuz Molodëzhi* positioned itself as heir of Ivan's *oprichnina* and named Ivan as its spiritual leader. Some participants wore black armbands displaying the "Eurasian rose"; in general, everything looked like a theatrical performance.

---

[286] "Ob otvetstvennosti Putina pered Khristom i smene rossiiskikh elit," http://evrazia.org/modules.php?name=News&file=article&sid=1542 (as of 18 November 2003).

[287] Ernest Pliev, "Kuda zovët ukradennaia ideia," http://www.evrazia.org/modules.php?name=News&file=article&sid=2303 (as of 18 March 2005).

[288] "Putin's agenda. Interv'iu Dugina," http://www.evrazia.org/modules.php?name=News&file=article&sid=2363 (as of 13 April 2005).

The new organization had been implemented for the purpose of streetfighting. At least, this was the impression left by the words of its coordinator Pavel Zarifullin, who promised, in the near future, to commence with "direct actions" against "orange" revolutionaries.[289] The political history of the Union began on 16 April 2005, when its members took part in a "patriotic" (hear meaning "pro-establishment") and "anti-revolutionary" meeting in Ufa (Bashkortostan) which intended to confront the opposition to president Rakhmonov.

The style of covering the news at "Evrazia.org" resembles the forced optimism of youth organizations of the Soviet era. "The meeting was a triumph. The opposition, shocked, disengaged and fled. Hundreds of young people entered the ESM after the end of the meeting."[290] Evident preoccupation with numbers also reminds one of Komsomol, as in the statement: "The Union of Bashkir Youth joins the ESM: 10 000 bayonets more." All of the above-mentioned activities make the new movement look theatrical – very much like, for example, the "Falcons of Zhirinovskii."

Dugin's "unequivocal support" of Putin appears to be a self-defeating enterprise. It will not grant him any support from Putin himself while distracting, at the same time, many potential supporters of Dugin's radical Eurasianism. The reasons are as follows:

(1) Putin does not need the support of Eurasianists as long as the state can employ the regular police force, which is much more useful in the event of streetfighting.

(2) The niche of "a pro-Putin youth movement" is already occupied by *Nashi*. This is a Kremlin-initiated project and its existence leaves no opportunities for Eurasianists to serve the same function. To be sure, *Evraziiskii Soiuz Molodëzhi* may eventually be revealed to be a Kremlin back-project in support of *Nashi*. In this case Dugin seems to be following the path of Vladimir Zhirinovskii by ending up as a puppet of the government.

---

[289] "Russkii vzgliad na evraziiskuiu oprichninu," http://www.evrazia.org/modules.php?name=News&file=article&sid=2256 (as of 27 March 2005).

[290] "Evraziiskii miting v Ufe proshël triumfal'no: oppozitsiia v shoke, razobshchena i bezhala," http://www.evrazia.org/testlenta/shownews.php?0504166160522 (as of 16 April 2005).

(3) Dugin will not be able to find young people who are both capable of streetfighting while "unequivocally supporting" Putin. Young radicals would rather choose to oppose the regime and join Limonov's *National-bolshevistskaia Partiia* or some other left- or right-wing organization. Loyal conformists will not fight.

There is still no notable political movement or party based on Eurasianist ideology. *Partiia "Evraziia"* (which in December 2004 was renamed as *Partiia "Evraziiskii Soiuz"* – the "Eurasian Union" Party), after the expulsion of Dugin, is now headed by his former comrade-in-arms Pëtr Suslov. The latter definitely possesses neither Dugin's charisma nor his connections. The party from time to time joins electoral coalitions to take part in local elections, mostly without significant achievements.

Moderate Eurasianists participating in national elections experience constant failures. In 2003 a coalition calling its self *"Velikaia Rossiia – Evraziiskii Soiuz"* (Great Russia – Eurasian Union) based on Abdul-Vakhed Niiazov's *Evraziiskaia Partiia – Soiuz Patritov Rossii* received only 0.28% of the vote. Another moderate Eurasian party, *Istinnye Patrioty Rossii* (the Genuine Patriots of Russia), gained 0.25%.[291] When speaking about the influence of Neo-Eurasianism we should, thus, distinguish between Neo-Eurasianist ideas, which have been relatively popular, and the influence of organizations, which have been largely ineffecutal. The popularity of many Eurasian ideas apparently does not contribute to the strength and influence of organizations.

Meanwhile, Eurasianist ideas are being "sneaked" into political discourse by the other political actors, from the official ideologists to nationalists. We have already demonstrated how the emerging civil religion incorporates apparently Eurasianist concepts. Pan-Slavism and Orthodox Communism sometimes seem undistinguishable from Eurasianism. Even nationalists, when attempting to attract more public support, invite not only Russians, but also representatives of other ethnic groups to their meetings. For example, at the NDPR conference "Genocide of the Russian people in the 20th century" one of the presentations was made by "a head of Kharkov Judaist community" Eduard Khodos who "was speaking about the meaning of Judeo-Fascist policy, saying that Judeo-Fascists should not speak out on behalf of all Jews of Russia."[292] We regard such events as a sign that Eurasianist ideas gradually penetrate even the most extreme nationalist circles.

The appeal of Eurasianism is evident in electoral successes of the KPRF and other supporters of imperial resurrection (although most likely the supporters of this idea do not consciously define themselves as "Eurasianists"). The KRRF may be favorably compared with other Orthodox political organizations because of its numerous sympathizers from various social classes and wide network of local organizations. The party enjoys relative electoral success; its activities gather thousands of people and there are nation-wide Communist newspapers. Of even greater importance is the fact that the KPRF has a network of numerous grassroots organizations, which exist, unlike local units of many other parties, not only on the paper. The KPRF also has an electoral tradition behind it: there are families where *all generations* vote for the KPRF.

However, the KPRF did not build these resources and infrastructure on its own but inherited them from the Communist Party of the Soviet Union. So far the KPRF has done nothing to renew its human and other resources. In the near future this may well cause a loss of support, which actually happened during the parliamentary elections in 2003. (In 1993, it gained 12.4% of the vote, in 1995, 22.3 %, 1999, 24.3%, and 2003, 12.61%).[293] While it seems that under the leadership of Gennadii Ziuganov the party has drifted to some sort of political fundamentalism, it would be much more beneficial for the KPRF to put more emphasis on the Eurasianist elements of its ideology. If this had been the case, it could now occupy the vacant niche of a major Eurasianist political organization.

At the moment (as of January-May 2005) we have observed a noticeable radicalization of KPRF rhetoric and activities. Representatives of the party induced agitation among the participants of the spontaneous anti-monetization protests in January 2005 and tried to organize these protests;

---

[291] "TsIK oglasil ofitsial'nye rezul'taty vyborov v Gosdumu," http://www.vibori.info/news/article.php?id=398 (as of 19 December 2003).

[292] "Ostanovim genotzid russkogo naroda i politiku iudeo-fashizma," *Russkaia pravda* no. 37 (2005): 8.

[293] "TsIK oglasil ofitsial'nye rezul'taty vyborov v Gosdumu".

on May Day the KPRF held its meeting under the slogan "No to anti-people regime!," a phrase that, since Putin's inauguration, has been hitherto retired. At this time, however, we are not able to predict the future of these developments or their possible impact on KPRF ideology and political practice.

The nationalists' ability to influence the rest of society is very much in question (here we mean radical nationalists combining Orthodoxy with Paganism, not fundamentalist Orthodox nationalists). On the one hand, they demonstrate no significant electoral successes. Nationalist coalitions have never been admitted to participate in national parliamentary elections. For example, in 1999 neither the *"Za Veru i Otechestvo"* (For Faith and Fatherland), nor *"Spas"* (Savior) extreme nationalist coalitions were allowed to participate in the elections, most likely, because the state did not want to provide them with an opportunity to disseminate their ideas. When the RNE participated in local elections, it showed slightly better results (from 0.6 to 6%).[294] Boris Mironov who ran for Governor's office in Novosibirsk in 2003 won only 0.5% of the constituency.[295] Most nationalist organizations, however, never had a chance to try their electoral capabilities.

Nevertheless, along with fundamentalists, with whom they often overlap, nationalists have managed to build relatively wide networks of local units. The number of their supporters may be insignificant in Moscow and other big cities. However, in small provincial towns or former centers of industry where the majority of young people are jobless, taking part in nationalist activities becomes a popular way of killing time. Even when the head office of such an organization disappears (which actually happened to the RNE), its local units continue working because they depend more on local conditions than on an office somewhere in Moscow. Nationalists, like fundamentalists, also recruit young people through various militarized sport clubs teaching martial arts, summer "military-sport" camps, and so forth.

Many nationalist organizations are based upon numerous Slav-Gorits wrestling clubs, most of which have units for children (e.g., the Center for Ancient Russian Wrestling and Martial Culture *"Sviatogor"* in Kaluga, the Club of

---

[294] For details, see: Stephen D. Shenfield, *Russian Fascism: Traditions, Tendencies, Movements* (Armonk, N.Y.: M.E.Sharpe, 2001), 145.
[295] "Byvshii glava Minpechati ob"iavlen v rozysk," http://xeno.sova-center.ru/45A2A1E/ 45B96A4?pub_copy=on (as of 7 January 2005).

Russian Fighting "*Trigora*" in Sankt-Peterburg, the National Club of Slav-Gorets Fighting "*Svarog*" in Moscow and the "*Rus*" Club in Odintsovo near Moscow. In addition to fundamentalist military-patriotic clubs, nationalist organizations always combine fighting, shooting and survival with indoctrination (though in their official documents this mission may be euphemized as "studying Slavic philosophy and customs").

It should be mentioned that the influence and participation of the "native religion" followers (or Neo-Pagans) in extreme nationalist organizations constantly grows. This seems to contribute to their strength in the short-run because such people are mostly highly motivated; they are also non-conformists who are unafraid of publicity. In the long-run, however, the prevalence of Neo-Pagans does not appear to be beneficial for nationalists. The more openly Neo-Pagan nationalist organizations become, the less likely their chances are of winning mass support. The number of people inclined to Neo-Paganism is limited; even if all of them joined nationalist organizations their numbers would still remain diminutive. A more auspicious tactic for nationalists would be to conceal their adherence to "native religion," while declaring, instead, militant "Orthodoxism" (exactly what the RNE did). They nevertheless seem to emphasize their Paganism more and more enthusiastically.

Nationalist groups not intending to follow the path of the RNE (which became too visible and, hence, sensitive) revert to semi-virtual functioning. We suggest that they deliberately borrow from the experiences of various "white supremacy," Nazi and other paramilitary groups in the West. Bruce Hoffman indicates that the latter were the first to make full use of the Internet and other computer nets. Their community consists of "autonomous leadership units" able to operate independently from one another or in unison to create a nationwide chain reaction.[296] Since Russian nationalist organizations have long-lasting contacts with similar Western groups, it is no surprise that extreme nationalist organizations have become less and less visible.

Most of them support web-sites where all propagandist materials may be found in printer-friendly form. These web-sites encourage people to print out leaflets and to spread them without expressing any formal allegiance to an organization. Some leaflets carry no signs allowing identifying their source

---

[296] Bruce Hoffman, *Inside Terrorism* (New York: Columbia Univ. Press, 1998), 118.

(for example, a well-known leaflet with a photo of a girl and inscription: "Daddy, will you protect me from the blacks?"). Web-forums and mailing lists help to coordinate nationalist activities without any need to bring people together physically. Some nationalist sites are hosted outside Russia.

Paramilitary organizations, of course, are not able to attract a significant number of supporters. Not all youngsters like wearing uniforms and parading. Nevertheless, in the absence of alternative opportunities for sporting, learning martial arts, or other activities, young people become interested in such things, thus cooperating with nationalists in various form (we don't mean, of course, young people from rich families). This means that nationalists and fundamentalists can always count on at least some base of support.

In the foreseeable future paramilitary organizations may exhaust their resource base if all people interested in such activities join one of the groups. Nationalist and fundamentalist ideas, on the contrary, will most likely transcend the limits of a "subculture within subculture" and penetrate national political agenda. This will happen due to the fact that only fundamentalists and nationalists (Orthodox nationalist fundamentalists and extreme quasi-Orthodox nationalists are, in fact, undistinguishable from one another) have been able to build up networks of alternative social institutions (hospitals, schools, summer camps, etc.). Such institutions have been of extreme importance for all political religions because they permit them to win mass support at the micropolitical level. Success at the macropolitical level seems to be the next hurdle for these organizations.

Alternative social institutions have a dual function: first of all, they perform many social functions otherwise relegated to the state, and second, they become centers of propaganda and political activism. Social services attract people indifferent to religion and politics; they become indoctrinated by political religions in the course of interaction with these organizations. There is nothing new about these tactics; they were initially used by the Catholic Church and were later borrowed by communists. Social activities have done much to contribute to the popularity of Neo-Wahhabism in the Russian North Caucasus. Wahhabists have opened schools, summer camps, English language schools and other institutions, where youngsters have been indoctrinated with political Islam and provided with basic military training.[297]

It seems that approximately ten years of micropolitical activities have brought their fruits: political Orthodoxy in its fundamentalist-cum-nationalist version has become increasingly popular. Sociologists warn as xenophobia spreads across Russian society. According to Lev Gudkov (Iurii Levada's Analytical Center), since 1999 the number of respondents supporting the slogan "Russia for Russians!" has increased from 35 to 55%.[298] Gudkov theorizes that in spite of increasing nationalist sentiments, the electoral support of nationalist organizations has not grown because mitigated nationalist slogans are "tapped" by respectable politicians. As a result, the whole political spectrum gradually drifts towards nationalism,[299] while continuing social crisis contributes to the popularity of political Orthodoxy in Russia. (We suggest that court decision in favor of fundamentalists in 2005 also reflects this growth of influence of political Orthodoxy).

In 2003 an electoral coalition *Rodina* (Motherland) received 9.02% of the nation's vote.[300] This may be seen as the first macropolitical success of political Orthodoxy. Leaning upon nationalism combined with anti-capitalist rhetoric and backed by Orthodoxy (without too much emphasize on ecclesiastic issues) *Rodina* has gathered people and ideas from all segments of political Orthodoxy. Among them one may name several people who combine fundamentalist and Pan-Slavist approaches (such as Aleksandr Krutov or Nataliia Narochnitskaia) and people who can be defined as Orthodox Communists (i.e., Iurii Savel'ev, Valentin Varennikov and Nikolai Leonov). All of them, however, profess moderate, as compared with, for instance, Nazi, nationalism.

The role of fundamentalists in *Rodina* should not be underestimated in spite of the fact that it is headed by Dmitrii Rogozin, whose reputation among the "Orthodox patriots" is dubious. The hosts of *Russkii dom*, Aleksandr

---

[297] Ol'ga Bibikova, "'Vakhkhabizm' v SNG," in *Islam i politika* (Moskva: IV RAN; Kraft+, 2001), 95.

[298] "'Ia nenavizhu – znachit ia sushchestvuiu.' Gruppovoi portret ksenofoba v postsovetskom inter'ere. Interv'iu L'va Gudkova,' *Russkii kur'er*, 17 December 2004

[299] See: "Chto predstavliaet soboi russkii natsionalizm?" http://www.liberal.ru/sitan.asp?Num=3098 (as of 2 January 2005).

[300] "TsIK oglasil ofitsial'nye rezul'taty vyborov v Gosdumu".

Krutov and Nikolai Leonov, were once active participants of the electoral campaign. One campaign poster portrayed Krutov, Leonov and a Russian birch with the following caption: "Brothers and sisters! Today the real power in the country belongs to oligarchs. This power should be transformed. What should we do? Return the wealth of the country to people! Establish Russian television! Win the elections! 'Motherland' will set the Motherland to rights. '*Rodina*' No. 16."

Addressing the participants of the *Russkii dom* web-forum, Krutov wrote in November 2004: "I think that today we in Russia must have one *Rodina* party that would unite all patriotically thinking people and all Orthodox people."[301] While *Rodina* is clearly dominated by the nationalist-fundamentalist branch of political Orthodoxy, its red flag and anti-oligarch rhetoric add a tincture of Orthodox Communism. Eurasian ideas, as well as some figures associated with Eurasianism, are represented in *Rodina* but to a much lesser extent.

In spite of the Eurasian mission being, in fact, more acceptable for Russia (it does not dissociate ethnic Russians and non-Russians), only the fundamentalist-nationalist segment of political Orthodoxy has become politically successful in any meaningful sense. Moderate fundamentalists and nationalists (swayed by certain Eurasianist and Communist ideas), on the one hand, back the official nation-building project. On the other hand, they have transformed this project, thus making it more Russocentric and Orthodox.

Paramilitary fundamentalist and nationalist organizations will, most likely, join some bigger and more moderate Orthodox political movement instead of sustaining independent political activity. Such symbiosis between the moderate opposition and paramilitary nationalist groups was put into practice during the siege of the parliamentary building in October 1993, when nationalist paramilitaries supported politicians with whom they had very little in common ideologically.

---

[301] Aleksandr Krutov, "V Rossii dolzhna byt' odna partiia 'Rodina', kotoraia ob"ediniala by vsekh patrioticheski mysliashchikh liudei," http://www.rodina.ru/article/show/?id=183 (as of 19 November 2004).

Concluding Remarks

In conclusion, we would like to repeat that politicization is a process that fully changes the religion from which it is derived, transforming it into a "political religion" which is a mixture of religion and ideology. Thus, political Orthodoxy – the final outcome of politicization – should in no way be confused with canonical Orthodox Christianity, in terms of either rituals or dogmas. We have found that in spite of all formal disagreements among the several varieties of political Orthodoxy (from fundamentalism to Orthodox Communism and semi-Pagan nationalism) these factions, nevertheless, constitute an organic whole consisting of many interrelated and overlapping ideas.

People sharing the ideas of this political religion are not "Orthodox believers" in the strict sense. In most cases they observe no rituals and have poor knowledge of "their" religion. They profess their own brand of Orthodoxy and sometimes practice rituals of their own invention instead of those offered by the Church. Their attitude toward the Church and its leadership is mostly hostile or, at best, indifferent. This does not prevent them from calling themselves true Orthodox believers and from being militant supporters of their version of political Orthodoxy. The Russian Orthodox Church, thus, is neither responsible for ongoing politicization of Orthodoxy, nor, even more importantly, is it able to control or reverse this process.

Politicization of Orthodoxy occurs through the efforts of a lay intelligentsia that simultaneously produces and consumes Orthodox political ideologies. Having lost their spiritual grounding after the fall of Communism, these people have turned their minds to an ideological Orthodoxy. Producers of Orthodox political ideologies (i.e., the "new intellectuals") constitute a specific intellectual community standing in stark contrast to both the clergy and what may be called "traditional intellectuals".

Those who share all or some of these Orthodox political ideas clearly distinguish themselves from the mainstream, thus comprising a community of "the political Orthodox" designated as "Orthodox patriots," "national patriots" or simply "patriots." The very word "patriotic," which has become nearly monopolized by these people becomes a marker indicating the adherence to certain tenets of political Orthodoxy. While the political Orthodox do not compose a subculture in the strictest sense, their distinct language, symbols and codes of behaviour set them apart from the mainstream, thus making them an identifiable "subculture," loosely defined. This subculture of political Orthodoxy is held together by networks, constructed by a unique segment of the mass media and through regularly-held events, as well as by a counterculture that has emerged on the basis of political Orthodoxy. In this book we have tried to provide an empirical description of this subculture, refraining as much as possible from evaluations or theoretical generalizations. This topic has yet to be considered as the subject of a thorough critical analysis.

We have found that having had no significant successes in the sphere of macropolitics, the political Orthodox, namely, fundamentalists and nationalists, have managed within the last ten years to build numerous alternative social institutions and paramilitary organizations at the grassroots level. Leaning upon these institutions they have been able to influence larger and more moderate political organizations and to infiltrate them thus contributing to general "Orthodoxization" of the political discourse.

We would like conclude this book by mentioning that contemporary political Orthodoxy in Russia may be described in terms of two competing trends. On one hand, the political Orthodox community has in many respects become a closed political subculture. One may live within this subculture while virtually never encountering the outside world. While this subculture provide comfort and safety for many of the political Orthodox, their leaders, nevertheless, can not help noticing that this development leads to isolation and an inability to influence the society as a whole.

The second trend thereby involves attempts by Orthodox religiopolitical movements to break through the limits of their subculture and to impose their ideologies on the rest of society. So far they have worked out several strategies for transcending the borders of their community.

First, some organizations have endeavoured to influence the elite directly so as to transform the consciousness of those in power in accordance with their goals. We note that this strategy may produce some unexpected results: instead of influencing the elite the political Orthodox may end up becoming co-opted by the state for the purpose of maintaining the status-quo. Second, many paramilitary organizations have tried to establish a niche within the official nation-building enterprise in an effort to make it more xenophobic and ethnocentric. The success of this tactic remains doubtful in that official nationalism will never reach the level of radicalism that is demanded by these paramilitaries. Third, some organizations seek to head spontaneous mass protests for the purpose of indoctrinating people with their ideology in the midst of, rather than prior to political struggle. The latter approach is typical for many nationalist organizations who wish to indoctrinate skinheads; in recent months it was also actively employed by the KPRF.

We suggest that the third strategy holds the most promise in terms of successfully implementing an agenda. In this case the success of political Orthodoxy would depend upon its ability to become the only ideological alternative. However, it is not presently clear which ideological positions and organizations will be able to make full use of such tactics, thus gaining prominence and leverage in the political sphere. In any event, we are positive that the influence of political Orthodoxy will continue to grow in accordance with the increase of social and political unrest in Russia.

Glossary of Names, Organizations, Events and Mass Media

Agentstvo Russkoi Informatsii (The Agency of Russian Information) – nationalist web-resource close to Neo-Paganism (www.ari.ru)

Akademiia geopoliticheskikh problem (the Academy of Geopolitical Problems) – research organization initiated by the military; sticks to Orthodox communist and nationalist positions

AKIRN – *Assotsiatsia po kompleksnomu izucheniu russkoi natsii* (Association for Complex Studies of the Russian Nation) – research organization founded by Evgenii Troitskii

Aleksii (Vladimir Prosvirin, born 1961) – clergyman of the ROC; Orthodox patriotic author and activist

Arktogeia – historical and religious association initiated by Aleksandr Dugin; web-resource dedicated to philosophy and culture (www.arcto.ru)

Avdeev, Vladimir – nationalist and Neo-Pagan author close to *Soiuz Slavianskikh Obshchin*

Balabanov, Aleksei (born 1959) – film director

Baranov, Ivan – singer and political activist

Barkashov, Aleksandr (born 1953) – founder of *Russkoe Natsional'noe Edinstvo*, currently leader of one of its branches.

Belaruskaia dumka (Byelorussian Thought) – journal published by the presidential administration of Belarus; sticks to socialism and Pan-Slavism

Belov, Aleksandr – historian, Neo-Pagan theorist, founder of Slav-Gorets wrestling

Bichevskaia, Zhanna (born 1944) – Orthodox singer, leader of *Soiuz Pravoslavnykh Zhenshchin*

Blokhin, Nikolai (born 1945) – Orthodox writer, disciple of Dmitrii Dudko

Bocharov, Sergei (born 1953) – painter and Orthodox nationalist activist

Bogdanov, Nikolai – nationalist and Neo-Pagan author close to *Soiuz Slavianskhikh Obshchin*

Boiarintsev, Vladimir – nationalist and Neo-Pagan author close to *Soiuz Slavianskikh Obshchin*

Bondarenko, Vladimir (born 1946) – journalist, political activist, editor-in-chief of *Den' literatury*, deputy editor-in-chief of *Zavtra*

Borodin, Leonid (born 1938) – writer, editor-in-chief of *Moskva*; participated in the nationalist opposition in the USSR; was arrested in 1968 and 1982

Borzenko, Aleksei – film-maker

Budanov, Iurii (born 1949) – colonel of the Russian army sentenced to jail for raping and killing a Chechen girl; Orthodox patriots consider him innocent

Burliaev, Nikolai (born 1946) – film director and actor, Orthodox nationalist activist; head of *Mezhdunarodnoe obshchestvo kinematografistov slavianskikh i pravoslavnykh narodov*

Burov, Pavel – clergyman of the ROC, fundamentalist activist, moderator of *Propovednik* (Preacher) program at *Narodnoe radio*; in May 2005 the program was renamed as *Pravoslavnoe Voinstvo* (Orthodox Warriors)

Catechon, *Vizantistsko-Evraziiskii klub* (the Byzantine-Eurasian Club "Catechon") – Neo-Eurasianist cultural and political organization. Initiated in 1999 by a group of students of the State University of Humanities at the Institute of Philosophy; in 2004 renamed as *Vizantistskii Club* (the Byzantine Club)

Center for Special Metastrategic Studies, the – research organization founded by Aleksandr Dugin

Chebalin, Evgenii – writer, member of *Soiuz Pisatelei Rossii*

Chertovich, Vladimir – Byelorussian fundamentalist and Pan-Slavist politician; chairman of *ZAO "Pravoslavnaia initsiativa"*

Chislov, Il'ia – Pan-Slavist activist; chairman of the Society of Russo-Serbian Friendship

Chvanov, Mikhail (born 1944) – writer; vice-president of *Mezhdunarodnyi fond slavianskoi pis'mennosti i kul'tury*

Cosic, Dobrica (born 1921) – Serbian writer; president of Yugoslavia in 1992-1993

Danilevskii, Nikolai (1822-1885) – Russian Pan-Slavist thinker

Demidov, Ivan (born 1963) – host of *Russkii vzgliad* TV-program

Demin, Valerii – nationalist and Neo-Pagan author close to *Soiuz Slavianskikh Obshchin*

Den' (Day) – leading patriotic newspaper in 1991-1993; banned in 1993 and reborn as *Zavtra*

Den' literatury – patriotic newspaper focused on literary criticism

Dzhemal', Geidar (born 1947) – activist of international political Islam; Neo-Eurasianist theorist

Draskovic, Vuk (born 1946) – Serbian writer; the founder of the "Serbian Renewal Movement" party

Dudko, Dmitrii (1922-2004) – clergyman of the ROC; former religious dissident (arrested in 1945, 1952, 1980); ghostly father of *Zavtra*

Duel – secular nationalist newspaper (editor-in-chief: Iurii Mukhin)

Dugin, Aleksandr (born 1962) – political Orthodox writer and activist; leader of intellectual Neo-Eurasiansm.

Dushenov, Konstantin (born 1960) – one of the leaders of *Soiuz Pravoslavnykh Bratstv*; press-secretary of Metropolitan Ioann in 1992-1995; editor-in-chief of *Rus' Pravoslavnaia*

Elementy – Evraziiskoe Obozrenie (Elements. Eurasian Review) – illustrated journal published by Aleksandr Dugin in 1992-1997

Era Rossii (Era of Russia) – nationalist newspaper focused on the idea of the Russian Republic

Evraziia – party initiated in May 2002 by Aleksandr Dugin and Pëtr Suslov; headed by Suslov after the expel of Dugin; in December 2004 renamed as *Partiia "Evraziiskii Soiuz"* (the "Eurasian Union" Party)

Evraziia – web-resource dedicated to current political issues (www.evrazia.org)

Evraziia, obshchestvenno-politicheskoe dvizhenie (the socio-political movement "Eurasia") – organization initiated by Aleksandr Dugin in April 2001

Evraziiskaia Partiia – Soiuz Patriotov Rossii (the Eurasian Party - the Union of Patriots of Russia) – moderate Eurasianst organization lead by Abdul-Vakhed Niiazov

Evraziiskii Soiuz Molodëzhi (the Eurasian Union of Youth) – political Neo-Eurasianist youth organization initiated by Aleksandr Dugin in February 2005; led by Pavel Zarifullin

Fond natsional'noi i mezhdunarodnoi bezopasnosti "NIMB" (the Fund of National and International Security) – patriotic organization initiated by Leonid Shershnev

Glaz'ev, Sergei (born 1961) – patriotically oriented politician; one of the leaders of *Rodina* till 2004

Glazunov, Il'ia (born 1930) – painter; Orthodox political writer and activist

Grazhdanskii komitet v podderzhku Soiuza Rossii i Belorussii (the civil committee for promoting the Union of Russia and Belarus) – nonstructured network of Pan-Slavist activists and organizations

Hvala, Brzetislav – international Pan-Slavist activist

Iabloko (literary means "apple") – Russian party of liberal orientation

Ianukovich, Viktor (born 1950) – 2004 presidential candidate in the Ukraine supported by the Russian government

Idushchie vmeste (Walking together) – pro-presidential youth movement reported to attract supporters mostly with the help of direct monetary payments or free access to services (swimming pools, etc.)

Iliukhin, Viktor (born 1949) – Communist politician; leader of *Dvizhenie v podderzhku armii, oboronnoi promyshlennosti i voennoi nauki*

International public tribunal on NATO crimes in the former Yugoslavia – nongovernmental Pan-Slavist organization

Iskakov, Boris (born 1934) – economist specializing in statistics; president of *Mezhdunarodnaia Slavianskaia Akademiia*

Islamskaia Partiia Vozrozhdenia (the Islamic Party of Resurrection) – Islamist organization that existed illegally in the beginning of the 1990s in the USSR

Istarkhov, Vladimir (Vladimir Ivanov) – Neo-Pagan theorist and activist

Istinnye Patrioty Rossii (the Genuine Patriots of Russia) – moderate Islamic Eurasianist organization

Iushin, Evgenii (born 1955) – poet; journalist; editor-in-chief of *Molodaia Gvardia*

Ivanov-Sukharevskii, Aleksandr (born 1950) – radical nationalist; leader of *Narodnaia Natsional'naia Partiia*

Ivashov, Leonid (born 1943) – general; patriotic activist; vice-president of *Akademiia geopoliticheskikh problem*; one of the initiators of the patriotic movement of officers

Ioann (Ivan Krest'iankin, born 1910) – archimandrite, conservative Orthodox author

Ioann (Ivan Snychev, 1927-1995) – Metropolitan of St. Petersburg and Ladoga; Orthodox political theorist highly respected by the majority of the political Orthodox

K Bogoderzhaviiu (Towards God-Statehood) – occult political movement initiated in 1997; now represented by *Kontseptual'naia Partiia "Edinenie"*

Kadyrov, Akhmat (1951-2004) – president of the Chechen Republic (2003-2004)

Karadzic, Radovan (born 1945) – president of the self-proclaimed Republika Srpska within Bosnia (1992-1995)

Kara-Murza, Sergei (born 1939) – Communist and nationalist political writer

Kasimovskii, Konstantin (born 1974) – Orthodox nationalist activist; leader of *Russkoe Deistvie*

Kazakov, Vadim (born 1965) – Neo-Pagan activist and author; leader of *Soiuz Slavianskikh Obshchin*

Khalidov, Den'ga – head of the Center for Ethnopolitical and Islamic Studies at *Akademiia geopoliticheskikh problem*

Kharchikov, Aleksandr (born 1949) – singer and political activist

Khatiushin, Valerii (born 1948) – poet and nationalist activist

Khodos, Eduard – Jewish anti-Semitic author

Kirill (Aleksandr Sakharov, born 1957) − clergyman of the ROC (*edinoverie*); head of *Soiuz Pravoslavnykh Bratstv* till 1999; now its secretary.

Kirill (Vladimir Gundiaev, born 1946) − Metropolitan of Smolensk and Kaliningrad

Klykov, Viacheslav (born 1939) − sculptor; Orthodox and nationalist activist

Klimov, Grigorii (born 1918) − émigré; nationalist political writer

Kokukhin, Nikolai − fundamentalist and Pan-Slavist author

Kommunisticheskaia Partiia Rossiiskoi Federatsii (KPRF, the Communist Party of the Russian Federation) − major oppositional organization in Russia; in fact, serves an umbrella for political activism of various ideological origins

Kontseptual'naia Partiia "Edinenie" (the Conceptual Party "Unification") − occult political organization initiated by Konstantin Petrov

Kornilov, Leonid (born 1952) − poet and singer; political activist

Korroziia metalla (Corrosion of Metal) − nationalist rock-band

Kozhinov, Vadim (1930-2001) − Orthodox patriotic political writer and literary critic

Krylov, Aleksandr (born 1969) − singer and political activist

Krutov, Aleksandr (born 1947) − Orthodox nationalist activist; journalist; host of *Russkii dom*; member of parliament (*Rodina*)

Kuniaev, Stanislav (born 1932) − poet; editor-in-chief of *Nash Sovremennik*

Kuraev, Andrei (born 1963) − clergyman of the ROC; Orthodox political writer

Kurekhin, Sergei (1954-1996) − underground musician close to Aleksandr Dugin's circle

Kuznetsov, Mikhail (born 1940) − lawyer; Orthodox political activist; chairman of the International public tribunal on NATO crimes in the former Yugoslavia

Leonov, Nikolai (born 1928) − general-lieutenant (ret.); Orthodox patriotic activist and writer; member of parliament (*Rodina*)

Leont'ev, Konstantin (1831-1891) − Russian Pan-Slavist thinker

Leont'ev, Mikhail (born 1958) – TV-analyst; propagandist of "official nationalism"

Limonov, Eduard (Eduard Savenko, born 1943) – leader of *Natsional-Bolshevistskaia Partiia*

Lisovoi, Nikolai – historian, poet, fundamentalist author

Lukashenko, Aleksandr (born 1954) – president of Belarus (since 1994)

Makashov, Al'bert (born 1938) – general; Communist and nationalist activist; member of parliament (KPRF)

Maleev, Mikhail – clergyman of the ROC; painter

Maler, Arkadii (born 1979) – moderator of Catechon; in 1997-1999 participated in Aleksandr Dugln's Eurasianist activities; in 2005 founded philosophical and political center *Severnii Catechon* (Northern Catechon)

Mezhdunarodnaia Slavianskaia Akademiia (the International Slavic Academy) – patriotic organization initiated in 1992 by Boris Iskakov.

Mezhdunarodnyi fond slavianskoi pis'mennosti i kul'tury (the International Foundation of Slavic Writing and Culture) – Pan-Slavist cultural organization initiated in 1989

Mezhdunarodnyi Slavianskii Komitet (the International Slavic Committee) – international Pan-Slavist organization based in Prague and supervising national Slavic committees; headed by Ian Mlinarzh

Mezhdunarodnyi Soiuz Slavianskikh Zhurnalistov (the International Union of Slavic Journalists) – Pan-Slavist organization headed by Ol'ga Zarudnaia

Mezhdunarodnoe Evraziiskoe Dvizhenie (the International Eurasian Movement) – socio-political movement initiated by Aleksandr Dugin in 2003

Mezhdunarodnoe obshchestvo kinematografistov slavianskikh i pravoslavnykh narodov (the International Community of Film-makers of the Slavic and Orthodox peoples) – Pan-Slavist cultural organization

My ne slomleny (We are not broken down) – All-Russian Contest of Patriotic Movies and Videoclips initiated in 2004 by the Moscow Committee of the KPRF

Milosevic, Slobodan (born 1941) – ex-president of Yugoslavia

Mironov, Boris (born 1951) – writer; journalist; Orthodox nationalist activist

Mkalavishvili, Vasilii – ex-clergyman of the Georgian Orthodox Church; leader of anti-cult activities in Georgia

Mladic, Ratko (born 1943) – general; led the Bosnian Serb army

Molodaia gvardiia (Young Guard) – extreme nationalist literary journal; editor-in-chief: Evgenii Iushin

Molodezhnoe Demokraticheskoe Antifashistskoe Dvizhenie "Nashi" (the Youth Democratic Anti-fascist Movement "Us") – pro-presidential youth movement initiated in 2005; successor of *Idushchie Vmeste*

Moskva – Orthodox nationalist literary journal; editor-in-chief: Leonid Borodin

Moulatsiotis, Nektarios – clergyman of the Greek Orthodox Church; initiator of a monastic rock-band "*Eleftheri*"

NAMAKON (Nezavisimoe Agentstvo, Marketing i Konsalting) – patriotic analytical center initiated by former military

Narochnitskaia, Nataliia (born 1948) – nationalist and Pan-Slavist author; member of parliament (*Rodina*)

Narodnaia Natsional'naia Partiia (the People's National Party) – extreme nationalist organization imitating ideology and style of German National Socialism

Narodnoe radio (People's Radio) – oppositional broadcasting station

Nash sovremennik (Our Contemporary) – patriotic literary journal, editor-in-chief: Stanislav Kuniaev

Nasha strategiia – nationalist TV-program; most likely initiated by *Rodina*

National-Bolshevistskaia Partiia (the National Bolshevik Party) – organization initiated by Eduard Limonov and Aleksandr Dugin in 1992-1993; used to be extremely nationalist; by the 2000s has become leftist

National'no-patrioticheskii Front "Pamiat'" (the National Patriotic Front "Memory") – one of the first Orthodox nationalist political organizations in the former USSR; nearly ceased to exist at the moment

Natsional'no-Derzhavnaia Partiia Rossii (the National Etatist Party of Russia, the NDPR) – extreme nationalist organization officially declaring itself secular but close, in fact, to political Neo-Paganism. Leaders: Aleksandr Sevast'ianov and Stanislav Terekhov

Nazarov, Mikhail (born 1948) – former émigré; Orthodox nationalist author

Nesterov, Dmitrii – author of a seemingly autobiographic novel about skinheads

New University – educational organization initiated by Aleksandr Dugin

Niiazov, Abdul-Vakhed (Vadim Medvedev, born 1969) – moderate Eurasianist; leader of *Evraziiskaia Partiia – Soiuz Patriotov Rossii*

Nikiforov, Evgenii (born 1955) – former religious dissident; leader of "Radonezh" brotherhood

Obshchestvennyi komitet "Za nravstvennoe vozrozhdenie Otechestva" (the Public Committee "For Moral Resurrection of the Fatherland") – fundamentalist organization initiated in 1994; led by Aleksandr Shargunov

Oprichnoe Bratstvo – fundamentalist organization initiated by Andrei Shchedrin; members live together in a compound

Osipov, Vladimir (born 1938) – former religious dissident (arrested in 1961, 1974); Orthodox political writer and activist; leader of *Soiuz "Khristianskoe Vozrozhdenie"*

Panarin, Aleksandr (1940-2003) – political scientist and philosopher

Parshev, Andrei – author of a patriotic bestseller *Why Russia is not America*

Pchelkin, Nikolai – communist activist; initiator of the All-Russian Contest "Songs of Resistance"

Perin, Roman – nationalist Neo-Pagan author; head of *Slavianskaia obshchina* of St. Petersburg

Petrov, Konstantin (born 1945) – major-general (ret.); founder of several occult political organizations

Pichuzhkin, Viktor (born 1926) – clergyman of the ROC; communist activist

Platonov, Oleg (born 1950) – Orthodox fundamentalist and nationalist author

Poliakov, Iurii (born 1954) – writer; best-selling author

Polikarpov, Mikhail – author of an autobiographic novel about Russian volunteers in Bosnia

Ponomarev, Gennadii – fundamentalist poet; husband of Zhanna Bichevskaia

Popov, Vladimir (born 1968) – nationalist activist; editor-in-chief of *Era Rossii*; "Supreme Ruler of the Russian Republic"

Poznanovic, Zelko – Serbian nationalist philosopher and theologian

Pravoslavnaia kniga (Orthodox Book) – bookstore in Minsk (Belarus); headquarters of *ZAO "Pravoslavanaia Initsiativa"*

Prokhanov, Aleksandr (born 1938) – writer; journalist; editor-in-chief of *Den'* and *Zavtra*

Radonezh, festival of Orthodox films, TV- and radio-programs – fundamentalist cultural event held each year since 1995; Radonezh is a village where St. Sergii was born

Radonezh, Internet TV-channel – web-collection of Orthodox TV-programs and films

Radonezh, pravoslavnoe obozrenie (An Orthodox survey "Radonezh") – fundamentalist newspaper

Radonezh, pravoslavnoe obshchestvo (bratstvo) (Orthodox society (brotherhood) "Radonezh") – fundamentalist organization headed by Evgenii Nikiforov

Radonezh, radio – fundamentalist broadcasting station

Rezonans (Resonance) – Communist broadcasting station

Rodina, sotsial-patrioticheskaia partiia (Motherland, a social patriotic party) – political organization initiated in 2002; combines moderate Orthodox nationalism with anti-capitalist rhetoric

Rodionov, Evgenii (1977-1996) – conscript killed in Chechnya supposedly for refusing to convert into Islam

Roerichs, Nikolai (1874-1947) and Elena (1879-1955) – occult theorists; cultural and political activists

Rogozin, Dmitrii (born 1963) – moderate nationalist politician; leader of *Rodina*

Roman (Aleksandr Matiushin, born 1954) – hieromonk; singer and poet

Rossiiskaia Kommunisticheskaia Rabochaia Partiia (the Russian Communist Worker's Party, the RKRP) – radical communist organization

Rus' Pravoslavnaia, nezavisimaia patrioticheskaia pravoslavnaia gazeta (The Orthodox Rus, independent patriotic Orthodox newspaper) – extreme fundamentalist and nationalist newspaper published by Konstantin Dushenov

Russian Orthodox Television on the Internet – Orthodox patriotic web-resource disseminating "resistance films" (http://russtv.ru/)

Russkaia Akademiia (the Russian Academy) – patriotic organization headed by A. Lipatov

Russkaia Gvardiia (Russian Guard) – nationalist military patriotic club

Russkaia liniia (Russian Line. The Orthodox Information Agency) – Orthodox patriotic web-resource (www.rusk.ru)

Russkaia Partiia (the Russian Party) – nationalist organization, now ineffective

Russkaia Pravda (Russian Truth) – nationalist and Neo-Pagan newsletter published by *Russkaia Pravda* publishing house

Russkaia Respublika (The Russian Republic) – nationalist web-based organization headed by Vladimir Popov

Russkaia Trudovaia Partiia Rossii (the Russian Labor Party of Russia) – nationalist organization founded in 1997

Russkii dom (Russian Home) – illustrated monthly (editor-in-chief: Aleksandr Krutov)

Russkii dom (Russian Home) – Orthodox patriotic TV-program hosted by Aleksandr Krutov (till 2004)

Russkii vzgliad (Russian Vision) - Orthodox patriotic TV-program hosted by Ivan Demidov (since 2004)

Russkoe Deistvie (The Russian Action, former *Russkii Natsional'nyi Soiuz*) – nationalist Orthodox organization, headed by Konstantin Kasimovskii

Russkoe Natsional'noe Edinstvo (the Russian National Unity, the RNE) – nationalist Orthodox organization; now mostly exists as a virtual community

Savtskii, Pëtr (1895-1968) – Russian Eurasianist theorist

Semenko, Vladimir – Orthodox author; member of *Soiuz Pravoslavnykh Grazhdan*

Sevast'ianov, Aleksandr (born 1955) – nationalist activist; leader of *Natsional'no-Derzhavnaia Partiia Rossii*

Shamir, Israel – anti-Zionist Israeli author; emigrated from the USSR in the 1960s

Shargunov, Aleksandr – clergyman of the ROC; fundamentalist and nationalist author and activist; leader of *Obshchestvenyi komitet "Za nravstvennoe vozrozhdenie Otechestva"*

Shchedrin, Andrei (also known as Nikolai Kozlov) – fundamentalist activist; initiator of *Oprichnoe Bratstvo*

Shershnev, Leonid – patriotic activist; lieutenant general (in reserve); the president of "NIMB"

Shiriaev, Mikhail – host of *Nasha strategiia* TV-program; son of nationalist activist Nikolai Shiriaev

Shiropaev, Aleksei (born 1959) – painter and writer; nationalist Neo-Pagan author

Shishova, Tat'iana – practicing psychologist; fundamentalist author

Shmulevich, Avrom - radical Zionist; former Soviet dissident; immigrated to Israel in 1991

Sidel'nikov, Ivan (born 1979) – film director; son of film director Aleksandr Sidel'nikov

Simonovich, Leonid (born 1946) – fundamentalist activist, leader of *Soiuz Pravoslavnykh Khorugvenostsev*; now calls himself Simonovich-Nikshich

Slavianskaia obshchina of St. Petersburg (the Slavic Community of St. Petersburg) – extreme nationalist Neo-Pagan organization headed by Roman Perin

Slavianskaia Partiia Rossii (the Slavic Party of Russia) – Pan-Slavist organization headed by Anatolii Duvalov; aims at promoting the Union of Russia and Belarus

Slavianskii Komitet Rossii (the Slavic Committee of Russia) – Pan-Slavist organization, Russian branch of *Mezhdunarodnyi Slavianskii Komitet*

Slavianskoe Dvizhenie Rossii (the Slavic movement of Russia) – Pan-Slavist organization headed by Nikolai Kikeshev

Smirnov, Kim – rector of the International Slavic University

Smolin, Mikhail (born 1971) – historian and fundamentalist author

Society of Russo-Serbian Friendship, the – Pan-Slavist organization

Soiuz bor'by za narodnuiu trezvost' (the Union of Struggle for People's Sobriety) – nationalist organization focused on fighting alcohol, tobacco and narcotics. Leader: Fëdor Uglov

Soiuz "Khristianskoe Vozrozhdenie" (the Union "Christian Resurrection") – fundamentalist nationalist organization initiated in 1988

Soiuz Ofitserov (the Union of Officers) – militant patriotic organization initiated in 1992; ideology based on communism and nationalism; aims at provoking anti-governmental activities in the army

Soiuz Pisatelei Rossii (the Union of Writers of Russia) – patriotic organization of writers

Soiuz Pravoslavnykh Bratstv (the Union of Orthodox Brotherhoods) – fundamentalist organization; used to unite Orthodox brotherhoods; how is switching to individual membership

Soiuz Pravoslavnykh Grazhdan (the Union of Orthodox Citizens) – relatively moderate Orthodox political organization initiated in 1997

Soiuz Pravoslavnykh Khorugvenostsev (the Union of Orthodox Gonfalon-Bearers) – radical paramilitary Orthodox organization initiated in 1992

Soiuz Pravoslavnykh Zhenshchin (The Union of Orthodox Women) – charity women's organization ideologically close to fundamentalists

Soiuz Slavianskikh Obshchin (the Union of Slavic Communities) – radical Neo-Pagan political organization; lead by Vadim Kazakov

Soiuz Sovetskikh Ofitserov (the Union of Soviet Officers) – communist organization of the military operating throughout the former Soviet Union; headed by Vladimir Tkachenko

Songs of Resistance, All-Russian Contest – annual patriotic songs contest held since 1997 by *Duel* newspaper

Sovetskaia Rossiia, nezavisimaia narodnaia gazeta (Soviet Russia, independent people's newspaper) – Communist newspaper

Spas (Savior) – extreme nationalist coalition during 1999 electoral campaign

Stiag (Banner) – fundamentalist paramilitary organization established in 2004

Suslov, Pëtr – former supporter of Aleksandr Dugin; leader of *Evraziiskii Soiuz*

Tadzhuddin, Talgat (born 1948) – chairman of the Central Spiritual Department of Muslims of Russia and the European CIS Countries; recognized by some Muslims as the Supreme Mufti of Russia

Tal'kov, Igor' (1956-1991) – nationalism-oriented pop-singer

Tejkovski, Boleslav – chairman of the Polish Slavic Committee; leader of National Unity Party of Poland

Tereknov, Stanislav (born 1955) – nationalist and communist activist; leader of the NDPR and of *Soiuz Ofitserov*

Tikhon (Georgii Shevkunov, born 1958) – archimandrite; father superior of Sretenskii monastery; ideologically close to traditionalism

Tikhonov, Viacheslav – film director; author of patriotic documentaries "Russian Mystery" and "Listen to Russia" (not related to the actor Viacheslav Tikhonov)

Tiutchev, Fëdor (1803-1873) – Russian poet, diplomat and Pan-Slavist thinker

Triapkin, Nikolai (1918-1999) – Soviet and Russian poet

Troitskii, Evgenii (born 1928) – Pan-Slavist theorist, president of the AKIRN

Troitskii, Sergei (born 1966) – singer; leader of *Korroziia metalla*; nationalist activist; son of Evgenii Troitskii

Trubetskoi, Nikolai (1890-1938) – Eurasianist theorist

V podderzhku armii, oboronnoi promyshlennosti i voennoi nauki (In Support of the Army, Defense Industry and Military Science) – communist patriotic movement initiated by General Lev Rokhlin (1947-1998); now lead by Viktor Iliukhin

Varennikov, Valentin (born 1923) – general, communist activist, member of parliament (*Rodina*)

Vasil'ev, Konstantin (1942-1976) – Soviet painter

Velichko, Vladimir – editor-in-chief of *Belaruskaia dumka*

Velikaia Rossiia – Evraziiskii Soiuz (Great Russia – Eurasian Union) – a 2003 electoral coalition based on *Evraziiskaia Partiia – Soiuz Patritov Rossii*

Vernandskii, Georgii (1887 – 1973) – Eurasianist theorist

Vlasov, Mikhail (born 1953) – nationalist activist, leader of military-patriotic club *Russkaia Gvardia*

Voznesenskaia, Iuliia (born 1940) – émigré; Orthodox writer

Vsemirnyi Russkii Narodnyi Sobor (the World Russian People's Assembly) – assembly held annually since 1993 under the aegis of the ROC; serves a forum for Orthodox patriots of all orientations

Vserossiiskoe ofitserskoe sobranie (the All-Russian Assembly of Officers) – annual patriotic assembly of the military held since 2003; based on local assemblies of officers

Vseslavianskii S"ezd (the All-Slavic Congress) – international Pan-Slavist event held each 4 years since 1998

Vseslavianskii Sobor (the All-Slavic Assembly) – Pan-Slavist organization initiated in 1995

Web-ring of Patriotic Resources – web-ring uniting the majority of patriotic web-sites (www.patriot.rossija.info).

Za Rus' sviatuiu (For the Holy Russia) – a 2003 electoral coalition

Za russkoe delo (For the Russian cause) – a 1999 electoral coalition

Za Veru i Otechestvo (For Faith and Fatherland) – a 1999 extreme nationalist electoral coalition; never was allowed to participate in elections

ZAO *"Pravoslavnaia initsiativa"* (the stock-company "Orthodox Initiative") – Byelorussian Orthodox political organization headed by Vladimir Chertovich

Zarifullin, Pavel – leader of *Evraziiskii Soiuz Molodëzhi*

Zavtra, gazeta gosudarstva Rossiiskogo (Tomorrow) – "a newspaper of spiritual opposition" initiated after the ban of *Den* in 1993; since 1996 sold as "a newspaper of the State of Russia"

Zhdanov, Vladimir – deputy chairman of *Soiuz Bor'by za Narodnuiu Trezvost'*

Zhivotov, Gennadii – painter; employee of *Zavtra*

Ziuganov, Gennadii (born 1944) – leader of the KPRF

Zolotoi Vitiaz' (Golden Knight) – annual Pan-Slavist films contest

Zubov, Andrei – professor at the Orthodox University of St. John the Theologian; supporter of moderate fundamentalism

The glossary is partly based on: *Russkii patriotizm* (Moskva: Pravoslavnoe izdatel'stvo "Entsiklopediia russkoi tsivilizatsii", 2003)

List of Illustrations

1. Fundamentalists. *Soiuz Pravoslavnykh Khorugvenostsev*, 9 May 2005 (picture taken by Anastasia Mitrofanova)

2. "The Orthodox of the world, unite!", a slogan at ZAO *"Pravoslavnaia initsiativa"* headquarters, January 2005 (picture taken by Anastasia Mitrofanova)

3. "Lukashenko, Carry On!", a poster at May Day Demonstration, 1 May 2005 (picture taken by Anastasia Mitrofanova)

4. Mongoose RICI defeats the global snake (Artist: S.Sh., picture taken from *Bezopasnonst*, no. 7-8, July-August 2002, page 13)

5. Nationalists. The RNE, 9 May 2005 (picture taken by Anastasia Mitrofanova)

6. Igor' Tal'kov – a "political saint," *Soiuz Pravoslavnykh Khorugvenostsev*, 9 May 2005 (picture taken by Anastasia Mitrofanova)

7. "Freedom to Colonel Budanov," *Soiuz Pravoslavnykh Khorugvenostsev*, 9 May 2005 (picture taken by Anastasia Mitrofanova)

8. Modern Neo-Pagans meet with Valerii Demin (at the left) at Moscow Vasil'ev Musem. 29 April 2005 (picture taken by Anastasia Mitrofanova)

9. Aleksandr Kharchikov on the stage, 6 May 2005 (picture taken by Anastasia Mitrofanova)

10. A poster of Glazunov's Museum in Moscow, 28 May 2005 (picture taken by Anastasia Mitrofanova)

11. Utilization of religion by the state: "Respect Our Lady and State Fire Department," a poster in Moscow (June 2004, picture taken by Anastasia Mitrofanova)

12. "The Icon of the Victory" (Artist: Gennadii Zhivotov, picture taken from *Zavtra*, no. 18, May 2005)

13. An RNE girl. 9 May 2005 (picture taken by Anastasia Mitrofanova)

14. An icon depicting Evgenii Rodionov (not dated; picture taken from the web-site of *Soiuz Pravoslavnykh Khorugvenostsev*: http://istinnopycckie.narod.ru/Galereya/foto_gal_portret/Jun03-10.jpg)

15. New intellectuals are fond of diagrams. Vladimir Zhdanov, deputy chaiman of *Soiuz Bor'by za Narodnuiu Trezvost'* (the Union of Struggle for People's Sobriety), makes a presentation at the conference on genocide, 20 February 2005, (picture taken from the NDPR web-site: http://www.ndpr.ru/data/photo/050220-15.jpg)

16. "Red Easter", meeting of *Evraziiskii Soiuz Molodëzhi*, rightmost – Aleksandr Dugin, 1 May 2005 (picture taken from the web-site of *Mezhdunarodnoe Evraziiskoe Dvizhenie*: http://images.evrazia.org/images1/1_may_moscow/01.jpg)

17. Boys at the Orthodox military-patriotic club "*Rus'*" (not dated; picture taken from "*Rus'*" web-site: http://klubrus.narod.ru/rus7.jpg)

18. Instructors of the Orthodox military-patriotic summer camp in Zav'ialovo (2003, picture taken from Aleksandr Nevskii Brotherhood web-page
http://nevskiy.orthodoxy.ru/druzina/lager_voin_2003/index.htm)

THE POLITICIZATION OF RUSSIAN ORTHODOXY   225

19. Deacon Viktor Pichuzhkin at a Communist demonstration (2001, picture taken by Aleksandr Meller. By courtesy of Aleksandr Meller)

20. Aleksandr Krutov and Nikolai Leonov campaign for *Rodina*. A leaflet. (not dated; picture taken from *Rodina* web-site: http://www.rodina.ru/article/show/?id=66)

Illustrations

1. Fundamentalists. *Soiuz Pravoslavnykh Khorugvenostsev*, leftmost – Leonid Simonovich

2. "The Orthodox of the world, unite!", a slogan at *ZAO "Pravoslavnaia Initsiativa"* headquarters

3. "Lukashenko, Carry On!", a poster at May Day Demonstration

4. Mongoose RICI defeats the global snake (Artist: S.Sh.)

5. Nationalists. The RNE, 9 May 2005

6. Igor' Tal'kov – a "political saint," *Soiuz Pravoslavnykh Khorugvenostsev*, 9 May 2005

7. "Freedom to Colonel Budanov," *Soiuz Pravoslavnykh Khorugvenostsev*, 9 May 2005

8. Modern Neo-Pagans meet with Valerii Demin (at the left) at Moscow Vasil'ev Musem. 29 April 2005

9. Aleksandr Kharchikov on the stage. 6 May 2005

THE POLITICIZATION OF RUSSIAN ORTHODOXY   233

10. A poster of Glazunov's Museum in Moscow

11. Utilization of religion by the state: "Respect Our Lady and State Fire Department," a poster in Moscow

12. "The Icon of the Victory" (Artist: Gennadii Zhivotov, picture taken from *Zavtra*, no. 18, May 2005)

13. An RNE girl. 9 May 2005

14. An icon depicting Evgenii Rodionov

15. New intellectuals are fond of diagrams. Vladimir Zhdanov, deputy chairman of *Soiuz Bor'by za Narodnuiu Trezvost'*, 20 February 2005

16. "Red Easter", meeting of *Evraziiskii Soiuz Molodëzhi*, rightmost – Aleksandr Dugin

17. Boys at the Orthodox military-patriotic club *"Rus'"*

18. Instructors of the Orthodox military-patriotic summer camp in Zav'ialovo

19. Deacon Viktor Pichuzhkin at a Communist demonstration

20. Aleksandr Krutov and Nikolai Leonov campaign for *Rodina*. A leaflet

Dr. Andreas Umland (Ed.)

SOVIET AND POST-SOVIET POLITICS AND SOCIETY

ISSN 1614-3515

This book series makes available, to the academic community and general public, affordable English-, German- and Russian-language scholarly studies of various *empirical* aspects of the recent history and current affairs of the former Soviet bloc. The series features narrowly focused research on a variety of phenomena in Central and Eastern Europe as well as Central Asia and the Caucasus. It highlights, in particular, so far understudied aspects of late Tsarist, Soviet, and post-Soviet political, social, economic and cultural history from 1905 until today. Topics covered within this focus are, among others, political extremism, the history of ideas, religious affairs, higher education, and human rights protection. In addition, the series covers selected aspects of post-Soviet transitions such as economic crisis, civil society formation, and constitutional reform.

SOVIET AND POST-SOVIET POLITICS AND SOCIETY

Edited by Dr. Andreas Umland

ISSN 1614-3515

1   *Андреас Умланд (ред.)*
    Воплощение Европейской конвенции по правам человека в России
    Философские, юридические и эмпирические исследования
    ISBN 3-89821-387-0

2   *Christian Wipperfürth*
    Russland – ein vertrauenswürdiger Partner?
    Grundlagen, Hintergründe und Praxis gegenwärtiger russischer Außenpolitik
    Mit einem Vorwort von Heinz Timmermann
    ISBN 3-89821-401-X

3   *Manja Hussner*
    Die Übernahme internationalen Rechts in die russische und deutsche Rechtsordnung
    Eine vergleichende Analyse zur Völkerrechtsfreundlichkeit der Verfassungen der Russländischen Föderation und der Bundesrepublik Deutschland
    Mit einem Vorwort von Rainer Arnold
    ISBN 3-89821-438-9

4   *Matthew Tejada*
    Bulgaria's Democratic Consolidation and the Kozloduy Nuclear Power Plant (KNPP)
    The Unattainability of Closure
    With a foreword by Richard J. Crampton
    ISBN 3-89821-439-7

5   *Марк Григорьевич Меерович*
    Квадратные метры, определяющие сознание
    Государственная жилищная политика в СССР. 1921 – 1941 гг
    ISBN 3-89821-474-5

6   *Andrei P. Tsygankov, Pavel A.Tsygankov (Eds.)*
    New Directions in Russian International Studies
    ISBN 3-89821-422-2

7   *Марк Григорьевич Меерович*
    Как власть народ к труду приучала
    Жилище в СССР – средство управления людьми. 1917 – 1941 гг.
    С предисловием Елены Осокиной
    ISBN 3-89821-495-8

8   *David J. Galbreath*
    Nation-Building and Minority Politics in Post-Socialist States
    Interests, Influence and Identities in Estonia and Latvia
    With a foreword by David J. Smith
    ISBN 3-89821-467-2

9   *Алексей Юрьевич Безугольный*
    Народы Кавказа в Вооруженных силах СССР в годы Великой Отечественной войны 1941-1945 гг.
    С предисловием Николая Бугая
    ISBN 3-89821-475-3

10 *Вячеслав Лихачев и Владимир Прибыловский (ред.)*
    Русское Национальное Единство, 1990-2000. В 2-х томах
    ISBN 3-89821-523-7

11 *Николай Бугай (ред.)*
    Народы стран Балтии в условиях сталинизма (1940-е – 1950-е годы)
    Документированная история
    ISBN 3-89821-525-3

12 *Ingmar Bredies (Hrsg.)*
    Zur Anatomie der Orange Revolution in der Ukraine
    Wechsel des Elitenregimes oder Triumph des Parlamentarismus?
    ISBN 3-89821-524-5

13 *Anastasia V. Mitrofanova*
    The Politicization of Russian Orthodoxy
    Actors and Ideas
    With a foreword by William C. Gay
    ISBN 3-89821-481-8

14 *Nathan D. Larson*
    Alexander Solzhenitsyn and the Russo-Jewish Question
    ISBN 3-89821-483-4

FORTHCOMING (MANUSCRIPT WORKING TITLES)

Nicola Melloni
The Russian 1998 Financial Crisis and Its Aftermath
An Etherodox Perspective
ISBN 3-89821-407-9

Rebbecca Katz
The Republic of Georgia
Post-Soviet Media Representations of Politics and Corruption
ISBN 3-89821-413-3

Annette Freyberg-Inan
The Social Sciences in Romania
Research Conditions and the Role of International Support
ISBN 3-89821-416-8

Laura Victoir
The Russian Land Estate Today
ISBN 3-89821-426-5

Stephanie Solowyda
Biography of Semen Frank
ISBN 3-89821-457-5

Margaret Dikovitskaya
Arguing with the Photographs
Russian Imperial Colonial Attitudes in Visual Culture
ISBN 3-89821-462-1

Stefan Ihrig
Welche Nation in welcher Geschichte?
Eigen- und Fremdbilder der nationalen Diskurse in der Historiographie und den Geschichtsbüchern in der Republik Moldova, 1991-2003
ISBN 3-89821-466-4

Christian Autengruber
Die politischen Parteien in Bulgarien und Rumänien
Eine vergleichende Analyse seit Beginn der 90er Jahre
ISBN 3-89821-476-1

Sergei M. Plekhanov
Russian Nationalism in the Age of Globalization
ISBN 3-89821-484-2

Leonid Luks
Der russische „Sonderweg"?
Aufsätze zur neuesten Geschichte Rußlands im europäischen Kontext
ISBN 3-89821-496-6

Михаил Лукянов
Российский консерватизм и реформа, 1905-1917
ISBN 3-89821-503-2

Christian Ganzer
Das Museum der Geschichte des Zaporoger Kosakentums auf Chortycja
ISBN 3-89821-504-0

Robert Pyrah
Cultural Memory and Identity
Literature, Criticism and the Theatre in Lviv - Lwow - Lemberg, 1918-1939 and in post-Soviet Ukraine
ISBN 3-89821-505-9

Эльза-Баир Гучинова
Помнить нельзя забыть
Антропология депортационной травмы калмыков
ISBN 3-89821-506-7

Юлия Лидерман
Мотивы «проверки» и «испытания» в постсоветской культуре(на материале кинематографа 1990-х годов)
ISBN 3-89821-511-3

Dmitrij Chmelnizki
Die Architektur Stalins
Ideologie und Stil 1929-1960
ISBN 3-89821-515-6

Andrei Rogatchevski
The National-Bolshevik Party
ISBN 3-89821-532-6

Zenon Victor Wasyliw
Soviet Culture in the Ukrainian Village
The Transformation of Everyday Life and Values, 1921-1928
ISBN 3-89821-536-9

Guido Houben
Kulturpolitik und Ethnizität
Föderale Kunstförderung im Vielvölkerstaat Russland
ISBN 3-89821-542-3

Nele Sass
Das gegenkulturelle Milieu im postsowjetischen Russland
ISBN 3-89821-543-1

Series Subscription

Please enter my subscription to the series *Soviet and Post-Soviet Politics and Society*, ISSN 1614-3515, as follows:

❐ complete series   OR   ❐ English-language titles
❐ German-language titles
❐ Russian-language titles

starting with
❐ volume # 1
❐ volume # ___
  ❐ please also include the following volumes: #___, ___, ___, ___, ___, ___
❐ the next volume being published
  ❐ please also include the following volumes: #___, ___, ___, ___, ___, ___

❐ 1 copy per volume   OR   ❐ ___ copies per volume

Subscription within Germany:
You will receive every volume at 1st publication at the regular bookseller's price – incl. s & h and VAT.
Payment:
❐ Please bill me for every volume.
❐ Lastschriftverfahren: Ich/wir ermächtige(n) Sie hiermit widerruflich, den Rechnungsbetrag je Band von meinem/unserem folgendem Konto einzuziehen.

Kontoinhaber: _____ Kreditinstitut: _____

Kontonummer: _____ Bankleitzahl: _____

International Subscription:
Payment (incl. s & h and VAT) in advance for
❐ 10 volumes/copies (€ 319,80)   ❐ 20 volumes/copies (€ 599,80)
❐ 40 volumes/copies (€ 1.099,80)
Please send my books to:

NAME_____   DEPARTMENT_____
ADDRESS _____
POST/ZIP CODE_____   COUNTRY _____
TELEPHONE _____   EMAIL_____

date/signature_____

Please fax to: 0511 / 262 2201 (+49 511 262 2201)
or mail to: *ibidem*-Verlag, Julius-Leber-Weg 11, D-30457 Hannover, Germany
or send an e-mail: ibidem@ibidem-verlag.de

***ibidem*-Verlag**
Melchiorstr. 15
D-70439 Stuttgart

info@ibidem-verlag.de

www.ibidem-verlag.de
www.edition-noema.de
www.autorenbetreuung.de